Praise for *Injury Time*

'A marriage of prose and detail so fine and fastidious that it takes the breath away' *Independent*

'A convincing behind the scenes re-enactment of English football . . . Hamilton has a perceptively humane understanding of men for whom football was never just a game' *Guardian*

'A fictional look at action, on and off the pitch, past and present, that will leave you smiling' *Sun*

'Set in the last decades of the 20th Century and mingling real-life footballers with fictional characters, this is a thoughtful, entertaining debut novel by one of our finest sports writers, in which the beautiful game becomes a moving metaphor for the vicissitudes of human experience' *Mail on Sunday*

'With spare, sharp prose and knowing insights, Hamilton has written a heartwarming as well as heartbreaking winner' *Weekend Sport*

'An immersive character study of people damaged by sport and its temptations of glory, how some overcome, and how others are crushed by it' *Strong Words*

DUNCAN HAMILTON is a journalist who has won three William Hill Sports Book of the Year Prizes. He has been nominated on a further four occasions. He has also claimed two British Sports Book Awards and is the first writer to have won the Wisden Cricket Book of the Year three times. His biography of the Chariots of Fire runner Eric Liddell, *For the Glory*, was a *New York Times* bestseller. *Injury Time* is his first novel.

Also by Duncan Hamilton

Nottingham Forest FC: Thirty Great Years in Photographs

Provided You Don't Kiss Me: 20 Years with Brian Clough

Sweet Summers: The Classic Cricket Writing of JM Kilburn (ed.)

Fire and Ashes

Harold Larwood: The Biography

Old Big 'ead: The Wit and Wisdom of Brian Clough (ed.)

A Last English Summer

The Kings of Summer

Wisden on Yorkshire (ed.)

The Footballer Who Could Fly:
Living in My Father's Black and White World

Immortal: The Biography of George Best

For the Glory: The Life of Eric Liddell

A Clear Blue Sky (with Jonny Bairstow)

Sweet Summers: The Cricket Writing of J. M. Kilburn

Going to the Match: The Passion for Football

The Great Romantic: Cricket and the Golden Age of Neville Cardus

One Long and Beautiful Summer

INJURY TIME

DUNCAN HAMILTON

riverrun

First published in Great Britain in 2021
This paperback edition published in 2022 by

riverrun

An imprint of

Quercus Editions Ltd
Carmelite House
50 Victoria Embankment
London EC4Y 0DZ

An Hachette UK company

A CIP catalogue record for this book is available
from the British Library.

Paperback 978 152940 844 7
Ebook 978 1 52940 845 4

10 9 8 7 6 5 4 3 2 1

Typeset by CC Book Production
Printed and bound in Great Britain by Clays Ltd, Elcograf S.p.A.

Papers used by riverrun are from well-managed forests and other responsible sources.

For those who still love the FA Cup

Football can make a man more ridiculous even than drink can.

Arthur Hopcraft

The Football Man

PROLOGUE
TWENTY-EIGHT WORDS

I

OF COURSE, YOU'LL WANT to know about Frank Mallory: what it was like to play for him and then to sit behind the desk he occupied for nearly 25 years. You'll want to know whether Frank – another Scottish manager, who came after Bill Shankly, Matt Busby and Jock Stein but before Alex Ferguson – was just a bullying bastard, always desperate to get his own way, or a quixotic genius with an alchemical touch.

You'll want all the details and all the dirt. How Frank raged pyrotechnically but also cajoled and flattered us – often in the same sentence. How we, his players, swore by him but also swore at him – though never when he could hear us. How, on some occasions, he belittled us. How, on others, he made us feel like a team of Gullivers striding through Lilliput. How he was black-balled from the only other job he wanted – and ought to have got – because of the kind of man he was: human nitroglycerine.

You'll want to know how my life turned on a solitary goal – a fluke, really – and how it came to define me and also my relationship with Frank.

That goal, which gave him the domestic prize he most craved, hasn't been the blessing for me that you'd imagine. For one thing,

3

every season I played afterwards became merely a suffix to the season in which it was scored. Despite my few England caps, and despite the other medals that followed, I was always Thom Callaghan, 'The Player Who Won the FA Cup'. For a while I reckoned that my obituary would comprise only two sentences: 'He once scored the only goal in a Cup final. Then he died.'

I was a hero, the affection for me so strong in my own city that I knew it would even survive the end of my career.

You'll want to know about that Cup-winning team. How, as underdogs – a pack of ageing mongrels, really – we pulled off what no one thought possible. Not even us. You'll particularly want to know about Robbie Clayton, my mentor in those early days, and how we became inseparably linked on that spring day of sunshine and showers at Wembley in 1982. Most days fade to a shadow, existing in a hazy crowd of others, but I am still turning that one over in my mind, unable to let it go.

I came to realise that no man's life ought to be winnowed down to one shining moment. The glare it gives off obscures everything else. In saying that, I'm aware that without the Cup final I'd never have gone to Sweden to coach there and I'd never have come back again to be a manager here. So you'll also want to know about why I left the club so abruptly in the first place and whether Frank was to blame.

2

You'll probably dismiss the city where I made my reputation as small and dully provincial, an inconsequential smudge on the map that the M1 allows you to dash past without ever glimpsing. Southerners regard it vaguely as the North. True Northerners regard it as limbo. So you'll also want to know how Jack J. Munroe VI persuaded me – with hard cash rather than airy promises – to return there. Munroe is surely one of the most unlikely characters ever to own an English football club. You'll want to know about him too.

They say you can't go home again after a long absence, and that only a damned fool would even try. You're different. The place is different. You can't be reconciled.

I was determined to disprove that.

On that first morning back, I familiarised myself with the city again. The castle on its lump of sandstone rock. The grey slabs of the Market Square. The blue-grey dome of the Council House. The pair of huge stone lions flanking the steps to its entrance, a rendezvous spot for courting couples at the weekend. I walked the two and a bit miles from the Market Square to the bridge and then across the river.

I've always liked the fact that, journeying from the city, you don't properly catch sight of the ground until you step onto the bridge. The rise of the floodlights and the slope of the stands come as an astonishing surprise to anyone who isn't expecting them. You see swans glide across the wide, brown water. You see rowers chop their oars into that water too, the blades like knives. You see fishermen waiting on the banks for fish that seldom come.

Many of the old grounds, built post-war, had been smashed down, bulldozed and cleared, replaced with glass rather than brick and steel rather than corrugated iron. The ground I saw that day had hardly changed in the four and a half years I'd been away. The architecture was still modest: two low stands and some old terracing that was now covered in shiny plastic bucket seats. The only concessions to modernity were the 'big' stand, which Frank Mallory expected to be named after him, and a slim electronic scoreboard behind the far goal.

Looking at the ground that day, I immediately thought about my father.

You'll want to know about him as well. How he raised me alone. How he made me into a footballer. How passionately proud I made him whenever I pulled on that red shirt with its white badge – the same shirt and badge he had worn in the days when the ball had a lace in it and goalkeepers kept out shots with ungloved hands. How he and Frank rubbed along together, each tolerating the other.

6

Above all – and it's the reason I'm telling this story – you'll want to know about the very end of the 1996–97 season.

Why things happened the way they did. Who, if anyone, was to blame. What I might have done differently. It's taken me more than 20 years to confront those questions. Why? Because we live our lives forwards, but we can only understand them backwards. Enough time had to pass before I understood events properly.

Another, much smaller reason is that I've never been fond of footballers' autobiographies. Most of them are so swollen with self-importance, so obsessed with self-justification and so choked with platitudes, evasions, excuses and a lot of other crap. The rest is just pap and padding that patronises the reader: score-settling, chummy favours repaid, statistics that supposedly prove the player's omnipotence on the pitch. The line of truth? It gets blurred or distorted deliberately by the line of feeling, the need to pretend.

How you judge something depends on the perspective from which you saw it. Where you sit in a room determines the angle from which you view the scene, and the opinion you form of it is tainted by your own prejudices. The past can seem so close on the one hand and so incomprehensibly distant on the other.

Trust me, I've made allowances for all that. I'm a reliable narrator.

3

THE PAST STARTED TO throw things back at me. It all began with a clip on YouTube.

If you're a fan, especially of Liverpool, you'll have seen the thing a thousand and one times. If not, you'll still know it exists, waiting to be found.

I was searching for something else – a fragment from my own career – but instead I caught for the first time that TV interview Bill Shankly gave during his retirement. It's the one which is either famous or infamous, philosophical or fatuous, depending on what you think about him and also the value you attach to football as part of your life.

I watched it over and over again.

Shankly is being Shankly, his personality like a big house with all its windows lit. He's being the man who on official documents declared 'football' as his occupation and 'Anfield' as his home address. He's wearing a grey suit and a white shirt. His tie is vivid Liverpool red. His hair, the little of it that exists, is cropped to stubble. He is leaning forward in his chair. He is sombrely telling us about the game's place in the great scheme of things.

And he says:

Some people believe football is a matter of life and death. I am very disappointed by that attitude. I can assure you it's much more important than that.

Constant repetition has diluted the impact that quote originally made, reducing it to a cliché. But it still turns up in books. It still appears on T-shirts and posters, beside the hard folds of Shankly's face and those marble-bright eyes.

And some still believe it, taking those 28 words as gospel.

I know Shankly was being sincere. He wasn't showboating. He wasn't looking for a cheap headline. He merely told us what he believed.

Shankly said what he did because football consumed him. He was an addict, dependent on what he loved. I'm certain he didn't dwell on the possibility that anyone else would think differently or dismiss his remark as disproportionally zealous.

Frank Mallory admired Bob Paisley, Shankly's successor, but he worshipped Shankly, as though from the prayer mat.

I knew Shankly a little, which irritated Frank because he couldn't understand why his hero had an interest in someone who was then a nobody.

Not long after making my debut for Frank – it was only my fifth game – I came out of the dressing room at Anfield, my hair still wet from the showers, and found Shankly alone in the corridor. He'd been working as an analyst for one of Liverpool's local radio stations. He seemed a shrunken figure to me. His shoulders were stooped, his body slouched against a wall. There was a bewildered sadness in him, as if he felt he didn't possess a plausible reason for being there.

The indispensable element in any tragedy is some great misfortune. Shankly's was leaving football too soon. He was forever grieving for what he'd given up and could never have again, which was management. To have quit Liverpool at 60 years old, which he did in haste and confusion, was not just premature, but also incomprehensible, even to those who didn't know him well. Shankly, I think, hadn't imagined that the game, let alone his club, would go on without him. He never recovered from the shock of discovering that it could.

He glanced up, recognised me and shouted across. 'Son, I've something to tell you.' I was petrified. My mouth went dry. I was used to Frank picking minor faults in my game; I assumed Shankly had also spotted something amiss in the way that I'd played. Liverpool had wiped their feet on us that afternoon, so I braced myself for a blast of Shankly's criticism.

If you've heard him speak, you won't have forgotten the thick rasp of his voice. If you were lucky and he spoke directly to you, he did so as though addressing a crowd from a soapbox. The orator in Shankly even turned a request to pass the salt into a soliloquy.

He said: 'I watched you very carefully today. You have ability.

Now show you have the will. One without the other is useless. I tell every young player this: you'll never get anything out of the game unless you put everything into it. Promise me you'll do that. And never cheat, son. Never cheat. Cheaters perish in football. You've got a long career ahead of you. I'm sure of that because I'm never wrong. Not about something like this.'

He held out his hand to shake mine.

I ran into him half a dozen times that season. I always called him Mr Shankly, never Bill, and certainly not 'Shanks'; I didn't dare be too familiar. He'd always pay special attention to me. He'd always reiterate his belief in my talent. He thought success wasn't far away.

Shankly didn't live to see to his prophecy fulfilled: he died eight months before I scored at Wembley.

I loved Shankly and the warmth inside him. In fact, I loved him more than any boss I've ever met – including Frank.

I was born inconveniently too late to have played under him. At his funeral, though, held at St Mary's Church in West Derby, I looked around and saw those who had, and I wondered what it would have been like. How I would have fared. How differently my career might have gone if his influence, rather than Frank's, had steered it.

Sometimes even perfection wasn't good enough for Shankly, so I doubt whether I'd have got on to his team sheet in the 1960s when he was in his magical prime. I've seen the highlights and savoured all the colour of those days. I don't match up to Smith and St John or Yeats, Callaghan and Hunt. It wouldn't have taken the Kop long to realise that I didn't belong in company in like that.

Managers are always pleasant when you don't work for them. I still have no idea why Shankly singled me out for special attention, but I like to believe it's because he saw someone keen, wholehearted. I already felt like an 'old' young man then, an unremarkable player who had worked hard to get as far as he had and was prepared to work harder still to go even further. Perhaps that's what Shankly recognised. He'd been a similar sort of battler back in the day, aware of his own limitations and a slave to self-improvement.

You probably sense that there's a 'but' coming. There is.

I played and replayed the interview. Eventually, I could recite it like a verse of poetry learnt by rote.

I still can.

However much I respected Shankly, what he said about football and life and death isn't true. It isn't even half true. In fact, it's bollocks.

Football isn't the be-all and end-all of everything. If nothing else, I know that much. I've come a long way since the spring of 1997, but never far enough to forget that.

If Shankly was still with us, I'd have told him so.

Now I can tell only you.

PART ONE

BLUE BLOOD, RED SHIRT

I

I WAS A BOY WHEN I first met Frank Mallory. I can't give you the precise date, but it was about the midpoint between two World Cups: the one England won, fancifully thinking of themselves as almost invincible afterwards; and the next, in which the Brazil of Pelé and Carlos Alberto, Rivelino and Jairzinho disabused everyone of that notion.

I knew almost nothing about Frank. I knew only that my father was an ex-player and that footballers, both former and current, counted as his friends. My father's name was Martyn, but no one called him that. He was always Marty.

At home, we had a treasured copy of a magazine called *The FA Bulletin*, dated December 1946. He appeared on page 14. The portrait was posed, as if taken in a studio, and the colour was so richly wild – particularly his lips and his cheeks – that he seemed made-up, like a stage entertainer in rouge. He looked awkward, obeying the orders of the photographer, who'd tucked a brown ball under his arm. His head was turned slightly away from the camera, his gaze fixed somewhere in the middle distance. He resembled a Corinthian Casual from the late 19th century; the only thing missing was a moustache as thick as a privet hedge.

He was just 17 years old at the time, pushed into the team too early because of the scarcity of players after the war. Years later, whenever I studied that photograph again, I looked at my father, free of crow's feet, worry lines and other accumulated wrinkles, and almost didn't recognise him. He was a midfielder cum defender who was rated as sturdy and versatile. Not bad, but never outstanding. He could run all day, though: he had a pair of lungs that were the size of party balloons. Or that's what everyone told me. Though a shade under 6ft tall, he was also commanding in the air. His tremendous power was the result of a springy leap and constant practice. The first team trainer used to suspend a row of six balls from a long beam beneath one of the main stands. My father would spend hours going along the line, bashing his forehead against each ball in sequence to strengthen his neck muscles. He would get headaches, which were soothed only by strong painkillers and ice packs.

The future that awaited him was this: 159 league appearances and five more in the FA Cup. He was a peripheral player, remembered only by anyone fascinated by minutiae of the 1940s and 1950s. As the 1960s began, he was selling and collecting insurance door-to-door. He worked as a part-time scout, an ostensible act of benevolence by the club that had gently cut him loose as a player. In reality, it emphasised patronage on their part and dependency on his own. He became one of those ex-pros in an overcoat and a cheap pair of waterproof shoes who lurked as inconspicuously as possible on park touchlines or at non-league matches. Sometimes he'd watch four or five fixtures in a single weekend in exchange for a peppercorn salary and complimentary tickets to big matches.

My mother – of whom I'll say nothing more – did her moonlight flit when I was barely four years old. Her clothes and her jewellery vanished, but what lingered for umpteen weeks was the scent of her. The smell of her perfumes, her face creams, her powdery talc stuck to the air. We never heard from her again. No letters. No birthday cards. No word passed on. It's said that a man who's been his mother's favourite will feel like a hero all his life; I never had the chance to find out. Perhaps I was very odd, but I didn't miss her.

My mother's absence changed the relationship I had with my father. As ridiculous as this sounds, he was like the older brother I never had.

He came home one day with a new plastic football for me. Pelé once wrote: 'I close my eyes, and I can still see my first football.' I can still see mine too. It was the colour of a Belisha beacon and so light that you never knew where it would go after you kicked it. The moulded plastic had raised spots on it, like small pimples. If you closed your eyes and ran your fingers over the surface, you thought you were reading Braille. I took that ball everywhere with me – even to bed.

Every Sunday afternoon, I'd watch my father write out his

scouting reports in blue Biro while hunched over the dining table. In winter, an anglepoise lamp illuminated the paper he wrote on. It was laborious work for someone for whom clerical duties were a chore. It could take three hours or more for him to fill four sides of foolscap legibly and without crossings-out. He gripped the pen so hard that the bone at the top of his middle finger would swell and redden, like a welt, before the story of his weekend had a full stop. He was always smoking. He joked that he smoked so much in order to persuade me never to start.

On a Monday lunchtime, I'd occasionally go with him to the ground, where he delivered his dispatches from the grass roots. My father would rap on a frosted-glass window in the front office. The rat-a-tat rhythm of that knock sounded like a secret code, as though someone inside was waiting for a specific signal. The window would abruptly slide open and close again, a hand accepting the large buff-coloured envelope that was grandly adorned with the club's crest. Rarely was a word spoken or even a greeting exchanged.

My father would take me to the boot room, where the coaches, some of them his former teammates, sat in muddy kit, warming their hands on chipped mugs of tea. The room was ten by eight. It smelt of sweat, cigarette smoke and stale farts. Benches, covered in red plastic, were affixed to three of the walls. Pinned to those walls were myriad team sheets, fixture lists, training schedules, travel arrangements and notices from the Football League. I'd sit opposite the blackboard, staring at what I couldn't yet fully comprehend – the arrows, squiggles and sharp, short lines on a chalk-drawn football pitch, each player denoted by either an 'X' or an 'O'. On the one hand, it looked like an elaborate game of noughts and crosses without the grid; on the other, with each arrow sweeping under or across the next, it reminded me of the synchronicity of planes during an air display.

The time I spent in that room made me want to become a coach even before I wanted to be a player. I'm sure I learnt something integral there, as if by osmosis.

The coaches all wore blue nylon tracksuits with a high collar. It was from them – for the word seemed part of the official language of coaching – that I first heard the word 'fuck' and every derivative of it. Someone was always a 'lazy fucker' or a 'fucking waster'. Or someone else had 'fucked up' a part of his anatomy, which the physio, a doctor or even a surgeon was now trying to 'unfuck' so they could get him back on the 'fucking' field.

As if I were a pet dog, the coaches would say hello, make a fuss of me for two minutes and then either completely forget I was there or assume I couldn't hear them. Sometimes, though, my father would send me outside. I'd take my orange football and kick it about on the pitch, slowly creeping towards the centre circle. I pretended, as all boys do, that I was a pro in front of a crowd who were there solely to see me. By the time I was 11 years old, I knew every square foot of that pitch.

It was my back garden.

2

MY FATHER WAS A different man when he was among the coaches, striving to fit in and be one of them and to recreate the camaraderie of the dressing room, for which he still pined.

You could argue that, as a child, I couldn't possibly have noticed my father's anguish, balled up inside him, and the acute sense of separation he felt between his old life and his new one. But, honestly, I think I did somehow. Or at least I was aware that *something* – even if I couldn't be categorical about it – was off kilter. It was all to do with the way my father spoke – too defensively, and also too conciliatory on occasion – along with how the coaches spoke to him. They made an elaborate show of slapping my father on the back and pouring him tea, but their gestures were too loud and too showy to be authentic. There was an edge to everything said and done there, transmitted invisibly like a current. Again, I may have appreciated this only retrospectively, but my father was being silently pitied by those who felt superior in his company. Surely he, while collaborating in the charade, knew this perfectly well.

The longer I've contemplated this, the more layers I've piled onto these acts of one-upmanship that I witnessed and filed away. It helps me explain them. We all tell white lies. They make the world bearable for ourselves and for others. The lie my father told himself was that a coaching job, for which he was always implicitly campaigning, would come up if he hung around long enough; that he'd be first choice because of his amiability; that the other coaches would vouch for him enthusiastically; that a blue tracksuit would one day belong to him too; that he'd pour tea and patronise some other poor bugger.

Frank Mallory was in his mid-30s then, the youngest of the coaches. His playing career had ended ten years earlier, a sudden and damning experience from which he never entirely recovered.

Frank was playing for Bolton, a foil to someone much more famous: Nat Lofthouse, the 'Lion of Vienna'. That sobriquet was given to Lofthouse after he scored two goals for England against Austria in 1952. At the time, Austria were considered the slickest team in Europe, better even than the Hungarians. There's a short Pathé News clip of Lofthouse sliding the winner beneath the goalkeeper, who smacks against his body with the kind of thump that would have toppled a brick wall. On his way into the box – a run that began in the centre circle – Lofthouse had been elbowed on the nose and hacked at from behind. Still he had surged on. Frank was always grudging about Lofthouse, suggesting brawny strength alone got him the bulk of his goals. He was just jealous.

It was mid-January 1958, the bleakest of afternoons at Burnden Park. Thick smoke from a forest of chimneys, coming from homes and factories alike, rose indistinguishably against the slate-greyness of the north-west sky. The Christmas decorations had been taken down only a couple of weeks before, but the scene at the ground resembled the snowy festive cards that had recently adorned every mantelpiece. In those days, you played a match even if two feet of snow smothered the pitch. The groundsman shovelled off as much of it as he could and rolled flat what remained. The lines were painted bright blue.

It was an FA Cup third round replay. Early in the second half, the tie goalless, the temperature began to drop and the compacted snow started to freeze. The game became an inelegant slide across the ice, the ball hit hopefully long because close control had become impossible. In the 54th minute – Frank would never forget that – a diagonal pass was struck from the left touchline in Bolton's half. It climbed towards the 'D' of the opposition's box, dropping only a few yards short. Frank set off in pursuit, chased by his closest marker. Both players lost their footing simultaneously. Their studs were useless because the snow had become so hard and slippery. Aware that neither of them would get possession, the marker tried to avoid making a challenge. Frank banged into him, badly twisting his right leg. He went down and couldn't get up again. The goalkeeper came out, claimed the ball and cleared it upfield.

The opposition player went up to Frank, crouched over him and placed a consoling hand on his back. Frank stopped screaming in pain only long enough to yell at him: 'Fuck off. You've done me, you bastard. I won't forget it.' He left the field horizontally, four uniformed St John's ambulance men carrying his canvas stretcher like a guard of honour.

There were no substitutes; Bolton won the match with ten men. Lofthouse scored both goals. He did so again in the final against Manchester United. Everyone without an affinity to Bolton had been emotionally invested in Busby's Babes, devastated only 87 days earlier when their aeroplane, British European Airways Flight 609, crashed while attempting to take off for the third time on a slushy runway in Munich. Eight of the team were killed – including Duncan Edwards, who succumbed to his injuries in hospital. Matt Busby nearly died too. He arrived at Wembley with a limp and a walking stick.

So did Frank. The collision in the snow at Burnden Park had shredded his cruciate ligaments so badly that no surgeon could fix them. Bolton kitted him out in a Cup final suit, but he wasn't allowed to travel with the team. He sat beside the Royal Box rather than on the bench. Those needless snubs brought a snarl out of Frank whenever he reflected on them.

This was the final in which his 'pal', Lofthouse, shoulder-charged

United's goalkeeper, Harry Gregg, in the way a desperate man might smash his way through a locked door. Gregg, attempting to catch a floating ball beneath the bar, had turned his back on Lofthouse, who battered him across the line and into the net.

At the end, after the Cup was presented, Frank came onto the pitch and stood forlornly on the periphery of the celebrations, like a wallflower at a dance. I've seen a photograph of that moment. The Cup, which Lofthouse holds, glints in the sun. The other players look at it and at him, anticipating the bottles of champagne awaiting them in the dressing room. Frank is as solemn as a mourner at a graveside. He is gripping his walking stick so tightly, steadying himself on the lush turf, that his knuckles are white. After seeing that photograph once, Frank was never able to look at it again. 'I look so undignified,' he said.

His attempt at a comeback, midway through the following season, lasted only four games. Frank was just 26 years old. The anguish of retirement, a future denied him, was compounded by the knowledge of what his past lacked: a gold Cup-winner's medal in a navy leather box.

3

AFTER HIS INJURY, AND despite being ridiculously young, hurricane-force persistence got Frank Mallory a youth coach's job at Rochdale, which was about as low down as you could go without falling out of the Football League. From Rochdale he went to Charlton. From Charlton he came to us.

The manager at the time was Jock Lockhead, who'd won medals as a centre half with Glasgow Rangers shortly before and after the war. He was most proud of once being named Scottish Footballer of the Year. Lockhead looked older than Moses, but his mantra was ultra-modern: he wanted his team to 'fizz it about', demanding that whenever possible the ball should be passed short and sweetly rather than hacked inelegantly long. He was a suit-and-tie, clean-shaven disciplinarian. His head, which was also clean-shaven, looked like a shiny bullet. He didn't walk so much as march everywhere, military-style, and his black Oxford brogues squeaked like mice. You heard him coming two minutes before he entered a room.

Lockhead, however, didn't lower the rope that hauled Frank out of obscurity. Instead, Frank was forced upon him.

The club's owner was Sir Charles Bembridge, an avuncular baronet who wanted everyone to refer to him as 'Uncle Charlie'.

Textiles were behind the fortune he inherited. The family opened its first mills, in both West Yorkshire and Greater Manchester, in the same year that the Duke of Wellington swapped the battlefield for Downing Street. Uncle Charlie was the aristocrat's aristocrat. Portraits of his ancestors – the framed faces of the dead – adorned his main staircase like trophies. I doubt he ever opened or drew his own curtains or knew where to find the taps in the kitchen. If a light bulb needed changing, he'd get one of his servants to call an electrician. His country house, which looked like a castle, stood on a hill among 7,000 acres and straddled the border of two counties. The central tower could be seen from twenty miles away.

Uncle Charlie was ungainly-looking. He had a slack, stringy body and was partly lame, the consequence of his 'good' war. A major in the Grenadier Guards, he won the VC after single-handedly taking out a German gun emplacement at Anzio, despite the 'bother' (his word) of being shot in the left leg three times.

Speed was Uncle Charlie's thing. Often he left the Bentleys he owned in the garage, gave the chauffeur a day off and tore about in a racing-green Morgan, his foot seldom off the accelerator, even at traffic lights. He loved the car so much that you'd see him stroking the bonnet in the way a groom strokes the mane of a horse. He always seemed to me to be slightly out of his time. He'd have revelled in the era of early Edwardian England. He belatedly got into football, which the rest of his family regarded as barbaric and beneath him. Uncle Charlie was 14 years old when he watched Alex James, after dribbling the ball in from the touchline, claim a goal for Arsenal in 1930. The game enthralled him from that moment onwards.

There was one problem with Uncle Charlie. He epitomised the old joke: *How do you make a small fortune? By starting with a big one*. He could live no way other than extravagantly; he walked about in a ticker-tape parade of banknotes. As though disdaining money as a triviality, Uncle Charlie spent indiscriminately on himself and neglected the upkeep of the house, believing it would repair itself. The house had a court for real tennis, which hosted important championships in the 1950s. Uncle Charlie let the roof rot. The court got wet when it rained and was usually covered in pigeon shit. It made no difference to him.

Uncle Charlie met Frank at a football dinner. From what I learnt later, Frank immediately marked him down as a soft touch, a man as malleable as wax. Within a week, Uncle Charlie had foisted Frank on Lockhead. For the next 30 years, he indulged Frank, excusing his worst excesses and forgiving everything else. He tended not to interfere, which was Frank's notion of the ideal boss. Board meetings, for example, lasted no longer than an hour because Uncle Charlie said it interfered with his lunchtime drinking.

4

FRANK MALLORY WAS A different man then. I don't think anyone would have predicted how wonderfully he'd reinvent himself over the next decade. You'll know Frank as someone who's always on the attack, his tongue like a blunt instrument, the forefinger of his right hand stabbing the air in an actorly manner. You'll also know he's capable of either charming the whiskers off a cat or being fantastically rude, mule-stubborn and unreasonably volatile, flaring up volcanically over something nondescript. The media feasted on his opinions. He appealed to the gallery. Acres of newsprint and hours of TV were devoted to Frank, who used both as a megaphone to condemn and castigate. The ubiquitous pundit, recognisable even to those unfamiliar with the game, nonetheless despised television, arguing that it fed parasitically on football, and deplored newspapers, thinking no clean hand ought to touch one. It was one of the many contradictions in his odd and singular personality. Lots of people tried to work Frank out. They attempted to take him apart, like a puzzle, and put him together again. They never could.

The Frank I observed in the beginning wasn't yet the kind of character who made a room look smaller as soon as he walked into it, filling the space from floor to ceiling with his ego. Back then he couldn't mesmerise anyone. In the coaches' room, he would prop his back lazily against one of the walls and loll across a bench. Frank didn't drink – not really – because, like my father, he was usually smoking. Many footballers liked a fag and were either unaware or didn't care about the carcinogenic dangers. In his day, Frank was as synonymous with the habit as Enzo Bearzot, with his pipe; César Menotti, taking drags even on stub ends; Johan Cruyff, with a packet of Camels in his jacket pocket; and Dr Socrates, seen taking puffs on a cigarette during the World Cup finals. Nowadays you'd think of Frank as another Maurizio Sarri, who faintly resembles him in appearance. Frank would take a gold Dupont lighter out of his pocket – a present from Uncle Charlie – and 'flame up', holding his cigarette low between his index and middle fingers.

His hair was short and very dark. His cheeks hadn't yet acquired the craters and pockmocks that a bacterial infection caused in his late 30s. I never saw him out of a sweatshirt and a pair of black boots or black trainers.

The most striking thing about Frank – and you'll think I'm making this up – is that he seldom spoke then. This was Frank before his empire-building phase. You rarely heard a thing from him, unless he had something specific to say. He took in everything around him, storing away what was useful and discarding what wasn't, like rubbish. And when he talked, he did so quietly, and his accent didn't betray his place of birth. Born in Stirling, Frank had left Scotland a year before reaching his teens. Only as he became more successful did he also become more Scottish, striking a pose.

The other coaches made the critical mistake of meretriciously lobbying against one another in expectation of succeeding Lockhead. Stealthier and craftier than all of them, Frank competed by feigning disinterest. He waited for them to trample over one another.

The team was relegated in 1972, and Lockhead got the sack. Up stepped Frank to take his job. He inherited a mess. The club was a ruin sitting on a patch of blasted ground. A rotten pitch. Three rickety stands, which were more like shacks, and an open terrace at one end where the clock and the scoreboard stood. The bookmakers tipped Frank as the first managerial casualty of the following season, reckoning a second successive relegation was almost certain.

No one saw the miracle coming.

5

H ERE'S THE THING.

In the boot room, my father and Frank Mallory would be as stiffly polite to one another as strangers on a train. The exchanges between them never amounted to much more than 'Hello, Frank' and 'Hello, Marty', and the offer of a cigarette or a light. This was difficult for my father because the recommendations he made to the club were immediately put into Frank's hands.

Nothing made sense until I learnt one thing. Frank had never forgiven the man who ended his career. That man was my father.

When Frank became manager, my father feared for his job. He expected retribution to arrive by post, and so he would jump whenever the letter box rattled. Only then, as if preparing me for that moment, did he share what had happened 14 years earlier. He did so nervously, protesting his innocence as though I might not believe him. Frank didn't sack him, but he made his employment dependent on the torture of an annual review.

If that FA Cup tie had been televised, if Frank could have seen a replay of the incident, he'd have known my father was never guilty of the charge levelled against him. I don't say that purely from filial loyalty. Over the years I've spoken to the players who were closest to the collision. Each one assured me that my father wasn't culpable. 'A terrible combination of chance and the conditions,' said Nat Lofthouse, whose reputation made him the most convincing witness. 'I told Frank all that when he was in hospital. I told him again when he came out. He didn't want to listen. He wanted someone to blame.'

The Cup consequently became a fixation for Frank. Denied it as a player, he sought it as a manager.

6

MY FATHER WAS CERTAIN I would make it as a pro. He knew it as soon as I began kicking that orange ball. I didn't toe-poke it, the way other boys did, and I headed it instinctively with my forehead rather than the crown of my head. I could put the ball where I wanted it too.

When the time came, he got one of the other scouts to tip off the club in case Frank Mallory cottoned on and my surname counted against me. It was an unnecessary precaution: I hadn't seen Frank close up for four years; he wouldn't have recognised me. He'd soon dismantled the old boot room, purging his former rivals, and rebuilt a new one in his own image. My father, who hadn't played with any of the fresh appointees, had stopped taking me there.

I'd also played for England schoolboys', which made subterfuge pointless. I often found myself in the local paper.

I featured in two trial matches for Frank. These came before and after a schoolboys' international against Scotland at Hampden Park. Playing there was like stepping into a suit that was three sizes too big for me. In the vastness of the pitch, and beside the enormous stands, I felt somehow diminished and out of place. The trial games were more to my liking. These were held on practice pitches near the river, overlooking a British Waterways building. It was a hulking rectangular block that resembled a prison, the windows barred and tiny. Anyone could abuse those pitches. You'd find walkers letting their dogs take a piss or a shit in the penalty box.

I longed to be a footballer more than anything on God's earth, but I didn't necessarily want to leave home to achieve that ambition. I didn't want to abandon my father. 'Don't worry if it doesn't happen for you here,' he kept saying. 'There are plenty of clubs – and plenty of other strings I can pull.'

Jonjo Whelan made sure it never came to that.

Some subtract from life. Some add to it. Jonjo was a man of palpable worth and also of forbearance, criteria imperative for being a foil to Frank. He was 12 years old when he came from the sunny warmth of St Kitts to the chill of the West Midlands, one of the *Windrush* generation. He found people, still ignorant, who thought shaking hands with him would turn their own hands black and who threw away a cup after he drank from it. He was called all those words that disgust us now. At one club, after scoring a late equaliser as a substitute, he heard his manager describe in a disgraceful, unforgivable fashion how the decision was made to put him on: 'I thought we were fucked, so I said to myself, "Why not throw the blackie on?"'

In those days, the mid-1960s, there was a brand of jam with a golliwog on the label. There'd always be someone in the crowd who'd shout at Jonjo: 'Get back on your jam jar.' 'I heard it a thousand times a season,' he said.

He got hate mail, unsigned and written in green or red ink, which he read and burnt. One letter threatened to fire-bomb his front door. Another promised to cut him. Plenty more said he'd be beaten up in the streets. Dog shit was stuffed through his letter box. At one game, against Newcastle, a policeman rode on the team bus as his bodyguard. On the field, he'd be pelted with objects: coins, cans, bottles and, of course, bananas by the bunch. They'd make monkey noises. They'd shake their fists at him, pretending to hold spears like the soldiers in the film *Zulu*.

Jonjo, the most dignified man I've ever met, turned both cheeks while smiling. He got on with the business of living, which meant silently putting up with much more abuse than I, or anyone else, ever found out about. He got on, too, with the business of scoring goals. Not only was Jonjo of formidable size, but he also possessed considerable skill, insight and the surest of touches under pressure.

He met Frank at Charlton. There, the two of them became matey and dependent on one another's friendship. It made sense. They were both goal-scorers. Ask them to independently write manifestos on the game, and in return you'd have got identical documents. Each had what the other needed too. There wasn't an ounce of vanity in Jonjo's body; he didn't like the heat of the house lights. Frank backed into those lights and then feigned surprise after finding himself there.

It's the lot of the dutiful assistant to be overshadowed or taken for granted. The credit for promotion, the league title and a League Cup was never evenly split. Nor, I think, did Jonjo's salary ever reflect his contribution. Frank was gracious enough to let Jonjo walk the team out at Wembley in the League Cup final, but still the cameras panned towards him, head down and striding out of the tunnel behind them. I'm sure he planned the timing of his entrance. Despite all this, Jonjo was fearsomely protective of his partner, doing his duty without dwelling on injustices.

Jonjo was the only man who could get away with calling Frank a fuckwit. I didn't know it at the time, but Frank didn't want to sign me. Jonjo did. When Frank offered some nonsensical reason about preferring someone else, Jonjo said, very quietly: 'Is all this bullshit really about your injury? It's a lifetime ago. Don't punish the lad for what you think his father did. Give him a chance.'

I was escorted into Frank's office. My father followed. Frank looked me up and down, like an uncle who hadn't seen his nephew for an age and couldn't fathom how fast the boy had filled out. 'I remember you,' he said. 'You used to sit in the boot room and stare at the tactics board. Well, bugger me. Get the photographer in here.' I sat behind his desk and signed my contract. Frank rested his hands on my shoulders, as if he might be about to squeeze them hard or strangle me. My father stood beside him. Frank couldn't help himself. 'I hear Thom's a bit like you, Marty. He can dish it out. I'd better be careful. I've only got one good knee left.'

Years later, my father told me that Jonjo had said one other thing to Frank: 'I know how much you want the FA Cup. Sign Thom Callaghan. You never know, Frank, one day he might win it for you.'

Frank huffed and said: 'He's more likely to get me the fucking sack.'

It sounds too much like a fairy tale to be true, but I've always wanted to believe it.

So I do.

7

I WAS 19 WHEN I made my debut. I came into a team of which
nothing much was expected.

Frank Mallory had done something wondrous by taking
a minuscule club like ours and making them into champions,
knocking aside Leeds and Liverpool, Arsenal and Tottenham.
Both at the time and afterwards, it seemed almost hallucinatory.
You blinked a thousand times and still didn't quite believe what
you'd seen. Frank set a standard for us, and also for himself, that
couldn't be sustained. The club didn't have the cash. He hadn't
won the title for four years. He hadn't won a trophy at all for
three. He hadn't qualified for Europe since 1977. Today, when
clubs demand repeat successes and a barren season is a fatal blight,
Frank would have got the heart-shaped bullet. Back then, purely
because of Uncle Charlie Bembridge, he instead received votes
of confidence that counted as guarantees of the board's support.

The silver-spoon rich always believe that money and privilege
afford them an insight into things that the less well-off, and especially the less well-connected, can't possibly understand. Uncle
Charlie considered himself sharply intelligent, someone who knew
a lot about everything. You preserve that sort of façade through

silence; just don't make the mistake of opening your mouth. But Uncle Charlie was always pontificating. On each occasion, he showed how dim he really was – especially regarding football matters, his knowledge still elementary.

Frank didn't like 'kids'. You had to come of age as a player – reach 20 or 21 – before he'd pick you. We'd had a wobbly start to the season. One game won. Another two lost. A couple of draws that ought to have been defeats. If you tacked those results on to the end of the previous season's, Frank's recent record was shot through with a lot of big holes. Doubts about his future were expressed. Out came Uncle Charlie, determined to crush them. It was the usual stuff: 'every belief in Frank . . . pulling together . . . standing by him . . . recovery all in hand.' He didn't anticipate the follow-up question and so stumbled over the specifics of his answer. Pinned down on who might come into the team to refresh it, easing us into that promised recovery, Uncle Charlie didn't know. 'I don't watch the reserves much,' he said in a fluster. In truth, he didn't watch the reserves at all. It looked, however, as though the club didn't possess a youth policy. The newspapers, sympathetic for so long, turned on Uncle Charlie, portraying him as an out-of-touch toff who'd escaped from the pages of a P. G. Wodehouse novel. Having stuck the knife in, they then twisted it with the most unflattering of photographs. His eyes were half closed, as if he was also half cut. He looked a prize arse. Frank felt obliged to repay one of the many debts he owed him, so he threw me in – not to prove the club had talent in waiting, but to allow Uncle Charlie to slink back into the wings again.

I made my debut at Villa Park on a Wednesday night. I was 18 years old.

I remember walking down the corridor to the away dressing room. I remember the frosted-glass door, which let in plenty of light, and the profusion of mirrors, like a minor Versailles. The floor, made with wooden blocks, was dull and badly scratched from the studs that were constantly scraped across it.

We drew 0–0. I barely got a kick.

8

IN FOOTBALL, ALMOST EVERYONE has a puerile nickname, because footballers generally aren't the most inventive when it comes to dreaming them up.

We didn't have a Divine Ponytail or a Baby-Faced Assassin, a Romford Pelé or even a Flea. We had two Kellys, whom everyone assumed were brothers – until they saw them together. Our right back, Carlton Kelly, got called 'Ned' after the outlaw. He was short and wide and solid. His hair was bright ginger. Our left-sided midfielder, Stuart Kelly, was all bone, thinner than a hatstand and 6ft 2ins tall. Our names were stitched onto the back of our training tops, which is why S. Kelly became known as 'Skelly'. The goalkeeper, Sean Ramsey, naturally became 'Alf' and then 'Alfie'. Andy Wharton was 'Sweets,' a moniker that, like Ned Kelly's, became established even in newspapers, making the name on his birth certificate almost redundant. Sweets heaped three and a half spoons of sugar into his tea; you felt as though your own teeth were rotting when you watched him drink it. Nat Carson, a block of destruction, was 'Scarecrow', the hard glaze of his face enough to scare a pit bull and his upturned nose like a snout. John Slater was 'Tracksuit' because we seldom saw him dressed in anything else. Alec Taylor, obsessed with fashion, was 'Oscar', in honour of Oscar Wilde, from the moment he arrived at a Player of the Year dinner in a crushed red velvet jacket and a cravat. Of our overseas players, Moritz Bleibtrau was 'Brian' because we considered his Christian name laughable and couldn't pronounce his surname without spitting. We were unoriginal enough to call the Dutchman Arend van het Hoff 'Van Gogh', before shaving it down to 'Goughie'. The winger Jimmy Bradley moved as fast as a quadruped and sweated like a thoroughbred, so he was 'Horse', which led profitably, if disingenuously, to the crudest possible chat-up line: he claimed his cock was the size of a Christmas stocking. Davie Collins anointed himself 'The Man'. We called him 'Big Head'. Collins had been signed from Liverpool, where he'd been unable to break past either Kevin Keegan or John Toshack, eventually finding himself as the understudy to Kenny Dalglish. He belly-flopped into the small pond Frank Mallory had allowed him to swim in. Collins didn't give a cow's fart about what anyone thought. He was an agitating presence because he thrived on being obnoxious. He didn't mind being unpopular; he just didn't want to be insignificant. The sort of man who had opinions rather than convictions, he nonetheless expressed a defiant belief in himself. He always thought his calf niggle was more important than someone else's broken leg. He surveyed the rest of us from a lofty angle and would turn his gaze upward and away from you, as though warming his face in the sun.

For a while I was 'H', but it and nothing else ever caught on, apart from 'Cally', which the newspapers also used because it fitted into a headline. My Christian name was often spelt wrongly in the newspapers and the match programmes of the away teams I faced. It began with that first game at Aston Villa. Even when my name was spelt correctly, almost everyone assumed the 'h' was a misprint. Those who didn't derided it as a haughty affectation. I had to explain that the name originated in Aberdeenshire. I'd been named after my Scottish maternal great-grandfather, who, improbably at 34, had played half a season for Aberdeen in the Scottish Second Division. He was a centre half. In photographs he is broad-shouldered and bulbous, with an unruly beard that partly obscures a top lip as thin as a blade. He was a bruiser, inclined to rely on sharp studs and sharper elbows, the pitch like a backstreet to him.

As soon as I signed for the club, I was looking for someone to follow; someone, moreover, from whom I could learn.

Robbie Clayton was just 'Captain', a blue blood in a red shirt.

9

I WAS A LONER, A bit of an oddity. You could say, if you were being kind, that I was a singular man. I stood a little apart from those I played alongside and never conformed to the common preconception of what a footballer is supposed to be like. I avoided the places most players frequent: the bars and the betting shops, the racetracks and the snooker halls and the nightclubs. I didn't go in for bling. No ostentatious loop of jewellery, as broad as naval rope, hung around my neck or wrists. No latticework of tattoos decorated my flesh. I've known a player or three who weren't prepared to run ten yards for the ball, but would dash two hundred to catch a woman, especially one with too much make-up and too few clothes. With women, I was a little shy, a little cautious, a little naïve. The older pros nudged one another, suspicious about whether or not I was 'a fucking queer'. When I was 17, one of them asked me to confirm or deny it. He'd found me reading a copy of the *Daily Telegraph*, regarding that as highly dubious.

On my days off I'd sit at home and read a lot about the history of the game. For umpteen hours, I'd study imperfect recordings of old matches. Some of these, pre-dating *Match of the Day*, were spooled through a projector. I bought the film in flat silver cans from the BBC. If I wasn't playing midweek, I'd go to a game, buying a ticket like everyone else. I was not only trying to be a better player, but also preparing myself eventually to become a coach, a factotum for someone like Frank Mallory or Bill Shankly.

I did all that work because of Robbie Clayton. He was a pro's pro, the quintessential leader. He did everything *just so*. Robbie would clean his own boots rather than let an apprentice do it. He'd use cotton wool, polishing the leather with the fastidiousness of a Buckingham Palace guardsman. He'd iron his laces. He'd iron the ties that held up his socks. He'd iron his underwear. He'd comb his short, curly black hair and wax it stiffly. Robbie even carried a handkerchief in the pocket of his shorts. He was immaculately groomed off the pitch too. He wore bespoke suits, silk ties and shirts of Egyptian cotton. He'd brush down those suits before he went to bed. The night before away games – I always roomed with him – Robbie relaxed in a silk dressing gown. One of his favourite sayings was: 'You're a better player, a better person, if you dress well.' Another was: 'What you do as a man off the field, how you act, reflects the player you'll be on it.' In one game he got kicked in the head. His shirt became blood-soaked. He was more upset about his disorderly appearance than the four-inch gash in his scalp.

Robbie was already 32 years old when I first got to know him. One afternoon I got to his boots before he did. I cleaned them the way he would have done. He began to treat me like a kid brother and invited me to his home.

The only mark on Robbie's skin was a tattoo on his left shoulder blade. It was of a small heart, the size of a 50p piece. The name of his wife, Beth, was inked beneath it. Beth didn't care for football and seldom went to a match. She was only 5ft 5ins tall. Her eyes were brown and she wore her black hair in a pixie cut. She was eight years younger than Robbie, which made her only five years older than me, but she seemed very mature, as though she'd been through a previous life before this one and could remember it. At first, she intimidated me, and I didn't know what to make of her. She was more flamboyantly unconventional than anyone I'd ever met.

Even in winter, she'd walk around the house in bare feet and summer dresses, impervious to the cold. She played music – mostly punk – very loudly; you could still hear the beat of it when she wore headphones. And she was fond of abstract art, which she painted with a decorating brush on canvases that were the size of a goalmouth. You wouldn't have put Robbie and Beth together.

Beth's father was a High Court judge. She was unmistakably highfalutin, a cut-glass girl with a cut-glass accent. Robbie was born in London's East End, the son of a Tube driver. The area in which he grew up was a bomb site, purple flowers growing out of rubble that the Luftwaffe had left behind, but he wasn't a jellied-eels-and-whelks cockney. All the slang, all the 'cor blimeys' had been slowly shaved away. Still, beside his wife, Robbie was perpetually out-shone, which I think partly explained his liking for smart clothes.

The man who influenced me – certainly more than Frank Mallory did – was influenced himself by Bobby Moore. Robbie had been on West Ham's books, remaining in the reserves longer than he should have done. He did so because Moore was there – despite knowing that he'd never break through, never get a chance, for that very same reason. He was proud to share a Christian name with Moore, not minding that everyone at Upton Park shortened it to Robbie to differentiate one from the other in conversation. He was prouder still to share a training pitch with him.

I was a teenager when I saw Robbie make his debut for us. Soon, he was an exemplary captain. He'd never shout. It was enough for him to wave a hand or even raise a questioning eyebrow to get a response. Tucking in beside whoever else was playing centre half, he'd move gracefully around the pitch. He had more speed than Moore, but then nearly everybody did. He just had to graft harder in order to be able to do what came as naturally as breathing to Moore, who rarely had to make a sliding or inelegant tackle because he always seemed to know where the opposition was going. How good was Robbie in comparison? You need to know only one thing: after a European tie, Johan Cruyff came into the dressing room and politely asked to swap shirts with him.

You didn't question Robbie's authority any more than you questioned Frank's. When Davie Collins tried, he ended up sprawled on the grass. In training, there is always barging, skirmishes, full-on scrums and even fisticuffs in which blood is spilt. Collins had played all sorts of schoolboy practical jokes: snipping the heels out of your socks; cutting out the crotch of your trousers or the silk lining of your pockets; putting fish in your bag or your hotel bed. He would sign photographs of other players with his own name.

Rather than trade imbecilic jokes with him, Robbie waited until Collins got the ball. He ankle-tapped him and sent his body spinning. He did this three times in less than a quarter of an hour. After the fourth time, Collins got up and tried to put Robbie down. It was a swing and a miss. He tried again. This time Robbie side-stepped the punch and thumped him in the stomach. He winded him completely, and Collins puked up his breakfast.

These days we've turned practice into a mathematical equation. We're told 10,000 hours of it will make anyone world class. Robbie knew that in the 1970s. He would arrive at training an hour and a half before anyone else. He was also the last to leave. 'It's all about repetition,' he'd say. 'You have to do the same thing over and again. Some people find it boring, but you don't improve any other way.' He perfected his control, his positioning, his passing. A pass from Robbie was like someone flicking a gold coin into your hand.

He believed researching the history of the game could be beneficial. You can profit from the past, he explained, if you could be bothered to research it. 'Most players ignore history. They don't care what happened yesterday. I learn from it,' he said. At Robbie's home, we'd talk about tactics and watch matches together. It was like being back at school. Without him, I don't know whether I'd have been confident enough to make it as a player. Not under Frank anyway.

I was regarded as a bits-and-pieces performer. I wasn't sure, despite what Bill Shankly had told me, that I'd have much of a career to grow into. I reckoned my ration of the First Division might be two or three seasons. I'd earn a decent wage and the odd, lucrative bonus, before the drop to somewhere less respectable became inevitable. Dozens upon dozens of players had more ability. I wasn't silky on the ball. I didn't ping 70-yard passes and receive 'ooh's of admiration in return. I didn't move lithely. I wasn't especially quick. I was only 5ft 9ins tall, which didn't make me a threat or a deterrent in the air.

But I could play anywhere. I had multiple uses, like a Swiss army knife. What lifted me above the ordinary was the way in which I judged the game.

I once saw a short reel of film in which a precocious chess genius, a grandmaster in the making, had beaten his opponent in a few rapid moves. After each one, his palm thumped down hard on the push button of the clock, without him even looking at it. The gesture was like a provocation. His eyes were dark and glassy; he didn't blink. His unblemished face betrayed no emotion – not a twitch of it. His upper body was absolutely still until the moment when his unusually long fingers reached for a piece. His hand obeyed his mind and then claimed a square so swiftly that the act itself was a blur. The film astonished me. I identified with that chess player. I pictured how the wooden board surely looked through his eyes. It was lit up and glowing. The permutation of possible moves down and across it was lit up too, a cross-hatching of firm lines. The pattern resembled a cat's cradle of different, very bright colours. I knew this must be true, for sometimes I saw a football pitch in exactly the same way, every space and the angles within it mapped out. I anticipated what was going to happen next, always one step and two thoughts ahead of everyone else. I saw where a pass might go before it was hit. I saw the run a striker would make – even before the striker himself knew it. The opposition would think they'd split open the belly of our defence . . . and then I'd appear to stitch it cleanly up again.

This was my superpower.

I remember startling Frank with it. I'd covered 40 yards to be in the right place to block a pass by Liam Brady before he even lifted his left boot to strike it. In the same game I saw – five seconds before he did – the only attacking space into which Graham Rix could go. I body-checked him to the floor like a grid-iron line-backer; the referee didn't notice.

Afterwards Frank asked: 'Are you fucking psychic?'

This made it difficult for those who didn't know me – and even a few who did, such as Robbie – to reconcile how differently I behaved on and off the pitch. My temper, especially in my early years, didn't take long to reach boiling point. I would bite off your ear and spit in the hole. It's probably because I grew up in the era of Hunter and Harris, Storey and Smith and Stiles. 'He makes any of those seem innocently seraphic in comparison,' was a back-handed compliment the *Guardian* once paid me. *The Times* paid me another: 'The body is 60 per cent water. Not Callaghan's. His is 60 per cent concrete.'

I went over the top in tackles, leering over the unfortunate player I'd just kicked. The newspapers thought I relished the brutality a tad too much. Perhaps I did. In one season, I picked up enough bookings to be banned twice. Some of those I chopped down and stomped on dabbled with revenge. I got the odd 'flying fist' in the face, always off the ball, when the referee wasn't looking. I got a rabbit punch in the kidneys. Someone tap-danced across my legs. You have to pretend you don't care and that you're not hurting. Jack Charlton horrified the Football Association by claiming he owned a 'little black book' containing the names of two players who had wronged him. Charlton promised he would get even with them before retiring; he wanted to make them 'suffer'. He was idiotically honest. You don't advertise the crime with menaces that you're about to commit. You do your work surreptitiously, carrying out your retribution when the miscreant least expects it. That was another lesson Robbie taught me.

At that stage of his career, he and Frank had the same aim. More than anything, Robbie was chasing the one thing that had eluded him, which was the FA Cup. He'd assembled a collection of Cup finals on tape. We'd sit together and watch them, constantly pressing the rewind button. His favourites were West Ham's win over Preston – his claret-and-blue loyalty the reason for that – and Everton's against Sheffield Wednesday. He'd not only been to that final, but had sat behind Paul McCartney, Beatle-mania at screaming pitch back then.

The Everton–Wednesday final epitomised the essence of the Cup for Robbie. He spoke of it endlessly. Everton, who hadn't conceded a goal on the way to Wembley, were 2–0 behind after 54 minutes and 3–2 ahead after 74. We'd count the strides Derek Temple ran between collecting the ball and ramming it past Ron Springett for Everton's winner. Robbie liked, as I did, the formality of the occasion. The fact you had to 'dress up' for it, he said. The fact half the world was watching. The fact everyone, even if they forgot the rest of your career, would remember that you'd won a Cup final.

Two semis, narrowly lost, were as close as Robbie had ever come. He took his hope of something better into every season.

By the 1981–82 season, he and Frank, who'd won every other domestic honour together, hadn't been beyond the fifth round since the mid-1970s. 'I've given up,' Robbie confessed to me. 'It's not happening.'

I O

THE FA CUP.

It's difficult to convey, especially to the generations that never witnessed it, the command the competition once had on the heart and the imagination. That seems far off now, belonging to the age of rosettes and wooden rattles and concrete terracing. But when I was just an ordinary fan, and then once I became a player, the Cup final was like another Christmas Day, always held on a soft spring afternoon. We spoke of Cup fever, as though it was a recognised medical condition. Restless with excitement, you could never sleep the night before the final. You rose early, wanting to miss nothing of the build-up. You consumed everything the TV fed you, even the highlights on *Match of the Day*, where the winners were feted, the distraught losers already half forgotten.

Today, most managers regard the Cup as an irritant, a chore to be tolerated and endured like torture. They put out weakened teams, protecting their glittering stars for bigger things, and then feebly roll out excuses for doing so. Even bosses in the lower leagues are more hung up on promotion and the play-offs. Giant-killing has gone out of fashion because it doesn't pay as handsomely as it once did.

In a heyday that went on for a century, the Cup final was part of the great panoply of English life. The two captains appeared on the cover of the *Radio Times*. The city of each finalist, especially in the provinces, was decked out as though the monarch's coronation was coming: the pubs and storefronts a blaze of colour; bunting strung between lamp posts; banners hanging between the pillars of the grandest buildings. Getting a ticket for the final was like getting eight score draws on the pools – something else almost no one bothers with now.

I've met hundreds of ex-pros who told me that *the* Cup – no one ever had to explain *which* Cup – was not only the climactic moment of their career, but also the summit from which they judged their entire life. Some of these men, wizened when I met them, had won at Wembley thirty or even forty years before. The Cup meant more to them than the League Championship.

It defined them. 'You wanted to win it more,' Stanley Matthews once said to me, 'because you were playing on behalf of tens of thousands of people and because not winning felt so horrible at the end. You were crying inside. You know what my fear was? That a career without a winner's medal would leave a hole that nothing afterwards in life could ever fill.' Matthews was in his mid-70s, a lean man with a sunken face. His hair was the colour of hoar frost. He wore a natty leather jacket, the length of a Victorian frock coat, and a white silk scarf, knotted stylishly. He spoke with relief but, from its opening words, I knew where his little speech was going. It was planned, not spontaneous. He was going to remind me about something of which I was already aware: how grateful I ought to be. For I'd claimed what Matthews saw as 'the top prize' without having to toil for it. 'You were just a babe,' he said. 'A lot of players envied you. Some will have resented you – especially those who never got the chance or failed when it came. You got lucky.'

Matthews said it all in an amazed rather than malevolent way. I didn't blame him for that. For one thing, it's bad manners to dispute the word of a legend, a player, at 38, who went into his third and last Cup final with the whole nation, including the Queen, willing him to flourish and hand them a happy ending. For another, he was right.

I *was* lucky.

11

I WAS LUCKY BECAUSE I benefited from someone else's misfortune. I was lucky because I went into the team at the right time. I was lucky because Frank Mallory saw something in me that he hadn't spotted before. 1981–82 was the season I came of age. My 21st birthday even fell between the fourth and fifth rounds.

On a Wednesday night in mid-December, the weather bitter beyond belief, I was playing for the reserves against Birmingham City at St Andrew's. The first team were nearly 200 miles away at Brighton. My career at the club had stalled and then gone into a slow reverse. I didn't see much future for myself there. I felt forgotten. I thought about asking whether I could go out on loan, hopefully into Division Two. That move, designed to remind everyone that I still existed, would be merely the prelude to another. A month or two later, as the March deadline loomed, I'd demand a transfer. In two seasons, I'd played in only 29 league games, appearing in three different positions – right back, left back and on the right side of midfield. I was the understudy, the player you only called on to fix something or whenever some minor emergency occurred.

The temperature dipped at St Andrew's. At the end of the

scrappy match, I pulled off my boots simply to count my toes. It was a miserable night. The cold . . . a hard, untrustworthy pitch . . . the empty, black stands . . . a defeat.

We heard the news on the radio.

The first team had won at Brighton, but the victory was a pyrrhic one. In the last ten minutes Sweets Wharton had taken the ball over to the corner flag, protecting our 2–1 lead. For his trouble, he'd got himself trodden on, breaking three bones in his right foot. I learnt later that his shin, even with pads on, looked as though someone had taken the skin off with a cheese grater.

That's why I found myself, on the last shopping Saturday before Christmas, facing Liverpool at Anfield. I was back on the right-hand side of midfield. This is the only thing you need to know about *that* Liverpool side in *that* particular season: they won the title.

The turning point for me came in the 78th minute. We were 3–0 down, striving to preserve our dignity and our goal difference.

You wouldn't need more than a couple of beads on an abacus to count the number of 50/50s that Graeme Souness lost in his whole career. Your bones jumped out of their sockets when he tackled you. So did your teeth. I don't know how I did it – probably with my eyes closed – but I took the ball from him on the halfway line after we both slid into one another. I looked up, surprised to find myself in possession rather than on the floor and in several pieces. Before Souness had a chance to recover, I swept a 30-yard pass that bisected Hansen and Lawrenson. Davie Collins plonked it past Grobbelaar. It was a token goal, but in the dressing room afterwards Frank Mallory made a show of calling me 'his boy' in front of everyone. Robbie Clayton cupped a hand to my ear and whispered: 'You're in, my friend.'

I was – and the third round of the Cup was only three weeks away.

If I had to define the 'magic' of the competition, I'd say it is its unpredictability. Get the wrong draw on the wrong pitch, or think of yourselves as invulnerable against lesser sides, and you'd be ridiculed after coming a cropper.

In the third round, we'd been drawn to play at non-league Enfield, one of those postage-stamp towns that people out-side London can't find on a map. We played in front of a full house at Woodside Park. At half-time, their team a goal up, the Enfield fans in the stand above our dressing room stamped their feet. We thought they were about to crash through the ceiling. Frank erupted. 'Listen to that? They think you're so feeble that you're pissing yourself in here. I haven't spent nearly 30 years in this profession to lose to a bunch of part-timers. I'm not going to be a cheap headline in tomorrow's papers. Rouse yourself or the lot of you aren't coming home with me. I don't want the embarrassment of being seen with you. You can all fuck off.' Within two minutes of the restart, Collins headed in the equaliser from a route-one ball that I thumped towards him on the cramped, cut-up pitch. Enfield folded and we beat them 4–1.

On the way home, our coach driver turned left rather than right at a junction and we got lost. We headed west, when we ought to have been going north. We passed within a mile of Wembley, the twin towers dominating the landscape. 'See that, Frank?' said Robbie. 'It's an omen.'

Soon we began to believe it.

Getting Enfield had felt as though the FA had taken a pin out of a grenade and tossed the thing into our laps. From then on, the draw was kinder. In the fourth round, we went to Molineux. Wolves were ailing, scrambling to stay up. We edged the tie with 10 minutes to go. We needed a replay, at home, to beat mid-table Manchester City 2–1 in the fifth round. Then a solitary goal saw us beat Leicester in the quarter-finals after we fluffed five or six other openings.

One of the tabloid newspapers cast Frank's horoscope, predicting he'd win the Cup. Frank threw the paper aside. 'So Mercury's in conjunction with Venus on the dark side of my arse. It's all crap.'

In those days, the draw was always made on a Monday lunchtime and broadcast on the radio. You'd hear the clack of wooden balls in a velvet bag, before the posh voice of some anonymous FA official put you out of your misery. I listened to it with Robbie. The opposition we didn't want was Spurs. Not with

Hoddle and Archibald and Crooks. Not with Clemence in goal. We got Queen's Park Rangers, then of the Second Division. 'I was joking when I told Frank that seeing Wembley that day was an omen . . . but I think there's something in it,' said Robbie.

After we beat QPR at Villa Park, scoring twice in the first half, Robbie sank to his knees and cried. He looked like a man in anguish. At 36, he'd be the oldest Cup finalist since Jack Charlton won the centenary Cup with Leeds ten years before. 'At last,' he kept saying. 'A Cup final. At my age. Fucking hell, fucking hell.' Frank celebrated eccentrically, diving fully clothed into the sunken bath and splashing about as if learning how to swim.

Seven weeks separated the semi-final and final. The football writers handed Robbie their Footballer of the Year award, a reward for his longevity and service as much as his achievements. Robbie's ecstatic reaction was encapsulated in one sentence: 'Bobby Moore once won this.'

Safely mid-table, we wallowed in the attention lavished on the finalists. Everybody wants something from you, and usually it's a ticket. There were autograph sheets to be signed, laborious interviews to be done and photographs to be posed for, functions to attend, decent money to be made from short-term sponsorships, public appearances and advertisements. The company supplying Robbie's boots designed a new pair for him with a distinctive orange cross on them. They asked him to wear the boots for the first time at Wembley. Initially reluctant, he agreed after the company's rep arrived with £3,500 in crisp banknotes, furtively handed over in a manila envelope. For a month, Robbie broke the boots in. I'd go to his home and find him running about in his back garden in them. Sometimes, he even wore the boots while watching TV.

You were the media's property before a Cup final. You'd be asked about your favourite meal or your favourite film. You'd be asked about your wife and what she'd be wearing on Cup final day, and whether or not you had a dog. The trivia mounted up, meaninglessly. In the week of the match, an exasperated reporter, having exhausted every angle, said to Robbie in desperation: 'What question haven't you been asked yet?' Robbie didn't know.

You were always thinking about the Cup, which is why we played like a pub team in the league. At one stage, we lost three matches in a row without scoring. We won just four out of 13 games. Fear of injury was partly to blame. Sweets Wharton was the only player not scared of missing out because someone in the opposition – either by accident or design – might slice into one of his limbs. What preoccupied Wharton was proving his fitness, which he did by mid-April. The place he claimed was mine. As a permanent substitute, I didn't play more than a quarter of an hour of any match after his belated return. No reporter wanted to know about the wife I hadn't got or the dog I didn't own. I became downcast. My father had to remind me that even being a substitute at Wembley would be an honour.

The club had last won the Cup at the end of the 1950s. My father didn't get close to appearing in that final, which is another reason why watching me play in one meant so much to him. The club had released him 12 months earlier. His departure came at the end of the season in which he and Frank got tangled up together at Burnden Park. He went to Second Division Lincoln, who picked him up for next to nothing. Nine of his former teammates went to Wembley. Still living in the city, he felt like an outsider during the build-up. 'I was a little boy with his nose pressed against the shop window,' he said.

The team stayed in Russell Square. My father visited them the night before the game to wish his friends good luck. The following afternoon he queued with his ticket at the turnstiles like an ordinary fan and found a space near the halfway line, opposite the Royal Box.

'It won't matter if you only get the number 12 shirt,' he told me. 'You'll be a part of things. I never was.'

When the season finished, we were 17th. Spurs were fourth, qualifiers for Europe. It was their highest league placing for a decade. The league table wasn't the only evidence pointing to what everybody believed would be our certain defeat. We'd eked out a draw with them in early October. In late February, we'd been hammered 5–1 at White Hart Lane. Hoddle's mastery of the ball had been imperious. We should have all stood in the mouth of the tunnel and applauded him off. Also, Spurs had already been to Wembley that season, losing to Liverpool in the League Cup.

On the Saturday before Wembley, our hearts and minds elsewhere, we lost 4–1 at Everton. Our odds of winning the Cup were longer than that scoreline: we were 5–1 in a two-horse race. Ned Kelly, who could have claimed squatter's rights in his local bookmaker's, persuaded us all to chip in. 'We'll put a bag of sand on that,' he said. I didn't understand bookmakers' slang. 'A grand,' he said. 'It'll be beer money after we win.'

My father was friendly with Danny Blanchflower. He knew Blanchflower well enough to chat with him on the phone every few months and exchange Christmas cards. He owned a signed copy of Blanchflower's autobiography *The Double and Before*, which told of how Spurs won both the league and the Cup in 1961.

It was ironic that Blanchflower, writing for the *Sunday Express*, was in the press box during our final. It was also ironic that we were facing his team. It was more ironic still that Spurs were striving to imitate the success Blanchflower had brought them 20 years earlier by claiming the Cup in successive years, a feat that had eluded every side since then. 'I have to say that your boy's lot have got no chance,' Blanchflower told my father. 'I don't see any way they can win it – or even come close to winning it. Spurs are too good.'

12

YOU'RE NOT SUPPOSED TO recall much about a Cup final. The day is reckoned to be the shortest of your life, the crowded hours condensed into what most players describe as a 'few hurried seconds', an incredible speeding-up of time that defies explanation. The build-up, the game itself, the presentations and your lap of honour? They're all said to pass in a few rapid blinks. Afterwards, what's left in your head is nothing but a handful of loose, random images – most as still as photographs – that you constantly shuffle about, trying to patch together a linear story from them.

It wasn't so for me. I can tell you everything about the Cup final I played in. I can see it with a depth of colour that is effulgent.

Most struggle to remember. I struggle to forget. My memory, though not strictly eidetic, is fairly extraordinary. I take it for granted. I watch managers produce a pocket notebook and a ballpoint pen during a match. I see them scribbling down observations and drawing the odd stick diagram, afraid that whatever thought has struck them will soon evaporate, like a message on a misted-up window. I never have to write anything down to summon it back. I can recall inconsequential details and sharpen

them into specificity. Once people realise this isn't a party trick –
I don't need mnemonic devices – I seldom get contradicted. My
version of events tends to stick, the veracity of it unchallenged.

On Thursday, we went to Hendon Hall, a Palladian villa set
in grounds so huge that you could have got lost in them. Frank
Mallory, despite his nationality, chose it as our base because
England had stayed there before the 1966 World Cup final. It
was only five and a half miles from the hotel's vast portico, held
up by four rusticated Corinthian pillars, to Wembley.

On the eve of the game, after some light jogging and an
improbable game of cricket on the lawns, off we trooped to the
stadium to inspect the pitch and decide where to park ourselves
in the dressing room. We were merely following tradition. We
had an hour and a half until Spurs arrived to do the same thing.
Protocol demanded that, like bride and bridegroom, we didn't
meet before our big day.

Only five years before, my father had taken me to my first
Cup final, the game in which Manchester United, beaten the year
before, denied Liverpool the treble of championship, European
Cup and League Cup. We took the Tube to Wembley, our car-
riage full of Liverpudlians carrying cardboard cut-outs of the
Cup coated in silver foil. We arrived at the same time as United.
Tommy Docherty waved at me from his seat, thinking I was a
United supporter. So many fans spilt onto the road that the wheels
of the coach could only move in half-turns before stopping again.

My father and I hurried on, bustling past the hawkers selling commemorative souvenirs, and zigzagged around people who had already drunk too much and would probably remember only half the match. After a long wait, we got through the turnstiles and up the steps, which I took two at a time. I stood in deep shadow and stared across the bare pitch, so vividly green that it stung my eyes.

As a player, it was different.

Large, castle-like doors, with a smaller door within them, took you to the top of the tunnel, which was as dark as a bunker. I saw ahead only a flash of green and a slither of sky. The pitch seemed a long, long way off, like another country. I ignored the dressing room – as we all did – and headed along the tunnel, which sloped upwards. The heels of my shoes made a scraping noise against the concrete. I came out of the semi-blackness into a fantastic burst of bright light. I thought: *This is how a baby must feel when it's born.*

The turf was very spongy. I felt as though I could bounce on it the way astronauts bounced across the moon. Sweets Wharton stood on the centre spot and shouted 'Hello, Wembley' simply to hear his voice echo around the empty stands. Most of us said nothing for a while. I leant against one of the goalposts. Sean Ramsey rested against the other, leaping up to twang the bar occasionally.

'You won't hear yourself think in here tomorrow. We might not even hear ourselves scream,' he said.

'That'll help, won't it?' I asked. 'Won't it shock us, like freezing water, and then we'll just get used to it? You nervous?'

'Of course I'm fucking nervous. When you're a goalkeeper, everyone says one thing to you: "Don't be another Dan Lewis. You'll never live down that kind of mistake. You'll carry it with you, like a scar or a birthmark on your face." I'm not going to be another Dan Lewis. No fucking way.'

Ramsey and I walked in silence to the centre circle, where Frank Mallory stood. He lit a cigarette and flicked stubs of ash on the pitch. A yard away, Robbie Clayton glared at him disapprovingly, as if the act were akin to spitting in church. 'It's just strips of turf, Robbie,' said Frank.

He took another puff and told us to gather around him. Jimmy Bradley had taken a ball out. He and Alec Taylor passed the thing between them, marvelling at the way it skimmed smoothly off the surface. Davie Collins, the last to arrive, said: 'I thought about pissing in all four corners. It's supposed to bring you luck.' Frank just ignored him. 'You've been playing on shitholes for the past three months,' he told us. 'Tomorrow you'll be in paradise and you'll want everything to be perfect. It won't be – and don't try to force it. You'll be thinking of your family sitting up there.' He pointed to the seats to the right of the Royal Box, the cigarette still burning between his fingers. 'Give a wave and then forget them. You'll want to be all fancy because it's a fancy day. Don't do that either. If you're defending, lump it into row R if necessary. If you're up front and you have the chance to shoot, then do it. I know it doesn't look like it, but the goals are the same size as everywhere else, and so is the penalty box. Don't let the scale of the stadium make you feel small or insignificant. One last thing for now – and you'll have to trust me on this: when the game starts, you'll forget all about where you are.'

In hindsight, I appreciated how perfectly Frank had judged the mood and the match. He knew what we needed. He put us in a frame of mind to fight like billy-o, but to do it calmly and calculatedly, and with a confidence outsiders presumed we'd lack against a cultivated team such as Spurs. He was never the kind of manager to lecture you about other players. He didn't dwell on what damage the opposition could inflict. His view – a sensible one – was that we had to prepare mentally. If we did, everything else would dovetail.

Playing in a Cup final is a lot to take in, which is why Frank gave only informal team talks prior to kick off. What's more, he did so in instalments. Ten days beforehand, he asked Kenny O'Connor to speak to us. Kenny, a left half, had been a member of the team that had triumphed in the 1950s. He brought his medal with him, allowing each of us to hold it. 'Here,' Kenny seemed to be saying, 'is what could be yours.' He was a stocky man with a beaky nose, rough hands and a rougher voice. It sounded like gravel being tipped out of a plastic sack. He told us that his bonus for lifting the Cup had been £5; that a local butcher had fed the team on free steak between the semi-final and the final; that his Cup final suit still hung in his wardrobe (it didn't fit); and that he knew of at least five players who had used the Cup as a silver chamber pot ('and not always to piss in', he said).

At the end, Frank didn't have to say anything more to us than 'You don't want a losers' medal, do you?'

The night before the game, we went to the cinema. Uncle Charlie Bembridge had reserved the whole place for us. Somehow, he'd got hold of a film that wasn't due for release for another month: *Rocky III*. Even those of us slow on the uptake understood the symbolism in that.

We got back to the hotel at 10 p.m., expecting lights out half an hour later. Instead, Jonjo Whelan told us that Frank wanted to see all of us in the bar. We found glasses of beer and wine and tots of whisky and brandy waiting for us on a long trestle table. 'No one goes to bed,' said Frank, 'until each of you has had at least two of these. Take your pick. Jonjo and me are going to watch you drink them too. No slacking. No complaints. Get them down your neck.'

I thought it was a leg-pull or a piece of elaborate psychology, the meaning of which escaped me. So did Robbie. 'You're not serious? You want us to knock back that lot?'

'It's an order,' said Frank, very sharply.

'But, Frank,' he persisted, 'I have a routine. A way of doing things. I don't drink the night before a match.'

'You do now.'

'Why?'

'Because it'll get you to sleep. You'll float up those stairs, through your door and flop into bed, straight into fucking dreamland. You won't be lying awake, staring into the darkness and thinking about nothing but the final. You'll feel a lot better, and less stressed, in the morning. I bet Spurs aren't doing this. They'll be tucked up between the sheets – thinking of you, thinking of Wembley, thinking of the ways you might beat them. They'll be worrying about it too. Herbert Chapman, a fucking legend, used to let his players have a glass of sherry before a match. I'm giving you the run of the whole bar.'

Frank signalled to a waiter, who was dressed in a scarlet jacket and a pair of black trousers. He looked like a tin soldier. He began picking up the drinks from the table and putting them on a silver tray. Robbie shook his head.

Frank said: 'You'll all have heard about Arthur Ashe, the tennis player? The night before his Wimbledon final against Jimmy Connors – the final no one thought he could win – Ashe went to the Playboy Club and stayed there. He didn't want to be stuck in the silence of his room. He didn't want to pace the floor until dawn. So he ate. So he drank a bit. So he played the tables. Ashe was 31. Connors was 22, supposedly unbeatable. Well, Ashe beat him. That upset, one of the greatest in tennis history, began in the Playboy Club at 3 a.m. For the next hour, boys, this room is our Playboy Club. Get drinking.'

Robbie was still protesting when Frank, his temper a little ragged by now, picked up a glass of red wine and forced it on him. 'Take a sip. Then take another sip. Keep going until there's nothing left,' he said. 'There's another one of those to follow.' Robbie did take a sip, though rather tentatively, like someone offered a cup of hemlock. 'You're supposed to drink it, not lick it,' said Frank.

I went for brandy. The first went down easily and warmly. The second was a double. The neurons in my brain began to dance. A wonderful sense of well-being, a kind of conquer-all assurance, washed over me. I didn't even consider how I'd feel when I heard the morning papers being slid under the door.

When I went upstairs, Robbie was already in the bathroom. He was shoving two fingers down his throat to make himself sick. The sink, over which he was retching, looked as if someone had cut their throat in it. The floor, too, had thick spots of regurgitated red wine on it.

'I'll be fine now,' he said, wiping his mouth.

13

IN HIS BOOK, DANNY Blanchflower writes about waking up on Cup final morning. He says that at first he 'heard a door slam somewhere'. What I heard, from beneath a stack of bed-clothes, was Robbie Clayton. Robbie was ironing his kit, which he'd been downstairs to fish out of the hamper. He stood there in his underwear and those boots with the orange crosses. I blinked twice, making sure that the brandy from the night before hadn't been spiked with something hallucinogenic.

It was 7.30 a.m.

Robbie said to me, as though proud of it, 'I haven't slept for the last three hours. I've been going through the match in my head.' His eyes were sore-looking and reddish. They darted everywhere. After he finished his ironing, he began pulling things out of his case and putting them back in again. He brushed down his battleship-grey suit, which the club had paid for. He walked around the room. He put on the TV and then switched it off. He did the same to the radio, cutting off mid-sentence a story about warships, aircraft and the Falkland Islands. The papers arrived. He couldn't bring himself to look at them. He put more polish on his new boots, which didn't need it, and shined them obsessively. 'These are moulded to my feet now,' he said, holding them up for inspection. 'They're like slippers.' He had the look of someone possessed.

By now, it was 8.15 a.m.

If the final were to kick off in half an hour, Robbie would have been ready for it. The fact it was still six and three-quarter hours away troubled me. If I'd been older, wiser and much more self-assured, I'd have recognised the signs of anxiety. I'd have forced him to sit down, drink some tea and compose himself. But I didn't feel as though I had the authority to suggest such things. Not to him.

When he announced, 'I'm going for a run around the hotel grounds,' I was relieved. His fidgeting, his pacing, his inability to stay still was annoying me. I wanted to be alone, contemplating everything in silence. I held the door open for him. Robbie pulled on his tracksuit and laced up a pair of white trainers. 'See you at breakfast,' was all he said.

It was 8.30 a.m.

I wanted a Cup winner's medal like Kenny O'Connor's. I also wanted to earn it. Earning it meant playing, for at least 15 minutes, instead of sitting behind Frank Mallory and Jonjo Whelan on those red leather benches. You don't want anyone to get injured. Nor do you want to come on because your team's hopes are disappearing down a sinkhole. But swirling around in my head was some kind of cruel black fantasy: that one of our team would pull or break something very early on; that I'd be warming up before my arse got numb; that, after a rusty few minutes, I'd be King for a day. I felt guilty about that; it was almost as bad as wishing someone dead so you could inherit something from them. I just couldn't help it.

The BBC's coverage began at 9 a.m. On the screen was an aerial shot of Wembley, taken from a helicopter. I counted the stripes on the pitch. The picture cut to some recorded film of supporters' coaches setting off shortly after dawn. They were full of crates of beer. Many of the bottles were already open. A row of talking heads – Jimmy Hill, Bob Wilson, Bobby Charlton – discussed the possible outcome of the match. Only Charlton gave us the faintest glimmer of a chance. He pointed out, very pertinently, that he'd backed Sunderland to beat Leeds in 1973. His prediction had been scoffed at, considered preposterous, until Sunderland actually did beat them. I thought of Arthur Ashe and Jimmy Connors.

It was 9.30 a.m.

At breakfast, which was nothing more than tea and toast, I couldn't find Robbie, and no one else had seen him. Afterwards, I walked around the front lawn of the hotel. Jimmy Bradley had gone to look for a Catholic church and a priest to take his confession. John Slater and Stuart Kelly intended to wander off down the high street to buy themselves a shirt each. Just for something to do, I decided to go with them. On the way out we passed Frank, who was sitting beside Jonjo. He was smoking, of course. 'Don't be late,' he said.

We were on the bottom step of the hotel entrance when we saw Robbie. His head was thrown back, his mouth gaped open. He wasn't able to put any weight on his left foot. Two men we didn't recognise were giving him a fireman's lift across the lawn. They were Americans on a business trip. Knowing nothing about football, they didn't recognise Robbie and weren't aware of the significance of what had just happened to him.

'Fuck me, fuck me,' was all Bradley could say.

'We found your friend when we went for a run,' said one of the men. 'His foot slid into a hole or something. His ankle is smashed up pretty bad, I think.'

Robbie was in too much pain to speak to us.

We followed the sad party into the lobby. Frank, looking up, dropped his burning cigarette into his lap. The men laid Robbie on a sofa and placed a cushion behind his head. We had a physiotherapist known as 'Dr Ice'. His first response to any injury was nearly always to call for ice and a towel in which to pack it. When he saw Robbie, he rang for an ambulance.

None of us knew what to say. All we could offer Robbie were platitudes and condolences. 'I'm sorry. The ankle's broken. I heard the crack. I'm fucked,' he eventually said to Frank, flinching through both his explanation and his apology. Frank said nothing meaningful in response. He turned to Jonjo: 'Wait with him until the ambulance comes. Let the physio go to the hospital. I've got work to do.' Frank turned away, abandoning his captain.

I'd like to say that I displayed some chivalry and knightly honour. That I was different, less obviously callous. That the pull of friendship and old dependencies persuaded me to stay with Robbie.

But I can't.

It was 10.10 a.m.

14

THIS IS WHAT I remember about the five hours that followed.

How Uncle Charlie Bembridge got dressed up, in a jacket of brilliant red, as though he was about to tell jokes in a holiday camp. How phlegmatically Frank Mallory gave the thumbs-up to the crowds from his front seat on the coach, as if bestowing his approval on them. How nonchalantly we walked around Wembley, hands stuffed in the pockets of our club suits. How we sniffed the air and checked the position of the sun and the direction of the wind. How I waved to my father, who waved back like someone signalling at a distant ship. How, since everything else had already been said, Frank spoke so briefly and so quietly. 'This is a day you're going to remember as long as there's breath in your lungs. Make everything you can of it. Not for me. Not for the club. For yourself.'

How the loudness of the dressing room buzzer was startling, telling us we had ten minutes before we had to go into the tunnel. How only then I put my shirt on and combed my hair. How, as we waited to walk onto the pitch, I looked down the line of Spurs players and saw the black number 10 on Glenn Hoddle's slender back. How, coming out into the mid-afternoon glare, I did something I'd never done before: I threw the ball up and began to head it.

It was warm and sultry. The cloud, a lot of it mottled grey, hung above the twin towers, low enough that I thought it might drop further and obscure them. Standing beside the red carpet, the national anthem blaring away, I felt fantastically calm. 'You're right back,' Frank had said at our team meeting, adding none of the frills other managers would have tacked on to that curt statement, such as 'Don't worry. I know you'll do a job for me.' I couldn't put my thanks into words. I would have played in goal for him.

Frank shifted Nat Carson to centre half and rejigged the midfield. It didn't seem to bother him. He barely alluded to Robbie Clayton and his injury; it was as though the circumstances of redrawing the side didn't matter to him. Robbie now existed only in the past for Frank.

Before I made my league debut, it was Robbie who had warned me: 'You're used to playing in front of a few hundred people. A few thousand, if you're lucky. Out there, what'll hit you first is the noise. It'll knock you on your arse. It'll take you a quarter of an hour to get used to it.' It had. Since then I'd played at Anfield and Old Trafford, but I'd experienced nothing like the noise at Wembley as we kicked off. It made my chest heave; I gulped for breath. On big occasions, though, the size of the stage makes you feel like a somebody. You know you're alive, and you also know you're relevant and important.

That's what playing in a Cup final is like.

15

NOTHING WAS EXPECTED OF US.

If we were beaten, so be it. We just didn't want to lose so badly, like some Sunday league Raggedy Arse Rovers, that it would embarrass us forever. So we were going to do what we always did: we'd be a sponge, soaking up Spurs' attacks and hitting them on the break when possible, grabbing what we could like thieves. We knew they would try to sledgehammer us into submission from the start. Any numbskull was aware of that. They'd aim to score early and then draw us out, taking advantage of the gaps that any adventure to seek an equaliser would create. Then they'd score again. In that scenario, the second half would be irrelevant.

Their plan went awry from the start. With only the third touch of the match, Micky Hazard misplaced his pass, slightly under-hitting it. Arend van het Hoff intercepted the ball, with ten yards of turf to call his own. If van het Hoff had been able to freeze the scene at that moment, he'd have realised how much time and territory belonged to him. I was so far back that I couldn't get forward in support. Alone, every red shirt behind him, he made the rashest of choices. You had to be a fool to think you'd beat Ray Clemence from long distance. Your shot would have to curve exactly beneath the angle of post and bar. Van het Hoff tried anyway. He spooned the effort six feet over; Clemence watched it whistle over his head.

We had a second chance after 15 minutes and a third shortly afterwards, jarring Spurs again.

In Robbie's absence, Davie Collins had been made captain. He was the worst possible choice. Collins never stopped yapping. He also never stopped hogging the ball. When I got my first touch, just inside Spurs' half, I chipped a pass over Paul Price. The ball fell into the gap Collins was running into. He kept on running, his arms moving like small pistons. Past Hazard, tracking back. Past Steve Perryman, who was surprised by how quickly and how far Collins' momentum had taken him. He could have gone on further. Instead, like van het Hoff, he had a Niagara Falls-like rush of blood to the head. He drove a hard, skiddy shot that evaded Clemence's dive but kissed the outside of the post.

Our next opening came from our first corner. Again, it fell to Collins. Jostling in a congested box, he wrestled himself free of Graham Roberts and took two steps back. For half a second, as the ball came into the box, I was convinced he'd score. I drew in a huge lungful of air, ready to acclaim the goal. But he dipped too early, pushing the header wide, when the centre of the target was easier to find. Clemence berated his defence with a lot of arm-waving. Glenn Hoddle began to clap and I heard him give a plaintive plea of 'Let's get in this game.' Knowing he ought to have scored, and perhaps thinking he could muddy that fact, Collins bullishly shouted: 'We've got them now.'

If only . . .

It's a moot point whether we became too cocky or Spurs shook themselves awake. A little of both, I suppose, but for the next half-hour we were corralled inside our own half. If we'd have been pushed any deeper, we'd have found ourselves back in the lobby of our hotel.

I wasn't quick enough to play at right back. Not against a left winger such as Tony Galvin, who was fast enough to have run in the greyhound derby and possibly to have won it. Galvin had begun his footballing life in non-league – a mystery when you consider what he could do with the ball and a minimum of space. A year before, when Spurs had beaten Manchester City in a replay at Wembley, we'd all gone into raptures about the corkscrew run Ricky Villa made inside the box, whipping the ball this way and that and bamboozling the City defenders before scoring. The goal was so astonishing we overlooked the assist that started it. Galvin had picked up possession midway in his own half and taken the ball midway into City's, showing the sort of speed that suggested he'd been drinking rocket fuel by the litre. Without him, there'd have been no goal for Villa and no win for Spurs. I was afraid of Galvin. Even if he wore pit boots, I knew he'd outpace me. I had to drop back an extra yard.

My first mistake: I missed a tackle on him.

In training, you work constantly on one-against-ones. You're told to wait, wait and wait again, before committing yourself and making a challenge. Go in too early and you risk opening up a swathe of the pitch. I went too early. Galvin broke down the channel, stretching us, and I let him escape. I gave pursuit, as pointlessly as a man chasing his hat in a gale. Galvin looked up and knocked the ball over. Garth Crooks met it cleanly on the volley, the ball making a crisp sound as it flew off his boot. Sean Ramsey, who had so far only touched the ball when we passed it back to him, made one of those Jim Montgomery-like stretching saves with his fingertips, twisting his body upwards to get to it. Crooks was aghast. So were the rest of us.

We were reeling from that punch when another hit us. On the turn – he'd got in front of Nat Carson – Steve Archibald struck a shot from the penalty spot. I waited for the roof of the net to bulge, but the ball's trajectory changed half a yard before it reached the line. It rose suddenly, grazing the top edge of the bar.

Then came my second mistake: I missed Galvin again.

He hurdled over my attempt to rob him near the touchline. This time, choosing to go it alone, he shot from an acute angle, but Ramsey blocked easily with his feet. We were defending the tunnel end, which meant I was patrolling the touchline where Frank Mallory was sitting. It was just as well that the crowd noise drowned out his criticism of me. I couldn't hear what the TV allowed me to lip-read when the highlights were televised: he was telling me to 'get a fucking grip'.

By now we were throwing ourselves at everything, chasing everything too, and just about clinging on. One spectacular block followed another. I took a free kick from Hoddle full on the chest; I'm surprised it didn't stop my heart.

Danny Blanchflower believed everyone was 'brain-washed' about Cup final day. He was a little sour about 'the majestic twin towers . . . the majestic green turf . . . the royal greeting . . . the crowd singing "Abide with Me"'. He likened the whole thing to 'some distant religious ceremony'. Blanchflower thought that the crowd was too far from the pitch to 'breathe fire into the game'. He also thought it contained too many people who 'do not care enough about the result', because 'too many of them' weren't passionate, prejudiced supporters of the two clubs. He insisted the final was 'more of a social occasion, a showpiece, a soccer match in tails'.

Blanchflower was wrong.

You're rarely conscious of your surroundings when a game starts. You're in what sportsmen call the Zone, that state of grace in which nothing disturbs your concentration or intense focus. You're *in* the moment completely. I've never been hypnotised, but I guess the Zone is like that. You do everything without being conscious of it. What snapped me out of the Zone, late in the first half, was a thump Davie Collins took on his back. He rolled over, clutching the base of his spine. He needed treatment for a few minutes, breaking the ebb and flow of a match in which we were being battered. I stood very still and looked around me. At the scoreboard. At the manicured acres of pitch. At the crowd. At the Royal Box. The stands at the old Wembley formed the sweep of a perfect oval. That shape, coupled with their height, appeared to shrink the sky into a small pocket of cloud. You could fool yourself into believing that nothing existed beyond the stadium. *This is surely what playing in heaven must be like*, I thought. I wanted it to go on forever. I also, paradoxically, wanted to take refuge in the dressing room before Spurs, always on the edge of taking the lead, broke through and did the kind of damage we couldn't possibly repair.

16

AT HALF-TIME, FRANK MALLORY refused to dwell on our disarray. I was expecting him to go off on one of his infamous rants. On those occasions, you'd get a display of performance anger. Frank's body would change, as if something venomous were running through it. You'd hear his teeth grind. You'd see the veins in his neck thicken, like ridges in a landscape. But, as he'd done before kick-off, Frank spoke with surprising meekness, instructing rather than ordering us. 'Don't think you're beaten. In case you've forgotten, or haven't noticed, it's still o–o,' he said.

'Just keep the ball,' he went on. 'Use the width of the pitch. Have an awareness of space. Quicken the play. Sometimes we've been a bit slow. Operate as though you've got wing mirrors – know who's behind you – rather than like a race horse with the blinkers on. Frustrate them for as long as you can – and then we'll strike. Honestly, we'll strike.'

We were just about to go back out when Frank said the most inspirational thing of all.

'At half-time, as we come off, I always look into the eyes of the opposition's best player. I can tell from those eyes what he's thinking, how the match is going. I looked into Glenn Hoddle's eyes. He's worried. He's worried that all their pressure hasn't brought them a goal. He thinks we might nick it. Know what? *I* think we're going to nick it. When you get back into this dressing room, you're going to be bringing the Cup with you.'

I knew what Frank had said was a lie. I'd followed Hoddle off the pitch. Frank had been nowhere near him. The psychological effect of his words nonetheless sent us sprinting out of the tunnel.

I felt sorry for the armchair watcher. Grit came before glory or purity of purpose. The second half, like most of the first, was about Spurs' advances and our retreats. The strangest thing occurred, however: for all their possession, Spurs didn't manufacture much in the way of openings; nothing substantial came from them to suggest our imminent doom. In fact, Sean Ramsey didn't have to make a save at all until an hour had gone, when Garth Crooks tried to lob him. Ramsey went back on his line, tipping the ball safely over with a single finger. Much to my relief, Spurs stopped using the flanks, preferring to plough a furrow down the centre with Crooks and Archibald.

In the weirdest way, it helped that Nat Carson was wearing Robbie Clayton's shirt. Robbie had a habit of wanting to be like

Beckenbauer. He'd take a roll-out from Ramsey and dally with it, as though promenading a bit. Frank always said that 'the best players only do things once – that's one touch and *boom*'. Carson was like that. He got rid of the ball speedily and accurately, giving us a respite from the pressure. We had time to compose ourselves and regroup before Spurs came back at us.

The match went into a dreary limbo. I began to think about the possibility of extra time and even a replay.

I hadn't noticed – since I was back in the Zone – that the clouds had turned black, blotting out the sun. A heavy shower began. We were an 'old' group of players. Four of us were over 30; three others were in their late 20s. The average age of the team was nearly 29 and a half, older even than the Southampton 'Dad's Army' side that had beaten Manchester United to win the Cup in 1976. When that statistic got pointed out and then picked over during the week of the final, Frank was criticised either for being too sentimental, clinging on devotedly to those he trusted, or for being out of step with the modern game. You'd have thought we were pensioners, wheeling ourselves about in bath chairs. Spurs' average age, 27, was seen as being just about right. The rain freshened up the pitch and our 'old' legs too. We began to pass the ball and hold it, making Spurs play fetch. They became a bit snippy about that. They also felt, I think, that every decision was going against them. A shout for a penalty turned down. A free kick in the 'D' not given. A free kick awarded to us. With twenty minutes to go, I thought: *We've been the more effective side in this half. We can do it.*

A minute later, as if to slap me down for boasting, we had our Great Escape. Crooks, just inside our box, belted a shot so thunderously that I saw the ball only as a blur. It bounced off the underside of the bar and came out again. The ricochet hit Alec Taylor on the back. It would have gone in – the cruellest of own goals – if Ramsey hadn't leapt a yard and a half to his left and pawed it away. Another Montgomery-like miracle.

There were five minutes to go.

If you'd forced a confession out of every player on that field, I'm sure each of us would have conceded that we were resigned to another half an hour. Sweat rather than skill, endurance instead of flair were going to determine who won. We'd slog our way through it.

Thanks to Robbie – his belief that the past teaches us about the future – I knew all about late goals that had won the Cup. I could recite most of them: Mutch for Preston in the 119th minute. Perry for Blackpool in the 92nd. Griffin for West Brom in the 87th. Boyce for West Ham in the 90th. Sunderland for Arsenal in the 89th.

My goal was a beautiful accident – a moment that chance chose to be mine. When we won a corner, I wasn't even tempted to hang back. Instinct told me to stand where I did, shoving me onto the right spot. Why do some things always feel as though they were waiting to happen? Afterwards, you say it was meant to be. I was where I shouldn't have been, but somehow I knew the ball would find me there. On the left-hand side of the box, waiting for it, I felt unnaturally confident. If I'd turned around, I'd have seen Frank pointing and telling me to go 10 yards deeper and another 10 yards squarer, in case Spurs broke away and Galvin skinned me.

Over came the corner, flighted in by Jimmy Bradley. I saw the ball spinning against the great bank of the crowd. Up went half a dozen heads. There was a scramble. Spurs tried to clear the danger but couldn't. We stabbed at the ball, constantly blocked by a line of bodies in white shirts. Then a Stuart Kelly mishit, aimed towards the bottom corner, struck Davie Collins on the knee. The ball came towards me, the pace of it slowing as I moved to meet it. I knew where to hit the shot. I imagined it going in even before I put my laces through it. The gap between the post and the nearest defender wasn't much wider than the circumference of the ball. Oh, it flew off my left boot – hard, true and perfectly straight. The ball billowed the net before Clemence, who was unsighted, could scramble across to stop it.

The noise was like a detonation. I ran towards the corner flag and then dropped backwards onto the turf, spreading my arms like someone landing on a feather bed. The sky was blue again, flat and beautiful. Everyone piled on top of me.

When I got up, I saw Frank, dancing on the touchline, and the

Spurs players, dragging themselves upfield for the kick-off. I tried to look for my father, but everyone in the crowd was standing up and I couldn't find him. I bowed, hoping he'd noticed the gesture meant for him.

The game lasted another eight minutes. It was like living through an entire year. Time plodded on – one second forward and two back. Or so it seemed.

In 1970, when Leeds scored what ought to have been the winner against Chelsea, Don Revie was so far away from the pitch that he couldn't make himself heard. His instructions to his team were lost in the hubbub. Frank couldn't make himself heard either. 'Possession,' he kept shouting, aimlessly.

I had to force myself to concentrate. I'd started to think about the presentation, collecting my medal, lapping the pitch. I was thinking, too, about collecting the newspapers next morning, my face all over them. I knew that, if we held on, the Thom Callaghan of tomorrow would be seen and treated differently from the Thom Callaghan of today.

I kept looking at the referee. 'Blow the fucking whistle,' I said to myself.

Spurs poured forward, not caring now about protecting Clemence. We had a chance to make it 2–0, a smash-and grab breakaway. Collins steamed down the middle, expecting me to push a pass through to him. But my goal had taken everything out of me. I was breathing hard. My legs felt like two bags of sand.

I hit the ball over him (I don't think Collins has ever forgiven me for that) and watched it hop out of play.

That was the game's last kick.

I fell to the floor. Frank sprinted across the pitch towards me, the tails of his jacket flapping behind him. He dragged me up by the arms. He was crying, a happy haze of tears.

Nat Carson swapped shirts with Hoddle, a hero of his. When he went up for his winner's medal, one of the FA 'blazers' turned him away, thinking he was a Spurs player. I took my shirt off and tied it around my neck, but Frank told me to put it back on. Collins, once he'd been handed the Cup, wouldn't give it to anyone else for a while. He kept kissing and hugging it.

The Milk Marketing Board, paying for exposure, made sure there was milk waiting for us. When you walked into the tunnel, you were handed a pint in a glass bottle. You were supposed to hold the bottle while you were being interviewed on TV. I didn't even drink milk. I held the thing without even breaking the top. I was asked to describe my goal. There's a *Monty Python* sketch in which John Cleese plays the stereotypically stupid footballer, unable to speak in anything but the shortest of clichéd sentences. Asked about one of his goals, he essentially grunts: 'I hit it and it went in.' I sounded like Cleese's character, unable to say anything coherent.

All of us own an 'hour' of something. That day was my hour. I looked at my reflection in the Cup. I took my medal out of its box and held it aloft, the way Stanley Matthews had done in 1953. I was given a Golden Boot, encased in a wooden frame. I was so busy being the hero that I forgot one thing. It was only when Frank announced that he wanted the team to go to the hospital, taking the Cup with us, that I remembered why I'd been picked to start in the first place and the blow history had landed on my best friend.

I'd forgotten all about Robbie.

I 7

NEXT MORNING, THE NEWSPAPERS used a three-column photograph of us all gathered around Robbie Clayton's bedside. Robbie held one handle of the Cup. Beth held the other. Robbie was either smiling weakly or grimacing; I couldn't decide which.

We stayed for an hour, milling around and trying to find enough chairs to sit on and also somewhere to put the Cup when no one wanted to hold it. We cleared the top of Robbie's bedside table, placing it there. Someone pulled off the lid and stuck two bunches of daffodils into the trophy without arranging them. The room was white-walled and private. A single wide window overlooked a courtyard with flowers and wooden benches. Nurses, doctors and even some patients, who weren't supposed to be there, came in to claim autographs and take photographs, and to tell us that everyone on the wards had watched the match. Robbie's TV, suspended from a bracket on the wall, had been switched off. Propped up on a throne of five pillows, he lay quietly, hardly moving and staring into nothingness. He was groggy, glassy-eyed and very pale. Whether this was from the anaesthetic, the pain-killing medication or just the confusing trauma of the day, I can't say.

His hair was a tangle. His gown was crumpled. He didn't want us to see him like that. Everything was very awkward, and our clumsy, fumbling attempts to make things less so only made them worse. We were jubilant, but also aware that we had to tone down our celebrations out of respect for him. We tried to find a rigmarole of words to convey that and acknowledge how he felt. It was a bad situation for us but a tragedy for him.

He wouldn't be part of our celebration dinner or the home-coming parade on Sunday, the city coming to a standstill as everyone swept into the Market Square. The best thing we could do for Robbie was to leave him alone, but of course we knew – and so did he – that protocol demanded we turn up and put on a show. But I noticed how most of us – even Frank Mallory – avoided making eye contact with him because that would have meant finding something to say too.

'You scored the goal,' he said to me. 'Well done.'

'Thanks. I don't know how it happened.'

That was it. What other words could I have offered? 'How are you feeling?' 'Sorry you missed out on the greatest moment of your life'? 'How will you ever recover?' 'How can things ever be the same again?'

No. In that hospital, on that day, silence was the medicine Robbie most needed.

One small moment summed up his misery for me. Jimmy Bradley shoved his medal into Robbie's hands, thinking he would want to look at it. Robbie opened the lid of the box, closed it again and passed it back to Bradley, while turning wordlessly towards someone else. I thought he was about to weep. Beth put her hand across his forehead and then ran it through his hair.

I was relieved when we left. It was an escape from an ordeal that had been too much for all of us. I also think Robbie was glad when we retreated, leaving him in private. He wanted to be alone. He no longer had to pretend to be pleased for us. He could cry out all the sorrow he felt without any spectators.

We stood at the door and waved goodbye. We were desperate to get out of the hospital. Beth came up, kissed me on the cheek and promised to come to the banquet. I promised to dance with her, which I had no intention of doing.

I never dance.

18

ALL WE WANTED WAS alcohol, but we had to stay sober until eleven o'clock. *Match of the Day* wanted to interview us live. Only after the cameras were switched off and packed away did we begin to drink seriously.

The two Kellys went off into the West End with Sean Ramsey, who spent the early hours on a stranger's sofa. Sweets Wharton took out his guitar and wailed whatever came into his head. Davie Collins tried to piss into the Cup. Nat Carson walked into a door, cutting his cheek and bruising his forehead. Jimmy Bradley fell asleep on the floor outside his bedroom door. Frank Mallory and Jonjo Whelan bought a 30-year-old bottle of malt whisky and shared it between them, reminiscing about the old days. They drank it as though it was tap water.

I was so woozy that the hotel's staircase seemed to twist and double back on itself, like something Escher had designed,

I woke at 9 a.m.

Beth was in bed beside me. She was wearing nothing but my Cup final shirt.

PART TWO
HERE COMES THE HERO

I

I'M ALWAYS ASKED TWO things about Frank Mallory. The first is: 'What was he really like?' The second is: 'Did you like him?'

It's impossible to answer the first question in less than an hour. As for the second, I developed a pathetically flippant response to it. 'Everyone has a soft spot for Frank,' I'd say. 'You're forever looking for his approval, wanting to please him.' I would smile those sentences out, trying to camouflage the omissions in them.

I'd always tell a handful of stories about him, each one illustrating the unfathomable complexities of the man.

'He was capable of extraordinary acts of persuasion,' I'd say. Indeed, the most exceptional of these saved a stranger's life.

It was almost midday. With training over, Frank was returning to the ground. From the towpath of the embankment, he saw a woman sitting on the lip of the bridge, the river rushing beneath her. Already, a crowd had gathered, and two uniformed policemen were attempting to hold it back. The woman, in her late 30s, was threatening to jump. Frank could have walked away from something that didn't concern him. Instead, he chose to walk into it. Aware of the crisis, aware too of the urgency to act, he bounded up the steps to the bridge and took charge. He stayed there for half an hour, talking non-stop, until the woman agreed to be led to safety. If he'd miscalculated, if his intervention had gone horribly wrong, Frank would have been blamed for meddling. I and the other players, most of whom were FA Cup winners, watched him from below, knowing how insignificant our own achievement on a football pitch looked beside his bravery.

Frank insisted that his part in the rescue was infinitesimal. Today, of course, what he did would be broadcast on social media in a blink. You'd see photographs and film of it. Back then – 1984 – Frank could refuse to claim the role of Good Samaritan because few knew he had ever been one. He turned down a Citizen's Award, for which the two policemen nominated him. It was enough for Frank to know that we, his players, recognised him as a hero. He had no need for a framed certificate to prove it.

The drama on the bridge was not his only act of selflessness.

Frank could be extraordinarily generous. It was as if he'd created the bank of Robin Hood. He would provide funds for charitable causes or for someone in need – irrespective of whether he knew them or not. His largesse was distributed on the understanding that it remained strictly private. More money would be flung into the pockets of those – especially ex-players of whom he was fond – who were struggling to pay bills or meet other financial obligations, such as the cost of a wedding or private medical treatment. His benevolence arrived as cash in an envelope:

stiff new notes, as though Frank had just minted them. The sums could be anywhere between £500 and £5,000, I'm told. 'A little something from us all here,' he'd write in an accompanying note, anxious to pretend the cash was a whip-round donation from the whole club rather than from his own account. 'It's a gift,' he'd add, 'not a loan.'

He'd shower you with flowers on special occasions. He'd send invitations to matches – always the best tickets – and make sure a fuss was made when you got there. He'd pay for meals, nights out, weekends away.

Still, as many people loathed Frank as loved him. Those who hated him were suspicious of his kindness, thinking it was calculated. They thought he only dished out some treats so that others could be withheld later on, making their absence more conspicuous. They believed the deal Frank demanded in return for his favours was of the kind Faust offered. They believed, too, that his methods were an emanation of his personality. He relished the power he had. Or, more to the point, he relished the control it gave him and the way it made others feel powerless in his presence. In their eyes, this was not a fault that could be smoothed out or excused.

I saw both sides of him. I knew Frank as the paterfamilias, capable of smothering someone in love or turning on them. He could be like one of those spring days in which everything happens: sunshine, rain, thunder, sunshine again.

You could hold an opinion that conflicted with Frank's, but he would consider you to be a fool and seldom conceded even the possibility that you might have been right. Sometimes a downward turn of the lips, betraying mild dissent at one of his decisions, was sufficient to light the blue touchpaper within him. You had no choice then but to step back and duck for cover.

Frank was also particularly sensitive to slights, both real and imagined, which is why he went apoplectic over trivial misdemeanours. You had to do everything his way. A poor soul, spotted wearing white socks with black jeans, was fined and banned for a game for the sin of 'sartorial inelegance'; this, from a manager who slopped around in a baggy tracksuit. Another was hurled off the team coach and left on the rainy verge of the M62 because Frank considered his performance that afternoon had been 'completely fucking shit'. He had to shelter beneath his own jacket and thumb a lift home in a minibus full of beery fans. A third, chastised for 'doing nothing' in a league game, was promptly pulled out of an international under-21 squad because Frank believed he'd been 'deliberately saving himself' for that match. He invented an injury for the player, using it as an excuse to deny his release. A fourth, who hadn't 'trained hard enough', had to clean everyone's boots – even the apprentices' – and sweep the dressing rooms and also the corridor that led to them.

The very worst of Frank was that he could cut completely either those he thought were disloyal or anyone he considered to be superfluous to the club. He shook them off, dismissing them from his presence and seldom acknowledged their existence again. It was like an excommunication.

I never imagined it would happen to Robbie Clayton.

2

WHILE MOST OF US are prepared to admit our mistakes, we seldom confess — sometimes even to ourselves — to acts about which we're ashamed. It's pointless, of course. You can ignore, but never forget, them. However much you try to push them away, they always resurface, often catching you unawares. You churn over what you did or didn't do, searching for reasons why, but you always end up back where you started, which is a place you can never leave unless you can forgive yourself. You did something for which there is no absolution, and so it stays with you — a haunting, a punishment, a life sentence.

My betrayal of Robbie Clayton is all of those things.

I can't separate the memory of the FA Cup final from the memory of what happened after it. What I also regret is that Beth and I never talked it out. She refused; and I was too weak, and felt too guilty, to argue with her.

It was almost a week after Wembley before I summoned the courage to visit her and Robbie. I hesitated even at their barred wooden gate, almost turning back. My hand hovered over the latch before I lifted it.

She came to the front door of the house in bare feet and wearing one of those short summer dresses. A thin gold chain, which I hadn't seen before, dangled from her. 'Cally,' she said, loudly. 'We didn't think you were coming.' Then she placed her index finger over my lips: 'He doesn't know. I'm never going to tell him. You shouldn't tell him either.' She said this in a whisper, but also so emphatically that her words were like a rebuke.

'I won't.' It was the easiest promise I'd ever made.

'Make sure you don't,' she said.

Over the previous five days, what had occurred between us had come back to me bit by bit. I gathered up the pieces like broken glass.

As she'd promised, Beth had arrived at the banquet, but only after the tables had been cleared and the TV cameras had gone. It must have been past midnight. She wore a backless black dress, cut so low that almost her whole spine was visible, and a pair of high heels. Like everyone else, I had stopped counting my drinks. I had reached the stage drinkers know so well: everything around you sparkles and the world is full of bonhomie.

Beth asked whether she could collect Robbie's clothes and his shaving kit. I said I'd pack them into his suitcase. I went up the staircase alone, taking another drink with me. Her knock on the door followed almost immediately. Beth came into the room, carrying two empty glasses and a bottle of white wine. Only the bedside lamps were switched on. She put the bottle on the table that stood between the two double beds and poured herself a drink. She sat down on my bed. 'Poor Robbie,' she said. 'I'm not sure he'll ever get over it.'

I was taking things out of drawers and off hangers. All I said was: 'I'm sorry.'

I'd laid my winner's medal, still in its leather box, on my pillow. She held the box in the flat of her hand for a while before opening it. Then she took the medal out and held it against the lobe of her left ear. 'Does it suit me?' she asked.

I ignored the question. I hurried to finish the packing, making a clumsy mess of it, and slammed the suitcase shut. Simply for something else to do, I went to draw the curtains, a classic example of displacement. As I did so, Beth clicked the radio on: Out came the opening bars of Al Green's *Let's Stay Together*. I turned around and found her standing just two feet away from me. She shook off her shoes and ran her fingers, comb-like, through her hair.

'I was promised a dance,' she said.

I can't claim in mitigation that drink was to blame. It wasn't; I knew what I was doing. I knew what the consequences would be.

I ignored them.

3

ROBBIE CLAYTON WAS STRETCHED out on the sofa. 'Here comes the hero,' he shouted.

He asked me all the questions you'd expect. How I was, mostly. How I'd coped with the clamour and attention. He also wanted to know whether I'd spoken to Frank since we'd brought the Cup back. 'He hasn't called me,' he said. 'Uncle Charlie came. He's offered me a benefit match. He's having a replica medal made too. Says that's the least I deserve.'

The last thing you should say to someone in Robbie's position is: 'How do you feel?' I didn't; I was too afraid he might tell me. His Footballer of the Year statuette sat on the middle of the mantelpiece. The Footballer of the Year himself looked vulnerable and disorientated. I understand now, which I didn't then, that Robbie had chosen to grapple with the trauma of what had happened to him with the stiffest of upper lips. That's what he believed his brilliant friend Bobby Moore would have done. But he was continuously living in the moment of his misfortune. He was also doing the arithmetic, totting up the odds of his freak pratfall. Was it 10,000–1 or 100,000–1? He would be asked about it for as long as I'd be asked about my goal.

Robbie was angry only with himself and the newspapers. He handed me a bundle of cuttings.

They say that when the legend becomes fact, the newspapers will always print the legend. The pieces he showed me were among the first examples I ever saw of that. The papers, wanting to ginger up the saddest of stories, had dramatised it still further. They claimed Robbie had 'fallen down a rabbit hole'. His foot had actually got trapped in a spot where a fence post had stood years before, but the detail of the rabbit hole, a brazen invention, allowed the journalists to describe Robbie's misfortune as his '*Alice in Wonderland* Injury'.

'That's going to stick to me. I'll never get rid of it,' he said.

He was right. Even after his career ended, Robbie had to live with the taunt of being called 'Alice' by crowds who liked to mock him.

I gave him back the cuttings. He was a friend for whom fidelity counted. I could barely look at him; I couldn't look at Beth at all. I wondered how long I would have to sit in his living room, drinking his alcohol, before I could leave without arousing suspicion. I decided three hours would be enough.

Those hours crawled by. I tried to act as normally as I could, but everything I did and everything I said seemed incriminating, my betrayal surely transparent to him. I prayed for any excuse to flee. For Frank to appear. For Robbie to say he was dog-tired. For an earthquake. He suspected nothing because the scale of my cruelty was unthinkable to him. I could have shown him the bedsheets from the hotel; he still wouldn't have believed me. He trusted me that much.

When the ordeal was finally over, Beth led me to the door. She took my hand for a second or two and said: 'Don't feel too guilty. Things happen.'

I walked down the path, aware that what I'd taken for granted – Robbie's friendship – was lost and irrecoverable. Pretending to be friends would have been a second betrayal, worse even than the first.

4

FRANK MALLORY HAD A policy about injured players: he pretended they didn't exist. He avoided the treatment room the way someone morbidly superstitious avoids black cats, ladders and going out on Friday the 13th. If a casualty hobbled past him, he would turn his head away. You were a non-person to him until he could pick you again. We used to say that anyone injured had been consigned to 'the dark side of the moon'. Only outsiders took it as a joke.

Unless your injury was particularly hideous, Frank had a tendency to believe you were either malingering, wanting to come off, or exaggerating the severity of the damage. One incident I remember emphasised that fact. I was playing in a Youth Cup match. I knocked a ball down the channel to a winger called Johnny Halloran. He got there early. The defender got there late. Halloran was face-down, motionless in a patch of mud. Frank liked to watch reserve matches from the directors' box, and his voice from there was like a sonic boom across the still night air: 'Get up! Get up!' Halloran continued to lie where he'd fallen. Frank climbed out of his seat and sprinted down the steps, along the corridor and down the tunnel. He stood on the side of the pitch. 'Get to your feet. There's nothing wrong with you.' Halloran pulled himself up and immediately sank back down again. Frank told the coaches to drag him off.

Halloran's left leg was broken.

Robbie Clayton didn't only snap his ankle in two places; he tore ligaments in his knee too. It was early October before he could start training. It was late November before he appeared on a team sheet again.

I could – and did – make excuses for neglecting him. The close season was short, and the new season came at me in a rush and all at once. I was young, which I thought allowed me to be so selfish and so stupid. In that ripe summer, life had opened up for me. I was my own man at last. I bought a house. I accepted invitations from those I didn't know. Robbie's boot suppliers wanted to sponsor me too; I'd wear those boots with the orange crosses. I had no idea that signing me meant the company was letting go of Robbie.

I convinced myself he would accept, without regret or rancour, that my career would rush on without him. Our friendship had been rooted in football, from which he'd become semi-detached.

We stole the Charity Shield from Liverpool in a rag-and-bone sort of a match. Davie Collins claimed a Wembley goal at last. I won an England cap. Bobby Robson had taken over from Ron Greenwood, who was one of those managers who looked better wearing a sober John Collier suit than an Admiral tracksuit. He was balding, urbane, reserved. Robbie, who had worked with him at West Ham, gave Greenwood nothing but high praise, but he seemed a slightly Dickensian character to me. I wouldn't have belonged in his teams. Robson was different. While technically modern in thought and deed, he also possessed old-school passion.

Robson called me into his squad for a European Championship qualifier against Luxembourg. It was target practice for us. We won 9–0. At half-time, already 3–0 up, I replaced Steve Coppell. I found myself in the company of Bryan Robson and Terry Butcher, Luther Blissett and Sammy Lee. On any given Saturday, I'd be trying to kick at least one of them into the week after next. I set up a late goal for Blissett, a tap-in. 'I could have put that one in with my cock,' was the first thing Frank Mallory said to me when I reported back to the club. The second thing he said was: 'If I'd played against that lot, you'd have needed a fucking big calculator to tot up the goals.' I waited for a 'well done', which never came. 'Start thinking about Saturday. It's far more important than England.'

Robbie and I had different schedules. Often, I'd find him in the gym, straining to lift the weights, or glimpse his figure from a distance. He'd be lapping the pitch alone, a towel wrapped around his neck and a bobble hat on his head. When we met, usually in the car park, Robbie always said: 'Frank hasn't come anywhere near me. If I walk one way, he goes in the other direction.' He said this as though pleading with me to do something about it.

Twice Robbie grasped the initiative. Both times he planted himself in the corridor outside Frank's office. On the first occasion, Frank came out in a hurry, insisting he was urgently needed elsewhere. On the second, he poked his head around the door and curtly dismissed him. 'Not today. No time to spare. Come back tomorrow.'

Robbie didn't bother.

He began his comeback in a reserve match at Bramall Lane. He asked whether I would provide some moral support. I went there alone and sat in the shadows at the back of the main stand. Sheffield United had two strikers young enough not to have been walking during the years when Robbie was palling around with Bobby Moore at West Ham. They were just kids, little slips of lads who didn't care about someone of Robbie's vintage. What he'd achieved in the game was medieval history to them.

It was a surprisingly mild, clear night, but there were only 1,300 fans in the ground. Robbie was heckled from the beginning. Two critics, unmistakably from South Yorkshire, took it in turns to rile him.

'Mind thyself, Alice, or you'll disappear down another hole.'

'You're a long way from Wonderland now, Alice.'

Robbie lumbered around the pitch, his discomfort so obvious that I found it difficult to watch him. The two young strikers, canny and quick, darted around each challenge he made on them.

On the turn he looked timid, afraid of putting too much weight on his damaged knee. As so often happens to players who are trying to protect an old injury, Robbie sustained a new one. In the 61st minute he tore a calf muscle.

'Alice is a goner,' shouted one of his hecklers.

As Robbie came off the field, I got up and left.

5

IT WAS MARCH BEFORE Robbie Clayton's benefit match was staged. The opposition was Manchester United, chosen because their fan base was huge enough to guarantee him a gate. It was a wretched night. Rain and sleet swirled in the wind. With the worst possible timing, we'd been knocked out of the FA Cup the Saturday before, losing feebly at home to Bristol City, a mediocre side. We were in a rut of indifferent league results too, wedged solidly in mid-table. When Robbie appeared before kick-off, holding the trophy he never got to parade at Wembley, the ground was only two-thirds full. We gave him a guard of honour onto the sodden pitch, and Uncle Charlie Bembridge presented him with a silver salver, the club's thanks for his service expressed across it in filigree lettering.

When the game was over, after shaking everybody's hand twice and waving to the fervent few who had paid tribute to him, Robbie hid in the dressing room for an hour. He was reluctant to go to the party that Uncle Charlie had arranged for him in the directors' suite. The players said the right things to Robbie. We proclaimed him as a legend . . . We promised not to forget him or lose touch . . . We pledged to do anything for him.

Frank Mallory sat in a corner, blowing smoke rings. He didn't want to be there, which is why he left early.

'Switch the lights off on your way out,' he told Robbie.

I remembered Frank's reaction to the sight of Robbie on Cup final morning. His face tightening in disgust. His silence, the words he ought to have said stuck on his tongue. His fleeing from the chaotic scene. The way Frank recoiled from any player's injury – a phobia from which he never recovered – was visible on his face that day. It was the cause of all the unnecessary cruelty that followed. But also I understood something else: Frank could feel no sympathy for Robbie. His brutality towards him had been deliberate. He blamed Robbie for being an idiot, for bringing all that bad luck on himself.

6

THE BEST ADVICE ROBBIE Clayton ever gave me came after the FA Cup final. 'A career can go one of two ways after a player achieves what you've done,' he said. 'It will soar or it will slide. Think of Bobby Stokes. Think of Alan Taylor.'

Stokes, Southampton's unexpected match-winner against Manchester United, played only 11 more matches for them. Taylor, the toast of London's East End after his two goals beat Fulham, left West Ham only four seasons later. The last of those seasons brought him just three goals and 15 appearances. 'Taylor was your age when he got those goals at Wembley,' said Robbie. 'Make sure your finest hour isn't your last one.'

You won't want to hear all the *David Copperfield*-like details of the next eight years, the tedious kick-by-kick account of games won and lost.

Most of them don't matter.

But I wasn't another Stokes or a second Taylor.

I got 13 more England caps. I won two more tin buttons: a League Cup winner's medal, after we beat Norwich City; and a UEFA Cup medal, against Valencia in Lisbon, on a night so hot that my red shirt clung sweatily to my skin and had to be cut off my back with a pair of scissors at the end of extra time.

We nearly won the title, failing only because Liverpool – Joe Fagan had taken over from Bob Paisley – were infinitely more talented than us. At Anfield, we lost 3–1. At the final whistle, I went over to congratulate Kenny Dalglish. It was the closest I'd got to him all night.

I was curiously dissatisfied, always more preoccupied with what I hadn't done or won. The thing that rankled was this: I'd never made the leap to one of the glamour clubs. I was linked with a few – Manchester United and Arsenal, for instance – but nothing more than newspaper gossip came of it. I never got one of those clandestine phone calls in which the instruction is to sit tight and wait. I never heard that a £50,000 signing-on bonus, tucked in 'the sky rocket' so the Inland Revenue couldn't trace it, would, with patience and a bit of jiggery-pokery, be all mine.

At 29, though, I was among Frank Mallory's favourites, his bluest-eyed boy. I'd signed a new contract at the end of the previous season. 'I'm going to be generous,' he'd said. 'I'm giving you *four* years because you deserve it and because your football brain is worth the money. You'll lose that last bit of kick in your legs when you go past 30. Don't worry. You were never that fast anyway and you won't lose your intelligence. I want you to stay here. Show the others how to think and act and play.'

My contract was financial protection. The homework I'd done – those hours watching matches on film or from a midweek seat in the stand – was advance planning for the coaching position Frank was going to give me. While he'd never said so explicitly, Frank had scattered hints that I'd never leave the club. I'd get all the complimentary patter from him: 'Somehow you see the game differently from other players . . . I'm going to school you, improve your education and add some polish . . . You'll have a degree in football by the time I've finished with you.'

Like Stein, Shankly and Busby, Frank's family tree was a people's history of coal mining. He saw himself as the archetypal self-made man, proof that academic achievement was superfluous. Frank bulked up his working-class credentials, which gave him a bond with the ordinary fan. I've never known anyone quite so proud of not having a scholarly background. 'Left school without a scrap of paper,' he'd say. 'My qualifications are the medals I've won in the game.' Frank nonetheless quietly admired anyone who possessed qualifications, while being slightly cautious around them too.

His teaching methods were rooted in catechism. He'd test me. 'What's our team on Saturday?' he'd ask, aware I'd have watched the opposition and would know as much, if not more, about them tactically than he did. I'd reel off the side I thought he would pick. Frank would nod at me and say: 'You could do this job.' After matches, I'd get a different set of questions. 'Who was our best player? . . . Who was our worst player? . . . What would you have done at half-time? . . . Tell me all the mistakes the opposition made.' He pressed me to spend close seasons collecting coaching badges. He encouraged me to contribute scouting reports. He even took me on the odd mission to watch a potential signing.

One winter's night, Frank and I went on a 750-mile round journey to Scotland's easterly tip to check on a left back. We shared the driving, taking Frank's red BMW. He smoked all the way there and all the way back. I opened my window and slowly froze. Frank seldom scouted talent from the cushioned comfort of a directors' box. He went to extremes to be anonymous, paranoid about not advertising his presence at a game. His reasoning? 'The price will go up if they think I'm interested.' He'd dress in disguise: a woollen hat, a scarf pulled up above his chin, a pair of heavy framed spectacles with clear glass for lenses, a long grey coat with the collar upturned. He would pay to get in, queuing with everyone else for a cup of something wet at half-time.

We got through the turnstiles only a quarter of an hour before kick-off. The players were warming up, languidly knocking cross-field passes to one another. The grass was damp and lush. The ball moved slickly off it, shining with a smooth whiteness under the lights. The left back was close to the touchline, conveniently allowing Frank to lean on the perimeter rail and observe him without being noticed. He studied him for three or four minutes, then turned to me and said: 'He can't play. He doesn't trap the ball cleanly or quickly enough. He doesn't strike it soundly either. There's no lovely crisp sound off his boot and his right foot is far weaker than his left. Come on, we're off.'

At first, I dismissed this as a little joke. I didn't move until Frank, becoming agitated, yanked at my sleeve and marched off without me. I had to quicken my step to catch up with him. The player never knew that Frank had used up a day of his life to watch him. Eventually, he moved to England, bought for a decent sum. He failed, abjectly.

On the way home, I asked myself: *What else had Frank immediately seen – or not seen – in that player? Why hadn't I seen it?* Attempting to make sense of our fruitless expedition, I knew there was only one plausible explanation: I *had* seen what Frank saw; I'd missed nothing whatsoever. The trip was actually a kind of initiation – a ludicrous one, admittedly. Frank had trapped me in his car for 12 hours to find out who I really was, what I thought and also what I'd tolerate from him. He was never interested in signing the player.

7

HOW EASILY THINGS CAN fall apart.

It began one afternoon, a very wet Thursday early in 1989, when my father left the ground to drive home. He got confused at the fork in the road where he'd routinely turned left for nearly 35 years. He turned right and got lost. His surroundings were unrecognisable to him. The road signs meant nothing. He parked the car haphazardly, got out and began to walk. Three hours later, soaked to the skin, a passer-by found him huddled on a park bench. He was staring blankly at his keys, holding them in the well of his outstretched hand, while rocking his body backwards and forwards to a beat no one else could hear.

In the year between diagnosis and death, aged 62, his dementia estranged us. It was almost as if he had already died, and I was awaiting confirmation so I could move on.

Shakespeare called what we now recognise as Alzheimer's as 'a second childhood'. Slipping back into it came absurdly early for my father. Even now, I am ashamed to admit that his forgetfulness, barely noticeable at the outset, was obvious to me only when it became so extreme that I had to confront it. I'd watch him leave a half-lit cigarette somewhere and then light another, unaware of the first. I waved those signs away because I was ignorant enough not to register them. I knew nothing then of the speckled plaques and tangles that were forming, incrementally, in the cerebral cortex of his brain.

Everything accelerated. The bridges linking one memory to the next were taken in the raids dementia made on him. His memories were stolen one by one while he slept. He would wake and find something more had been snatched away. He was adrift on a disappearing archipelago, tiny islands of things he could remember. He was soon living – if it can be described as living – in a care home that was a former Victorian country house, the windows high and leaded. The walls of his room were as white-bright as the inside of a seashell. I pasted up pictures from his past in an orderly timeline, hoping the sight of them would reignite something of his old self. Nothing did. He used to tell me that Laura was coming to visit him. Sometimes she had left only recently. 'You probably passed one another in the corridor,' he'd say. Laura was my mother. He saw her as she'd once been: petite, with short dark hair, the fringe chopped off just above her eyebrows.

In my father's final weeks, after he caught pneumonia, I watched him shrink in front of me. He went into a soft oblivion, a cushioned fall into death. I sat beside his bed, the line of his body barely disturbing the tight cotton sheets that were wrapped around him like a shroud. His eyes were closed. I listened to his ragged breathing. His last breath, however, came so gently that it made almost no sound. It was like the silent drop of a leaf from a tree.

When someone you love is diagnosed with Alzheimer's, you grieve from the start. The person you knew is already hollowed out and gone – there but not there. In the end their death doesn't sting because you've already experienced it day by day, as though in instalments. You are either left numb, unable to cry, or you react as if some curse has been graciously lifted.

I know how cold, even unfeeling, all that must sound, but that's the way you cope with it. For in the end there is no conversation between you. My father recognised neither me nor himself.

A month went by.

I looked into the bathroom mirror and saw him staring back at me. The same flat, sallow face. The same shallow cleft in the chin. The same brown eyes. The same dark hair, swept slightly forward to disguise the widow's peak. I looked at myself for a long time, his features and mine indistinguishable.

His possessions were stored in a spare room. I'd cleared his house after he'd gone into the care home, but I hadn't wanted either to curate or dispose of those private relics – the material remains of his life. Among them was a tan-coloured leather suitcase that I found at the back of the Victorian wardrobe that my mother once used. The wardrobe was tall and wide and deep, like a vertical tomb. I had only the faintest recollection of seeing the suitcase before. It felt light in my hand, and I assumed it contained nothing much. The paperwork that mattered had been stuffed into the drawers of a bureau, which was never used for writing but instead held bills, documents, letters, insurance policies, photo albums and a couple of scrapbooks.

The suitcase had gathered a thin layer of dust. I wiped it away with a swipe of my fingers, the leather dull underneath. The lock was stiff, and I had to force it open with a heave, the lid swinging almost flat. I discovered ephemera that my father had never got around to putting into a third scrapbook or filing away in a box: programmes from matches, ticket stubs and passes, a loose assortment of news cuttings. The paper on which these were printed had either foxed or gone yellow and was brittle to the touch.

Evidence of his life as a hunter of football talent was there too. There were a few pocket notebooks, bound with a rubber band. I turned the pages, recognising his handwriting: the sharp downward slash on a 'g' or a 'y', the long cross on the 't', the dot noticeably high above the 'i'. I searched those notebooks, hoping to find a name he'd discovered – a star born thanks to his eye. I found instead the players who, like him, didn't really make it.

I came to a black-and-white photograph. My father was standing outside the entrance to a ground that I didn't recognise. Beside him was Frank Mallory. They both held cigarettes, the air above a swirl of what I imagined was blue–grey smoke. Frank had placed a solicitous hand on my father's shoulder. I looked at the back of the photograph, expecting to find a place or date scribbled there. It was blank.

It wasn't the contents of the suitcase that affected me; it was the odour of the cigarettes my father had smoked. If I inhaled deeply enough, the reek of his tobacco was so powerful that it almost made my eyes tear. It was as if my father were in the room with me. I felt that if I turned around quickly enough, I would glimpse his ghost before it was gone.

From then on, I saw him everywhere – I almost became afraid to look in the mirror – and I thought about him constantly. I couldn't understand why dementia had struck and taken him with such indecent speed, for none of us knew anything then about the severe harm you could inflict on yourself by heading a football. The ball has barely changed in either circumference or weight since my father last took the laces out of his boots. The difference is that back then the ball's dark brown leather absorbed water, which meant it gained weight when it was wet. Heading it was like driving a nail into your skull.

I picked over everything I knew about my father: his setbacks, his small triumphs, the sacrifices he made, unselfishly and without complaint, on my behalf. How unfair that life had given him back so little, denying him even the reward of a rich old age.

I was experiencing grief, of course, but in such a different form that at first I didn't recognise the symptoms. And I didn't know where it would lead.

8

A T THE END OF the season during which he died, I played in a testimonial at the Abbey Stadium for one of the 'stalwarts' of Cambridge United. I've always baulked at that word, in the same way I baulk at the word 'gaffer' to describe a manager. 'Gaffer' is redolent of old-fashioned deference, the sons of toil tipping their flat caps at the boss. 'Stalwart' isn't a compliment, being less a term of endearment and more a polite, slightly patronising insult. It makes me think of a player who has stayed somewhere too long, been too loyal for his own good, refused the chance to better himself because of misplaced faith. The Cambridge player was a rough-house centre half who kicked the snot out of strikers. He'd climbed as high as the Second Division with them, but now found himself back in the doldrums of the Fourth.

The place depressed me. It wasn't a stadium. There was no abbey beside it either. There were only grubby warehouses, a garage, prefabricated industrial units with flat roofs and a few shops. The main stand, painted in the club's colours of amber and black, resembled a long wooden shed. Like every other surface in late May, the pitch was ready for reseeding: the grass was sparse and no amount of rolling could get rid of the bumps and holes. It was like playing on corrugated iron. My worn-down studs left no impression on it.

We all know that testimonials are supposed to be a show rather than a serious contest. The honouree just wants you to turn up with as much plucky enthusiasm as you can give. In goal, we had Pat Jennings, not long retired; he saved two penalties, catching one of them cleanly. In midfield, David Rocastle pushed the ball about regally. We let Cambridge win 3–2. Distinguishing the match was the player everyone had paid to see.

It was George Best.

I'd been tapped up for the game because of my Wembley goal, which was usually the only reason I got invited anywhere. I was stuck at left back. Best, who normally roamed around indiscriminately, decided to hug the right wing. I hadn't faced him before. George's wondrous days at Manchester United were over before I even made my debut. In his prime, I saw him only on TV.

Even standing still, George compelled you to look at him. Your eyes were sometimes never quick enough to fully appreciate the subtleties of what you had just seen – the drop of a shoulder, a swivel on his heels, that spurt over 10 to 15 yards that could have taken him past an Olympic sprinter. You had to watch him in slow motion to learn how those tricks were done and their nuances; how, indeed, he made defenders look so useless. He had impeccable balance, tensile strength in that slender body and beautiful balletic movement in his feet. His looks were beautiful too. If George had been pig-ugly, life would have been less stressful for him and his career would have been half a dozen years longer. The fact he was Hollywood-handsome complicated everything. Women used to congregate around the corner flags at Old Trafford in the hope of getting close to him. He had talent to burn – and so he burnt it, publicly and very quickly, while dancing through the midnight hour. But he'd done so in a style that cast a lovely light, which is why there were queues outside the turnstiles that Sunday.

Predictably, George was late, turning up ten minutes after kick-off. I guess he'd got out of bed barely an hour before that. He looked as though he'd slept in his clothes: a pair of jeans, a denim shirt and cream-coloured linen jacket that was crumpled almost to destruction. By then George was 44, a peripatetic wanderer of the globe, borrowing boots in which to dazzle. I don't know why he'd agreed to appear as a 'guest' player for Cambridge that day. As a favour? For cash? With George, you were never sure. He was always in between gigs.

He'd explored the bars and nightclubs of Spain, South Africa and America. He'd gone off to make a few quid in Australia. On each occasion, the outcome of his adventures was the same:

the fanfare of his arrival; the disillusion of his departure; the recriminations that followed. Unsettled and discontented, George was going round in circles. It was the shape that most suited his life because it always brought him home, which is where he wanted to be, without ever admitting it. Going from place to place, changing the scenery around him, was simply George's way of never confronting the reason that made all that travelling necessary in the first place.

The nocturnal life George lived – he considered sleep to be a scandalous waste of drinking time – was evident in his appearance. He was very paunchy. His bushy black beard was already flecked with grey. His hair was long and unwashed.

He received possession and came at me, tight to the line. I expected him to dodge inside and try a nutmeg. Not a bit of it. George chipped the ball over my head with a surprisingly deft flick and ran around me, dashing off the pitch and back onto it again. I was still on the half-turn. The George Best of the late 1960s would have been in the box before I managed to regain both position and poise; now, he couldn't escape. With two rapid strides, I got level and bulldozed him over with a shoulder charge. The portion of the crowd that had come specifically to see George hissed at me, the pantomime villain. He got up, gave me the dead eye and wagged his finger.

We came to an accommodation after that. For the next half-hour – he soon ran out of puff – George would nudge the ball

past me, and I would try to haul him down, sometimes suc-
cessfully, or pull the tail of his shirt, which hung outside his
shorts. Or I'd take a scythe-like swipe at his legs in a sliding
tackle and deliberately miss. We were play-acting, putting on
an improvised performance so good that it could have been
choreographed like big-time wrestling. At one stage, George
whipped off his shin pads, tossing them with a flourish against
the advertising boards, and rolled his socks down to his ankles.
He held the ball and beckoned me towards him with sly wink.
'Come on, Callaghan,' he said, 'this way . . .' George had what
the Spanish call *duende*. He evoked spirit and emotion that you
could actually feel.

At the end of the game, we shook hands and embraced. 'I'd
give you my shirt,' he said, 'but I've promised it to the testimonial
committee for a raffle. I'll buy you a drink instead.'

We went for what George promised would be 'one or two
beers'. We were still drinking at 4 a.m. After a while, at his
insistence, we peeled off from the others who had tagged along.
We crawled through the pubs and ended up in a dingy nightclub
where the frayed royal-purple carpet was sticky. I picked my way
across it, afraid that my shoes would be sucked straight off my
feet. On the edge of the dance floor was a red telephone box,
in which ornamental fish swam around surreally in the cloudy
water. George pressed his face against the glass.

We eventually found two stools at the end of one of the

nightclub's quieter bars and drank double vodkas. 'Vodka doesn't catch on your breath. No one can tell you've been drinking,' said George.

Can you get to know the essence of a person in a few hours? I think so. Here's what I learnt about George. He was an autodidact. He read books – history, philosophy, religion. One of his most cherished volumes was Viktor Frankl's *Man's Search for Meaning*. He was obsessed in a benignly mad way with the accumulation of knowledge and trivia. In one pub, he played – and seldom lost – against a quiz machine, shouting most of the answers out loud before the multiple-choice options appeared. After an hour, his jacket pockets bulged with pound coins.

I'd heard George didn't like to talk about football or the fame it had brought him. But, as the evening warmed up, he began to speak about both.

'I envy you,' he said.

It was one of those compliments you wish someone else had been there to overhear. George Best envied me?

'You scored the winner in an FA Cup final. I always wanted to play in one of those. Especially if the Queen was there. I had a plan, you see. I imagined we'd be 2–0 up with twenty minutes left. I'd start to show off. I'd trap a long clearance with my arse. I'd go down the left flank, bouncing the ball on my thigh, never letting it touch the ground. Time would almost be up when we got a penalty. I'd take it. I'd think about back-heeling it in, but then I'd tell the goalkeeper: 'The ball's going in off the underside of the crossbar.' And it did. Then, just when everyone thought the game was over, I'd do a headstand and volley a cross into the bottom corner. Don't laugh – I used to do that in training. As I said, I envy you. You did something I didn't.'

I wondered whether I'd been invited out solely so that he could tell me that.

As strange as this may seem, I came to the conclusion that George and I had similar personalities. We were ridiculously competitive, fanatically driven and prone to long bouts of intro-spection. Things struck us in a way they seldom struck others, but sometimes we thought about them too much. I knew his mother had died at an even younger age than my father. I thought he'd understand the disorientating grief that had suddenly taken over my life. I'd talked to no one else about it.

'My father died recently,' I told him.

'He was a pro too, wasn't he?'

'A while ago, and only briefly,' I said. 'I thought I'd got over his death. Now, I'm not sure . . . I can't stop thinking about it. I don't know how to cope with it.'

Out came the stories about my father's dementia, and about the bathroom mirror and the suitcase too.

George listened. When I finished, he said: 'You're starting to wonder what this life's all about . . . and what it's for and whether it's worth it . . . and how you'll get over this and go on from here. That's perfectly normal.' He put down his glass and looked straight at me.

'I can't explain it, but when I was 21 I thought I wouldn't live past 35. I wasn't sure I wanted to, either. I didn't want to get old. I certainly didn't want to be 40. The people who were 40 looked past it to me, a shell of themselves. That's why I squeezed every hour dry. That's why I was so restless, going in every direction all at once. But – and this sounds crazy – there were mornings when I didn't want to wake up or face anyone or anything. Everything was too much for me. Then, when I was 32, my mother died. She was 44 before she had the first drink of her life – a Pimm's and lemonade. She died ten years later, an alcoholic. I think I was the cause of that. She was a private woman who ended up living a public life because of me. Every bloody mishap and stupid thing I did ended up on her front step. The newspapers made sure of that. She dreaded hearing a knock on the door: she knew another bit of bad news was waiting for her. She dreaded leaving the house as well. Someone would recognise her and bad-mouth me. Even at the shops. Even at the local social club. So then she was gone, dead in her sleep, and everything became blacker than it had been before. I loved my father – I really loved him – but I was my mother's child. It was too harrowing for me to look at her in her coffin. I couldn't do it. What you're feeling now, I've felt for a long time.'

George picked up his glass again and held it in front of him. He looked like Hamlet about to address Yorick's skull.

'This got me through. Still does. I used to have six or seven drinks. Then it became eleven or twelve and a few more besides – so many more that counting them wasn't worth the mental effort. That's how I manage. It's a short life, and I know I'll very probably make mine even shorter than it ought to be. I decided I didn't want to miss anything and didn't want to be bored. I'll die when I die, and I'll be as content as I possibly can be in the meantime. I'll do that irrespective of the consequences and no matter what anyone says to me. If someone tries to get in the way . . . well, I'll either ignore them or tell them to fuck off. I've had managers and friends and agents and a lot of shitty hangers-on who've always been in my ear. They never knew what I was thinking, not really, but they handed out crappy advice all the same. Occasionally, I pretended to listen for five minutes and agreed with everything they said just to get them off my back. I resented the intrusion and I resented them. That's why I don't usually give advice myself. But I'll tell you this story . . .'

I discovered later, from others, that George had treated me to one of his favourite party pieces. It was a ghost story, acted out in a whispery voice as he held me in an unblinking gaze. 'The story is called "The Appointment in Samarra",' he said. 'You've heard of Somerset Maugham?'

I nodded.

'A merchant's servant goes to a market in Baghdad. There

he finds the figure of Death, who makes a threatening gesture towards him. The servant rushes back, asks his master for a horse and says: "I will ride away from this city and avoid my Fate. I will go to Samarra, and there Death will not find me." So he gets the horse and rides to Samarra. His master goes to the market, hunts down and finds Death, and asks him why he made a threatening gesture to his servant. "That was not a threatening gesture," says Death, "but a start of surprise. I was astonished to see him in Baghdad. For I had an appointment with him tonight in Samarra."'

His eyes still locked on to mine, George smiled very slowly.

'Invest all you have in the *now*. It's a mistake not to,' he said. 'You can't escape your Fate. It's out there – waiting for you.'

George looked away, staring instead into the bottom of his glass, which was almost empty. He gestured towards the barman for two more vodkas. 'I usually like to be on my own. I mostly avoid company,' he added. 'Think of yourself as a bit privileged. Let's drink a toast and then we can forget all this and talk about something else.' He reached across and clinked his glass against mine.

'To the dead. Forgive us,' he said.

I liked getting drunk with George – except for the way it made me feel the next morning. That toast in the dingy nightclub was the last thing I remembered. Whatever else we had shared vanished in another two rounds of vodka. I awoke at noon when the phone rang on the bedside table in my hotel: I ought to have checked out an hour before.

What I felt for George was the one thing he didn't want: pity. That would have appalled him. No one knew what it was like to be him. Not when the 1960s began whirling and giving off sparks, and George became a fashion icon, sex symbol, fifth Beatle and footballer. Nor did anyone know how the consequences of that decade still impacted on him malignly, the decisions he made even as a teenager responsible for a misshapen life. George was proof that the world didn't contain enough alcohol to drink away your miseries entirely. Booze was only ever a palliative, and you had to constantly increase the dose. What dispirited me most of all was George's tone – the weary, matter-of-fact resignation. He'd decided that there weren't any answers, and so had given up trying to find them.

In striving to help me, George had made things worse.

My response to that evening was so irrational that it's difficult to explain. Merely admitting it makes me seem half demented. Trying to explain it makes me sound certifiable.

I became convinced then that I would die young. This, I believed, was my destiny, and I lived with the absolute conviction, which became a fear, that every day was carrying me a little closer towards fulfilling it.

9

IN THE BEGINNING, MY lows were particularly bad, almost subterranean. A sense of dread overwhelmed me. When it was at its worst, I'd find myself contemplating my mortality at 3 a.m., the very loneliest of hours because it seems to exist between nothing and nothing.

I'd be wide-eyed, staring into the night, knowing a panic attack was coming and would have to be got through somehow. All I could do was brace myself for it. Each attack was like the one before. I would tremble, my muscles tightening. I'd pant for breath, the sweat gathering in the ridges across my brow and trickling down my temples. A sense of falling or being dragged down came next, and my heart would jump about, thumping against my chest as if trying to escape from it. In the minute or so each bout lasted, and before I was able to reach over and flick on the bedside lamp, I became convinced that the darkness had destroyed what it was concealing from me; that I was about to discover that everything firm and familiar had gone – even the bed I was in and the floor beneath it – leaving me to drift in limitless space. Only with the sudden glow of bright light would I start to feel calm again.

I'd sit up abruptly and gasp, tossing my head backwards. I felt like a swimmer resurfacing from a dive fathoms deep. My gaze would swivel into the shadowed corners of the room. There was the alarm clock, its tick barely audible. There was the Shaker dresser, the key to its double doors always slightly askew in the lock. There was the wide, striped chair, my clothes draped tidily over the right arm. Also there – my saviour – was a radio that had belonged to my father.

The radio was old. Emblazoned on the dial in small black letters were obscure spots, such as Hilversum and Graz, alongside more glamorous capital cities: Berlin, Paris and Vienna. As a very young boy, barely strong enough to kick or head that orange football, I would listen with my father to midweek football commentaries, creating pictures for ourselves out of someone else's fine words. Amid the crackle and spit of the broadcasts, those words floated towards us through the ether from Highbury or Maine Road, Anfield or White Hart Lane.

In the wee small hours of crisis, I'd heave myself onto the lip of the bed and press one of the buttons of the radio at random, desperate for any voice to fill the silence. With the radio babbling away, I'd lie back on the bed and close my eyes, hoping to find some kind of late, jumbled sleep. Dawn came as a blessing.

George Best was scared of ageing, protesting too much that it didn't bother him. You could gift George immortality, but what use would it be to him without eternal youth as well? I was scared of dying, which meant I lived my life in a kind of semi-paralysis. I didn't like crossing a bridge in case it collapsed. I didn't like driving a car, too afraid of someone driving into me. Whenever I passed a tall building, I would look up, expecting to find some object dropping darkly towards to me. I became a doomsday hypochondriac, sensitive to every ache and palpitation.

Right now, I was fortunate only in the fact it was early June. There was nowhere I had to be and no one I was obliged to meet. As debilitating as my condition became, I did a decent job of hiding it, never sharing my daily struggles because I was too embarrassed. I certainly couldn't confess them to Frank Mallory. In his eyes, I'd have been broken – irreparably so, the crack always visible to him.

Just before pre-season training was about to begin, I went to the club doctor. I complained only of listlessness, extreme lassitude and muscle pain. I told him it was impossible for me to do anything – even make a pot of tea – without feeling utterly exhausted afterwards. He diagnosed chronic fatigue syndrome. The doctor prescribed medication. I flushed it away. Frank told everyone that I had damaged an ankle.

When we'd been out drinking, George had revealed that Matt Busby once sent him to a psychiatrist, who wore a tweedy suit and studied him over the top of gold half-moon spectacles.

I found one of my own. She was in her mid-40s and knew little about football, and even less about me, which I preferred. Her interest in the game alternated between curiosity and disdain. I think she saw footballers as stereotypes: uneducated, vulgar and sweaty. Before our first session, she glanced suspiciously at my copy of *The Times*, perhaps thinking I had brought it with me as a prop.

Her clinic was in a Georgian house on a tree-heavy street in north London, where no one recognised me. Her body was thin, her joints like sharp edges that even her loose clothes couldn't quite disguise. She would wear a trouser suit, usually in Payne's grey, a white shirt buttoned at the neck and a pair of black, thick-framed glasses. Her hair, a kind of mousey blonde, was scraped back and fastened with a tortoiseshell clip shaped like a butterfly. She was polite but impersonal, her manner and voice as formal as a diplomat's. I didn't mind that – I wanted things to be business-like. We'd sit facing one another in identical chairs, the leather arms of which were cold but beautifully smooth to the touch. She would open a black Moleskine notebook and write with a Mont Blanc fountain pen, the nib silver. I noticed her fingers were extraordinarily long, like a pianist's. I soon learnt of her habit, of which she was perhaps unaware, of contemplating a point by staring up at the ceiling, as though the answer to the problem I'd presented her with might be found there. Other 'tells' gave away her mood.

In response to anything interesting I said, her head would tilt inquisitively to the right a little. Boredom was signalled with a sliding, downward glance to her left. When exasperated, she'd scratch two horizontal lines sharply in her notebook. Her office was almost as spartan as a monk's cell. Only one print hung on the wall. It was Lowry's *The Sea 1963*, in which a blank sky meets a wide slab of empty water, the horizon indistinct. The lone ornament on the corner of her desk was a Newton's cradle, a temptation I could never resist. I thought one thing ironic: the furniture in the room in which I spoke about death – desk, bookcases, sideboard – was cut in the same pale oak from which coffins are made.

I'd unburdened myself so freely to George Best because I was drunk; because he was a stranger I didn't think I'd meet again for a year or two; and because he was also drunk, so I didn't imagine he'd remember much of what I said.

But in the still silence of the psychiatrist's office, I found it difficult to speak.

Psychiatrists are like forensic experts in crime dramas, examining every fingerprint, boot-print and bloodstain for clues, before making imaginative leaps of deduction that close the case.

She asked me about my mother. I said I'd been so young when she'd left that, once the initial shock had settled, her absence became normal because I'd accepted it. In fact, if one day she'd walked back into the house, I would have asked her to walk back out again. She'd have disturbed the harmony of the place, the routine we'd established, the brotherly friendship that my father and I had created.

It took several sessions – six, I think – to go through every damn thing. My career. My success. My thoughts as I watched the light go out in my father, like a candle burning slowly to the wick.

'There's a name for your condition,' she said. 'Thanatophobia.'

Look up 'thanatophobia' in a medical textbook and you'll find this thumbnail definition: *Abnormal fear of death . . . often precipitated by personal trauma . . . derived from the Greek.* Thanatos was the god who carried the dead off to the underworld. His family lineage was behind his profession: his mother was Nyx, the god of night; his brother was Hypnos, the god of sleep.

The psychiatrist gave me a moment in which to absorb her diagnosis. After identifying the beast, she then pinned a tail on it. 'Everything was going so beautifully for you, and everything came so easily too, that I suspect you began searching for an explanation for it. You talk about your career as though the axis on which it's always turned has been luck rather than talent. Your father's death triggered a trauma you can't rationalise, never mind control. You came to a conclusion few would have reached. You think – unconsciously, of course – that the amount of luck you say you've enjoyed can't possibly come without a catch. That somehow it's left you in debt. And you think that debt is about to be called in. That's the trauma talking to you. Don't worry. There are things we can do to break your pattern of negative thinking.'

In the end, I didn't find the cure in her office. It came instead in the most unlikely place: Chelsea's Stamford Bridge.

10

YOU SHOULD NEVER MOURN a building the way you mourn a human being, but I miss Stamford Bridge as it used to be. The elliptical shape of the ground made it much bigger then, a poor man's Wembley. You were remote from the crowd because of the semi-circles of empty space behind each goal and also the width of the track, where greyhounds used to race, skirting the pitch.

It was a raw November night, the fans in coats and sweaters and woollen hats. The game was meandering on – grim and goalless. If you'd saved the match programme and dug the thing out now, I doubt the sight of it would prompt a single memory. Nothing memorable occurred. We and Chelsea were as dreary as each other.

Thanks to the psychiatrist, I had returned to training and

got back on the field in September. I'd played only three games when I cracked a bone in my foot. It was painfully slow to heal.

Stamford Bridge was my first appearance anywhere in more than a month. I was neither fit nor match-ready, but our treatment room was like a casualty station. I was wary about playing; I even told Frank Mallory so. In return I got one of his infamous ray-gun stares, which I think he sincerely believed would incinerate me on the spot. 'Play right back. We'll nurse you through it.'

A career ends in one of two ways: very gradually or very suddenly. Mine was the latter.

That afternoon there'd been some heavy rain, which made the turf shiny, as if a veneer had been applied to it. The white ball glistened under the floodlights like the cue ball on the baize of a snooker table. We were defending the Shed End. One Chelsea attack had broken apart and another was being put together. Pat Nevin came through midfield and overhit a high pass intended for Kerry Dixon. The ball bounced towards the corner flag. I pivoted sharply to retrieve it. No player was within thirty yards of me. I don't know whether the grass was slightly longer than it ought to have been or whether I'd screwed in the wrong studs, but my balance went awry, my right leg taking too much weight. The pain felt as though someone had taken a 12-inch needle, held it over a fire and then hammered it into my knee and out the other side.

You can be caught up in an event, even something crucial, and be unaware of the significance of it, but I realised the finality of my injury even as I was carried off the field, dazzled by the lights. I was already an ex-player, the announcement of my retirement awaiting only a date. In hospital, preparing for the operation, I received consoling telephone calls, telegrams, cards and letters. Even the players I'd once tried to scar sent messages of support. I still have them. There was barely an injury that Bryan Robson hadn't suffered while playing for either England or Manchester United. Nearly every part of him had been patched up, pinned, operated on or put in a cast or sling. He'd dislocated his shoulder twice in 14 months. Robson was getting over surgery for the second of those dislocations when he signed a note on United's headed notepaper that I suppose a secretary had typed for him: 'Never, never give up,' it said.

I didn't give up, at least not demonstrably, but I was aware that pressing on only delayed the inevitable. Yes, there'd be a few months of recovery before the futile effort at rehabilitation began. Yes, I would complete lonesome laps of bare pitches on blowy mornings and rainy afternoons. Yes, I would dash up and down the concrete terraces (some of which still existed then) and do more press-ups and squats than an army battalion. Yes, I'd go through the motions of physiotherapy. But all of that would be pointless. My knee was shot. It couldn't resist a hard tackle. It wouldn't survive a quick turn. The pugilist in me was at rest, gone forever.

In the oddest way imaginable, I felt vindicated and even

liberated. It was a mercy. I knew, without initially knowing why, that I didn't need a psychiatrist any more. I could move on, go forward. I had thought something horrible was going to happen to me and was convinced that my good fortune couldn't last; I had just overestimated what I expected Fate to mete out. I wasn't going to die prematurely; I had suffered a different death instead – the small death of my footballing career, at the age of 29.

I thought about Robbie Clayton a lot.

As a player, once you reach 30 you see the end of your career approaching. You're old enough then to look back. You do the maths and depress yourself as a consequence. Robbie had made me aware of this before I'd barely broken out of my teens: 'One moment you're a novice, still picking at the spots on your face. The next you're staring at the youth team training on another pitch. You're thinking about which one of those players will take your shirt. Your career after 30? You're playing in injury time – and there's not long of that left.'

I remembered Robbie had said that so many players don't contemplate retirement until the chance to prepare properly for it had passed. They mistake the game for their whole world, he'd complained. 'We've all heard of footballers who found themselves in piss alley,' said Robbie. 'They end up there because they can't imagine a life without football. Or they expect football to come along and save them.'

He'd told me the story of Tommy Lawton, for whom the

prefix 'Great' was no exaggeration. Lawton was twice the First Division's top scorer as a teenager and a League Championship winner with Everton in 1939, the year Hitler reorganised the fixture list. If the war hadn't stopped him, at a point when no defence could, he'd have broken every scoring record in the book. In just 23 internationals for England, he scored 22 goals. His talent made him wealthy for a while.

Robbie used Lawton's crashing descent from superstardom as a warning from history. Coming from him, the account had genuine clout. He was so friendly with Lawton that he could quote him verbatim.

For Lawton, leaving the game was like an amputation, explained Robbie. He found that rock bottom was further down than he imagined. 'Tommy, bless him, flogged his shirts and his souvenirs in pubs to stay solvent. Sometimes he was obliged to bum money from friends, who he couldn't pay back. He'd leave home every morning, pretending to head for work, and mooch around the Market Square because he was afraid his wife would discover the truth about his unemployment. When I first met Tommy, he was finally putting his life together again. It had taken him nearly 20 years.'

The irony was that Robbie didn't take his own advice. I'd wished for better times for him, but he kept saying goodbye to things: a sports shop that went bust; a clothing company that failed. He'd retreated to a pub on the Lincolnshire coast.

Robbie didn't advertise his past, meaning he couldn't cash in on it. When Sweets Wharton went to see him, he discovered Robbie had swept his medals and trophies into a box – even his Footballer of the Year statuette – and all his shirts into supermarket plastic bags. They'd been shoved into the attic. You went into the pub, said Wharton, and found nothing there that linked him to his past.

I wouldn't be another Robbie, for I had a role waiting for me. Frank Mallory wanted me to work alongside him. Or so I thought.

I I

INJURED PLAYERS TEND TO be ignored. The focus of the fans, fickle as it is, turns elsewhere. Journalists have other things to write about.

Only the local evening newspaper, *The Post*, was interested in chronicling my fight for fitness, which I knew I would never achieve. It usually printed one or two paragraphs every month about my progress. The paragraphs always appeared at the bottom of a much longer story, like the PS at the end of a letter. But the paper's reporter sat me down for a full-length interview once. It was published in *The Pink*, a Saturday-night miracle of results and league tables that used to arrive so quickly off the presses that reading it stained your hands with ink.

I trusted my gentle interrogator. We were the same age. I'd known him before I'd broken into the team. He had VIP access to the club. Frank Mallory allowed him to travel on the coach, the rarest of privileges even then. He ghosted Frank's weekly column and had his own chair in the corridor outside the manager's office.

We sat in the stand overlooking the pitch. We talked about what had happened at Stamford Bridge. For appearances' sake, I spoke about the resolve you needed to go through the slog and drudgery of getting fit and how difficult match days had become. I was part of the side, but also apart from it. He took me through the cardinal points of my career. The Cup final, of course. The goal (about which I had nothing revelatory to say). The international caps. The season we jostled with Liverpool for the title. As I heard myself speak, I thought I was dictating my obituary to someone taking it down in shorthand.

Finally, he asked: 'You study the game very well and understand it. If you can't play, will you coach or manage?'

A tincture of flattery had been dropped into the question. I succumbed to it, answering candidly because the stuff that had gone before was the truth only up to a point. 'I will. I've always wanted that. I'm a football man.' I explained, more fully and expressively than I'd originally intended, about the kind of coach or manager that I wanted to be and also, at some length, about the work I'd put in so far. When *The Pink* came out, the piece ran under the headline: 'CALLAGHAN: MY PLAN TO BE A MANAGER'.

The accompanying photograph showed me staring wistfully across the empty ground. I decided not to give the article another thought, not even a fleeting one. But then other offers to speak came in. Would I talk to this or that national newspaper? Would I appear on *Football Focus*? Would I fill in as an analyst on *The Big Match*? For two weeks, I accepted those invitations and others like them. They were a respite from the stale repetition of all my days.

One evening the phone rang. I assumed an offer of more work was coming. Instead, it was Frank. You couldn't describe what followed as a conversation because I wasn't allowed to reply. The only word I said was 'hello'.

'Hey, busy bollocks,' he said. 'You're supposed to be getting fit. I'm the only one at our club allowed to go on TV and give an opinion. I don't want to switch on my set and see or hear you again. You're crap at it anyway.'

He slammed down the receiver.

12

IT WAS MY 30TH birthday.

I knew I'd never play again properly, but I'd been doing some light exercise – a few sprints and some jogging – before I joined in a five-a-side game with the reserves. I was back on the same junior pitches, next to the British Waterways building, where my trial matches had taken place 14 years before. The match was supposed to be 20 minutes each way. I went into it exhilarated, grateful to have a ball at my feet again. I suppose it brought back something of my boyhood: a small pitch; the teams chosen by the two captains, one of whom was me; the game informal; shouted disputes over whether a goal had or had not been scored; fading afternoon light; everyone trying to show off a bit.

We were winning, and I was running through on my own. A defender slid into me, taking the ball. The tackle was fair, but I went over exactly in the same way as I'd done at Stamford Bridge.

I was carried half a mile along the riverbank, my arms draped across the shoulders of two other players. As I was taken to the dressing room, where I waited for an ambulance, I thought about Robbie Clayton and the Cup final morning.

A couple of days later, the specialist put the X-ray of my knee onto the light box in his consulting room. He took a pencil and pointed to the fresh damage. The specialist was a portly man in his early 60s. He had a trim moustache of the sort that had long ceased to be fashionable. He wore a blue pin-striped suit, a white shirt and a crimson tie. The neat tip of a handkerchief, also crimson, poked from his top pocket. With a flower in his buttonhole too, he looked as though he was about to leave for a society wedding.

He sat behind his desk and rested his fingers together in the shape of a steeple. 'I'm sorry,' he said. 'You could go through this whole business again – the rest, the strappings, the training programme – but I don't think it would be worth your while.' I shook his flabby hand. He gave me a set of X-rays in a brown envelope, and I noticed – a fact that becomes more peculiar the more I think about it – how immaculately clipped his nails were. Perhaps I was sensitive to the small things around me: the branches of the tree outside his window; the soft thud his door made when I closed it; the traffic noise.

I was sorry but not depressed. I'd be taken on as a coach. I expected Frank Mallory to ring and invite me to the ground. When my father died, he'd been on the phone within an hour, promising whatever I wanted.

Frank greeted my latest news with a great silence.

The phone went at seven o'clock the following night. It was Jonjo Whelan.

'It'll be no consolation to you, but I think you were a great player and you gave us everything you had. The fans won't forget that. You'll always be popular.' He paused, leaving a space in which I could thank him. I did my duty. Jonjo then said: 'There's something I have to tell you.' There was a nervous catch in his voice, as though he was afraid of the message he had to deliver. 'The club is paying up your contract. They're giving you a bonus too. All the paperwork will be posted on. Take your time. Pick up your boots and whatever else is yours whenever you like. Come and say goodbye to the lads.' His voice petered out in embarrassment.

'Where's Frank?' I asked. 'Why hasn't he rung?'

Jonjo spluttered out a cough, his way of stalling, before composing himself again. 'Frank's not here. He's on a short break. He's asked me to handle everything.'

Those three sentences came out so quickly that I had to ask Jonjo to repeat them. I thought I'd misheard him.

I didn't speak to Frank for another six years.

PART THREE
YOU'RE NO ONE IN THIS GAME

I'VE MET PLAYERS FROM the 1950s and 1960s who have a certain bitterness inside them. They always make long, hostile speeches about how good the game used to be in 'my day'. Back then a defender could come at you with his claws out and his studs like spikes. One ex-pro said to me: 'You could take a machete onto the pitch, chop off someone's head and stuff it into a hat box. You still wouldn't get booked.' You went out on a Thursday night, drank seven pints and sweated the alcohol out of your system the next day. A pre-match meal was a slab of steak and a plateful of chips.

Their nostalgia was merely a preamble that led to a lot of bleating about money. How you'd been paid only £50 a week even though 50,000 people watched your games. How you'd had to live in some new, three-bedroom house, drive a Ford Cortina and cut your own lawn on a Sunday morning. How, after your career was over, you took over a pub or a firm hired you as a salesman. You'd butter up clients who would bore you into stupefaction about a wonder goal you'd scored at Goodison Park on some dreary January night. At least eight times out of ten, you'd have to tell them:

It wasn't you but someone else who scored that goal.

It wasn't at Goodison Park.

It happened in April.

These old boys, some of them contemporaries of my father, cursed the generations that followed them. You'd get to hear about how – with better timing of their birth – their careers and lives would have been *so* bloody different. They tortured themselves – and they'd torture you – with all those maybes and what-might-have-beens and if-onlys. It was as though complaining out loud legitimised each grievance.

I ought to have told them, but didn't, that not all of us lived high on the hog. I wasn't poor by any means, but I had to quit a year before the Premier League began. I missed all the flashy hoopla of 'Here We Go' and 'Alive and Kicking', the promotional adverts and graphics and two-hour build-up to every live game. I missed the big wages, sponsorships and endorsements that even mediocre players got, giving them more cash in one season than Matthews or Finney, Puskás or Di Stéfano earned in a dozen. I regret that, but I'm not remotely sour about it. Not now, anyway. I came to realise that the world is what it is.

But, I confess, it was different during those first, difficult months, when football forgot me, the way it forgot Robbie Clayton.

Frank Mallory used to quote one of his old coaches, who had told him: 'You're no one in this game once it decides to finish with you.' That line spun around in Frank's head after he finished playing, taunting and motivating him in equal measure.

It did the same for me when the reality of retirement sank in.

The practical problems, the nuts and bolts of no longer being a player, are difficult enough. The psychological strain is worse. The feeling of being *someone* is gone. So is the feeling of being part of a family. Overnight you're an orphan. Going back to your club can bring more misery than relief. Your name's not in the programme. Your autograph isn't as valuable as it was before. Someone is sitting where you always sat in the dressing room.

You feel so lonely.

I didn't even bother to collect my boots and my few belongings from the ground. I expected the postman to hand them to me one morning in a brown paper parcel. He never did.

In a hopeful mood, I was convinced something would turn up. For a while I enjoyed my freedom, unshackled from a club that had previously ordered my life. You're cosseted as a player, everything done for you. Frank was adamant: 'You don't have to think. I'll tell you when to breathe and eat and sleep and shit.' You're told to turn up at a certain time. You're told when you can leave again. You're told which days you can take off. You're told how to behave and what to wear on match days. I knew one player who, a week after quitting, rang the club and asked: 'How do I book a holiday?'

I had no routine in that floral late spring. I wallowed in it, doing whatever I liked on a whim. I wasn't overly concerned as the weeks passed by, gradually becoming indistinguishable from one another. I made only a few phone calls, asking managers whom I thought I knew well whether I might work for them. I wrote letters, which either went unanswered or elicited standard replies of such terse politeness that you wouldn't have known I'd ever been in the game. I binned all of them but kept a mental note of each patronising snub. Every 'friend' I had in football believed I had an ulterior motive. The most insecure managers thought I was chasing their job. I got only one offer: coaching, part-time, at Lincoln City. I didn't want to slum it so low down.

By mid-summer, when pre-season got under way, I felt utterly lost. I had nowhere to go, nothing to do.

I knew 'my' team – for I still thought of them that way – would train on the embankment beside the river. They'd run across the bridge and down the stone steps that led towards two public pitches. The goalposts there would have been pulled up at the end of May. The grass would still be recovering from the season before. The sun would glint off the water. The trees would cast the kind of dark shadow into which you could hide without being seen.

One morning I opened up the local newspaper and saw a photograph of the players there. The next day, the sky cloudless, I decided to go to the embankment. I wanted to watch the training as unobtrusively as possible. I sat on a bench, facing the river, and pulled the stiff peak of a navy baseball cap over my eyes. From beneath its long brim, I saw the players cross the bridge and trot along the narrow dusty path. I waited five minutes before following. I stood behind iron railings that smelt of fresh paint. I was 50 yards away; I must have looked like a stick figure to them. I can't explain, even now, what my purpose was – or what I hoped to achieve. What did I expect? Was I waiting to be recognised? Did I want Frank to turn around and say: 'What are you doing here?' Did I think he'd beckon me over?

But Frank wasn't even there. I watched my former friends, transfixed for about half an hour, before turning for home.

Jealousy ripped through me.

Then sorrow.

Lastly, a humbling self-pity.

My playing career was truly over. It belonged, as I did, to the world of yesterday. My yesterday was less than three months ago, but as I walked away from the embankment it felt as though three years had passed – or even thirty.

You're no one in this game once it decides to finish with you.

I'd been a gullible, arrogant fool for believing that sentence didn't apply to me. My first mistake was putting my faith in Frank. My second was waiting to be courted. My third was holding out for something better than the game was prepared to give me. Modest as they were, Lincoln City suddenly had a certain allure. Sincil Bank, the cathedral close by, was now as lovely as Shangri-La.

The similarities between Robbie and me became clearer then. We didn't know how to live without the game because football defined us. With it, we had an identity. Without it, we were nobody. We needed the recognition it brought us, the worship it inspired. Unless you've played, you can't know what the purest form of exhilaration is like. When every pair of eyes is on you. When your name is on everyone's lips. When it's being chanted, every voice singing.

Brooding on this, I didn't blame myself. I blamed Frank. Indeed, I blamed him for everything. He'd duped me into thinking I was special – and then, like Robbie, he'd dumped me.

When you rule out the impossible, whatever is left – however improbable – is surely the truth. I was convinced the clubs I'd approached had contacted Frank. I was also certain he had refused to recommend me. Asked for a reference, I imagined him slipping negative words or faint praise into it, like knives.

In my head, I heard him say: 'He wasn't right for us. I don't think he'll be right for you. Not quite coaching material.'

It was the only explanation that made sense to me.

2

EVEN IF YOU'RE AWARE that Växjö is in Sweden, which you probably aren't, I doubt you'd know where to find it on the map. It's a dot of a place, 260 miles south-west of Stockholm.

I'd played against the local team, Östers, in a UEFA Cup tie in the early 1980s. It was shortly after that club's 'Golden Hour', in which three Allsvenskan titles were won in four seasons. I took a homely shine to Växjö, a 'walking city' that is intimate without being claustrophobic. I liked the neat, clean and civilised streets. I liked the small squares and the buildings planted around them, washed in vibrant colour. I liked the copper-clad roof of the cathedral, its thin twin spires resembling the upturned prongs of a fork. I liked the fact that the air was like a splash of cold water. In January, when ice could root you to the floor, the snowy whiteness of the landscape was gorgeously bright on the eyes.

Everyone I met spoke English. They all knew every detail imaginable about English football, both current and recent. Sweden had been showing English matches live on TV since 1969. A new channel, launched then, capitalised on our football to inflate its ratings. It screened games between November and March, during Sweden's close season. I came across people, among them Östers season-ticket holders, who didn't just follow English clubs avidly – particularly Manchester United, Arsenal, Spurs and Liverpool – but also made frequent trips, like religious pilgrimages, to watch them.

The day before the second leg of our UEFA Cup tie – we were 2–0 up from the first – I went sightseeing alone. Without knowing it, I passed Östers' three-storey 'clubhouse'. By chance, their coach, Noah Björklund, saw me from a window. I've never told anyone about this. How, if we'd lost, could I have explained away a private, two-hour conversation with the man in charge of the opposition?

Noah was very gaunt and very blond. He'd played for 14 years in Sweden without winning a trophy. He'd coached Kalmar, which sits beside the Baltic Sea, before Östers poached him. When I met him, he'd already claimed back-to-back league titles.

Noah was an Anglophile. He spoke English with only a smidgen of an accent. He drank English tea without milk. Every morning he bought the *Daily Mail*, which arrived in Sweden a day after it was printed in London. He wore shirts bought from London's Jermyn Street. He used a video recorder – new technology back then – to build a tape library of more than a thousand English matches.

He'd been 17 years old, the same age as the little-known Pelé, when his country staged the 1958 World Cup finals. He'd trekked from one ground to the next to be bewitched either by

Brazil – particularly Didi and the 'Little Bird' Garrincha – or
Sweden, who were improbably managed by George Raynor,
the Englishman from the South Yorkshire coalfields who had
already made his adopted country Olympic champions. It was
Raynor, ignored and scorned in England but treasured abroad,
who had inspired Noah to go into coaching. A framed black-
and-white photograph of Raynor hung on the wall of Noah's
top-floor office. That day, Noah charted for me the development
of Raynor's innovative 'G-man' strategy: the deployment of a
deep-lying centre forward, whom, in modern parlance, we'd call
a 'false nine'. 'Raynor was a prophet,' said Noah. 'But, like all
prophets, he had no honour elsewhere, which is how he found
himself in Sweden.'

Noah still carried his ticket for the World Cup final, tucked into
his wallet like a lucky charm. Standing behind one of the goals
in the Råsunda Stadium, he'd got soaked on that rainy Sunday
when Brazil beat Sweden 5–2.

'Ten years later,' he said, 'I went to visit Raynor in England.
He lived in a very modest bungalow in Skegness. Do you know
that town?'

I did; during my boyhood, my father and I went there sometimes on summer weekends. We'd catch a train, travelling on
the Poacher Line towards the North Sea. Noah had arrived in
Skegness uninvited. He didn't know Raynor's address, relying on
the locals to point the way. Raynor had recently been sacked by

Doncaster Rovers, then of the Fourth Division. Noah found him in the garden. Raynor was wearing a thick polo-neck sweater, like a seafarer, and a pair of wellington boots. He was digging a vegetable patch with a fork. The wind cut across the land from the sea. His cheeks were apple-red.

'Mr Raynor, I have come from Sweden to learn from you,' said Noah.

'If you're from Sweden, you'd better come in.'

For six hours Noah drank Raynor's tea, sitting opposite the ex-manager in a small living room, the wallpaper as colourful as a wildflower meadow. 'After that, I loved English football even more than ever,' he told me.

I'd met Raynor – only once, and very briefly. He had been sitting in Frank Mallory's office. By then he was 70 years old, a grey-haired man in a pale-grey suit that made him seem semi-invisible. 'Shake George by the hand,' Frank had ordered, stubbing out the butt of a cigarette into an overflowing ashtray. 'This man is a giant'.

Noah was startled by that story. He saw serendipity in it. 'I had no idea Mallory was a disciple of Raynor's,' he said. He wanted to know all about Frank. 'Mallory's unconventional, isn't he?'

'Most would go even further than that,' I said.

My patter about Frank was well practised. I offered Noah a compilation of anecdotes. His dislike of being late, which made him an hour early for everything. His love of Blue Note jazz, which he played at high volume from a record deck beside his desk. His meticulousness about our pitch; he'd sink to eye level to inspect it, before always telling the groundsman to shave the grass closer still. What fascinated Noah was Frank's attitude towards training. He'd flog the squad hard in the summer. As the season progressed, the physical demands made on us eased. If we had a midweek match, we'd train just twice that week. Frank also arranged jaunts to Spain or Portugal for 'holidays'. Sunshine and rest acted like a tonic to both us and him. I told Noah that Frank, though ubiquitous in the media, was often no more than a vaporous presence at the ground.

'For months he's like the Yeti,' I said.

'You mean fearsome?' asked Noah.

'No. Glimpsed but never seen.'

Frank was convinced that rationing his own appearances in front of us was beneficial. He thought we'd pay more attention to his voice, the stick that could beat you, if we didn't hear it every day. Sometimes he'd appear only half an hour before kick-off.

As a young player, Frank's coaches had starved him of the ball during the week to make him hungry for it on a Saturday. Like Raynor, he thought that approach was nonsense on stilts. For how does *not* practising with a ball make you better at controlling it? He'd walk into our dressing room carrying one. 'Don't forget,' he'd say, 'this ball is your friend. Treat it like one. Don't kick the shit out of the leather. Caress it.'

Noah's eyes widened. 'That's the extent of his coaching?'

'Not exactly. Frank is coaching all the time. If you meet him in the corridor, he might say you were a yard out of position for a goal . . . or you weren't tight enough to the touchline . . . or you didn't intercept a pass you ought to have done.'

Noah looked baffled. I offered another example to make my explanation clearer. I had once witnessed Frank coach an aspiring centre forward in the club's car park. Frank, who was thirty yards away, yelled at him: 'Stop and bloody well don't move. Not a muscle.' The centre forward, terrified of him, went rigid in mid-stride. Frank marched over, repeating his instruction to stay still.

Frank worshipped Jimmy Greaves, who was capable of disappearing on a pitch for two minutes, as if invisible, and then reappearing again where the defence didn't want to find him. With an unexpected surge of tenderness, Frank told the centre forward about Greaves' qualities.

'Most fans lucky enough to have watched him saw Jimmy Greaves whooshing past defenders. I see him standing still before that happened. No one stood still better than Jimmy Greaves. He was clever. He had a perfect awareness of what was going on around him. You have to learn to do that. I've been watching you, son. You're trying to go in 12 directions at once and getting nowhere. You're wasting your energy. *Stand still.* Let everyone else run around you. Let the defenders move towards the ball. Pick a pocket of space where you can gather up a pass on the half-turn. That's what Greaves did.'

Frank then swivelled on his heels, a bit like Greaves in the box, and walked briskly past me. 'That's coaching,' he said.

We beat Östers 3–1. Noah and I exchanged only a handshake afterwards and said our goodbyes, each of us never expecting to run into the other again.

It's easy to regard a moment that meant little or nothing to you at the time as a turning point later on. That's the trick hindsight plays on you.

3

IT BEGAN WITH BOBBY Robson.

Like so many others – players, coaches and managers – I owe a debt to Robson. I came back into his orbit when the Professional Footballers' Association arranged a coaching course at Lilleshall for ex-players who were desperate to stay in the game. Robson was the keynote speaker. It was early 1993. Apart from picking up piecemeal work – mostly punditry and coaching schoolboys at holiday soccer schools – I'd been unemployed for 18 months. I hadn't got rid of my cash frivolously, but I had worked my way through it to the extent that I could see the bottom of my savings the way a pub drinker sees the bottom of a pint glass.

I invested in myself. I wrote begging letters to coaches in Europe to ask whether I could spend a week or two following them about as a silent, surreptitious observer. I boldly laid out the details of my career and my circumstances to them. I wanted to improve my football education. I'd take nothing from them except their time. I'd pay for my travel and my board. I asked for only two things. To watch them work and ask questions afterwards.

I went to Belgrade and spent a week with Ljupko Petrović at Red Star. I went to Marseille for ten days, where the Belgian Raymond Goethals, one of the few former goalkeepers to become a formidable coach, had recently lost a European Cup final but was barely six months from winning the trophy; he quit afterwards. Goethals was a grumpier version of Frank Mallory. Fools weren't allowed within 50 yards of him. A chain-smoker, he walked about as though his upper body were trapped in a bank of nimbostratus cloud.

After Marseille, I went to Milan, Turin and Munich. I most wanted to go to Barcelona, where Johann Cruyff was coaching his 'Dream Team'. The previous May, I'd gone to Wembley and had watched Barcelona beat Sampdoria in the final of the European Cup. Cruyff's team included Stoichkov and Koeman, Juan Carlos and Laudrup.

Cruyff ignored my letter.

I knew only one man who was sufficiently influential to get to Cruyff directly and lobby him on my behalf. I rang George Best, who'd become a friend, and asked for a favour. Within an hour, I was talking to Cruyff on the phone. Within four days, I was sitting in his office. He apologised, mortified that he hadn't seen my letter. I believed him: the top of his desk was a swamp of paper.

Cruyff, like George, willingly shared his genius whenever I got half an hour to interrogate him about it. His training sessions were never held behind closed doors. I could have turned up, like any Barca fan, and watched Koeman sharpen his free kicks. Cruyff, as lean as ever, either sat on a ball beside the touchline or trained with his players. He even dug out a pair of boots for me. We struck passes to one another in a minor competition to find out who was quicker at killing a ball stone dead. He won, of course. Cruyff pulled another player across to join us. He was dark-haired. The short sleeves of his shirt were baggy around his thin arms. Cruyff and I played piggy-in-the-middle with this player, trying to trick him; he always worked out where the ball was going and intercepted it.

This is how I met Pep Guardiola.

George knew Cruyff and I had something in common. He shared it with me, knowing I would understand. 'Cruyff once believed he'd die young too,' George said.

In his car, chauffeuring me across Barcelona for a late supper, Cruyff told me that his father had died of a heart attack, aged 45. 'I was only 12 years old,' he said. 'I convinced myself I wouldn't reach 50. The older I got, the worse that feeling became. Now, like you, the obsession has passed. It ended when I got heart problems of my own. I decided I had to get on with life.'

He still spoke to his dead father, Cruyff added. 'I talk to him about my problems. I once tested him. If he could really hear me, I asked that he send me a sign to prove it. Make my watch stop, I said. The next morning, it did. I took it to the watchmaker's. There was nothing wrong with the mechanism. Next morning, the watch stopped again. My father had made his point.'

Wherever he went, Cruyff exuded authority because of who he was, and he wore that authority as lightly as a linen cloak. He had given up smoking, swapping his 20-a-day habit for fruit lollipops. Whenever his craving for nicotine returned, he'd dip his hand into a cardboard box, unwrap a lollipop and crunch the cellophane into a tight ball. After finishing the lollipop, he'd jam its thin white stick between his first and second fingers, as though holding a fag.

'Promise me one thing,' he said before I left. 'If you become a coach, you have to try to entertain. Winning is vital, yes, but you don't get the same satisfaction out of it unless you also play well, put on a show. Who wants to watch, week in, week out, a team that is dull? I could never do that.'

After the 1990 World Cup, Bobby Robson swapped the England manager's job for PSV Eindhoven, where persuasion and magnanimity held together a fractious squad. He won two Eredivisie titles. He'd since moved to Sporting in Portugal.

At Lilleshall, he spoke for an hour and then took questions for an hour more. He talked with the kind of enthusiasm that made you a convert to whatever cause he championed. He bubbled over, his spirit crackling around the big, bare room. Robson was a very human figure, someone in whom it was easy to confide because you felt the belief you had in him would be reciprocated. He wouldn't let you down. He wouldn't say one thing but do another. He wouldn't exploit you for his own ends.

Afterwards, I corralled him in a corner, asking one thing after another. He couldn't escape, but seemed content to let me monopolise him. I told Robson where I'd been and what I'd been doing, shamelessly dropping Cruyff's name into our conversation.

As someone who understood others so well, I'm sure Robson recognised desperation when he saw it. He kept giving me one of his friendly, 'aw shucks' grins, his face collapsing into creases. I think my commitment impressed him more than my talent or my track record, but he made me feel better about myself than anyone else I'd met since retiring. 'You're more aware of the game than some coaches who are working,' he told me. If someone could have embroidered that reference for me on a square of cloth, I would have framed it. 'Let's see what I can do for you,' he added.

I doubt Robson needed another dogsbody scout in England, which is the job he gave me. I also doubt whether Sporting were in favour of hiring me – especially not for charitable reasons.

Shortly after the 1993–94 season began, Robson invited me
to Lisbon. Sporting, conducted like an orchestra by Luis Figo,
were facing Celtic in the second round, second leg of the UEFA
Cup. I sat at the back of a stand in the Estádio de Alvalade. At
half-time, I picked my way through the crowd and found the
hospitality suite, presenting my ticket at the door. The first person
I saw there was Noah Björklund. He stuck out his hand to make
sure I was flesh; he could no more believe the coincidence than I
could. We hadn't seen one another in a decade. After the match,
which Sporting won 2–1, we trekked to a bar in Avenue 24 de
Julho. Noah was about to become manager of Finland. 'I want
to get out of club football for a while, and the offer is a good
one,' he explained.

The next stage of the conversation – the stage that matters –
went like this:

ME: *I'm waiting for a break. I can't seem to get one in
England. Without Bobby Robson, I wouldn't have got
one here.*

HIM: *There's a job at Östers. It's with the youth team. It isn't
much, but it's a start, isn't it? I still know people there
and I'm in touch with them all the time. I can give them
a nudge for you. The coach is called Edvard Bildt. He's
one of my ex-players. A decent guy. You'd get on well
with him.*

ME: *You'd do all that for me?*

HIM: *Of course. I have a long memory. Not many players would have spent so long in my office in those circumstances and then told no one about it. It's OK. I didn't tell anyone either. Go and make a little name for yourself in Sweden. That's what George Raynor did. Eventually, you might get a job you want in England. Just one thing: you won't make much money. In fact, you'll make almost nothing. Does that matter? I don't suppose so.*

ME: *Not at all.*

A month later, I was in Växjö again, an Englishman abroad.

4

THERE ARE NO FOREIGN lands. Only the traveller is foreign. But the country you leave behind usually seems to shrink in size or sometimes disappear completely after you move abroad. You hear only a little of what is going on back home: a small story in the papers or a picture flashed briefly across the evening news. That wasn't so in Sweden. There, Premier League games were analysed to exhaustion.

The news of my appointment made no impact in England. I hadn't expected to be given a brass-band farewell, but I did hope I would catch the peripheral vision of clubs who had previously ignored me. I got two lines in *World Soccer*.

It was near the end of the Swedish season, which gave me time to acclimatise. I began to research the Allsvenskan, borrowing recordings of matches.

Östers were strictly of mid-table stock, too far from the top to make a spectacularly late push for a glittering prize and too distant from the bottom to fret about crashing out. They were a safe bet for me, a decent place to start. I expected to stay for 18 months or so. I'd burnish my CV, do enough to attract another team, perhaps in the Championship, and then I'd start afresh.

Noah Björklund was right: my new boss was a 'decent guy'. Edvard Bildt was only 39. He'd been a part of Noah's first title-winning team, before moving to Germany, where he'd tried and failed to consistently win a place in Kaiserslautern's midfield. Bildt was as bulky as a bodybuilder. Alopecia also made him distinctive – his bald head shone like a light bulb. He was an affable, if lugubrious, man who, like me, saw Östers as preparation for something else. Both of us were passing through.

Bildt and I met in Noah's old office in the Östers clubhouse. I looked at the spot on the wall where George Raynor's photograph had once hung. In its place was a team picture from the 1980s; Bildt sat at the end of the front row.

'I won't meddle in what you do,' he said. 'You're a factory for me. You'll produce players. Do that and we'll never have an argument.'

In my first season, I won a youth cup for him.

Everything then happened at a confusing speed. I was made an assistant coach, my reward for that cup success. I got much closer to Bildt than before, which allowed me to discover the weakness in him. His playing career had ended with a series of sideways, crab-like movements that had taken him nowhere. Impatient to make headway in management, he threw himself into impulsive decisions. He was in too much of a hurry to leave Östers behind.

At the start of the following season, we lost four of our first five matches. After the last of those, I watched him thump his forehead against a panelled wall in frustration. Another defeat, only three days later, and Bildt went completely haywire, walking out on the club with nowhere to go and despite assurances that Östers had no intention of sacking him. The coach he most trusted walked out with him in friendly solidarity. Without identifying anyone, Bildt whined to the local newspaper that he hadn't been given sufficient moral support or the necessary money to build a side. He branded the job as 'impossible'.

There was only one candidate to become caretaker boss. After less than a year and a half at the club, I found myself in charge of it.

Two days later, a small, flat box arrived, wrapped in brown

paper. It carried a Finnish postmark. Inside, I found a handwritten message: 'You know where to hang this.'

Noah had sent me his photograph of George Raynor.

5

MY JOB WAS ONLY the second-most important thing to happen to me in Växjö.

'No one ever plays well when their personal life is a shitstorm. That's why I don't like drinkers at this club. That's why I don't tolerate gamblers. That's why I don't want anybody fucking anybody's wife apart from their own.'

I can still hear Frank Mallory giving me that speech.

My personal life had infuriated Frank. Not because I was boozing, betting and bedding my way around his city, but because I lived alone.

'Get yourself a wife,' he'd say. 'You've got lonely eyes.'

'I'm not lonely,' I'd reply. 'Only lonesome. I like it that way.'

There had been women in my life. They arrived and disappeared again, after a night, a week, a month, six months or – on one occasion – 14 and a half months. In the end, football always got in the way.

The psychiatrist had put an obvious question to me during my treatment: was my mother's abandonment responsible for the lack of any stable female relationship in my life? 'Do you subconsciously push women away before you think they're going to leave you too?' she asked.

I said I didn't think so. 'I just haven't found the right woman,' I added.

When retreating to Sweden still seemed uncomfortably like an exile, I finally did find the right woman. I met Freyja.

Östers were holding a retirement party for someone I had never met and whose name I didn't know, then or subsequently. I remember only two things about him: he had unusually clammy hands, and he held his neck and body very stiffly and straight. He was like someone wearing a top hat at a wedding, afraid it might slide off his head. The party was held in the chandeliered ballroom of a hotel. I was bored for an hour or more, moving from table to table, swapping polite, inconsequential chatter. She entered the ballroom through two vast oak doors, the panels of which were ornately carved with twisting vines and broad leaves. Perhaps Freyja had been in the ballroom all along, hiding in plain sight, and I just hadn't noticed her. But I prefer to believe – making the coincidence meaningful – that she made her entrance at the precise moment I was standing directly in front of those doors, there to greet her.

She'd arrived at the club only six weeks before me, taking a junior job in the commercial department. She dressed like my psychiatrist had done: smart trouser suits and plain, unfussy shirts. Her hair was often scraped back and she eschewed make-up, never bothering with a lick of lipstick or eyeliner. She made a show instead with her jewellery: silver necklaces and wide, loose bangles and rings that could open the top of a bottle. A diamond stud, no bigger than a full stop, sparkled on the left side of her nose.

Freyja was three inches taller and nine years younger than me. She could have been an artist's model. She looked like Lauren Bacall in one of my father's favourite films, *To Have and Have Not*. She was a strawberry blonde. Her skin was almost translucent, her body spindle-slim. Her prominent cheekbones gave her face a sculpted look. That night she wore a long grey satin dress, low-cut and with thin straps. She moved languidly through the room, from one bloom of light to another, like drifting smoke. She was almost apparitional.

In the very beginning I couldn't decide whether to think of what we had as a casual affair or a relationship. Freyja wasn't sure either. She thought that a discreet trip to Stockholm was my way of romancing her. She'd packed an assortment of dresses. Only when we got there did I produce two tickets for a Champions League game in the Råsunda Stadium. 'I'm not getting dressed up for that,' she said.

As newcomers, we were both nervous about whether the club would disapprove of our relationship, judging it as a minor scandal to be discouraged and then suppressed. We didn't flaunt the fact that we were together, but it made no difference. The small signs and the furtive looks were detectable. And so the rumours began and gathered pace until we stopped denying them.

Freyja lived in a single room in a gloomy house with only one shower that she shared with a group of university students. I gave her a key to my apartment. Soon she was practically living there. She would arrive and always ask, as though she needed permission, whether she could take a bath. Afterwards, wrapped in a towel, she would sit cross-legged in front of the fire and slowly drink a gin and tonic. She would tease me about how we met and then our night out shortly afterwards, a date that wasn't quite a date but turned into one. 'You kept staring at my bare shoulders,' she'd say. 'Yes,' I agreed, shy about admitting that I hadn't dared to look directly at her.

I knew what attracted me to her; I just couldn't work out – and still can't – why that attraction was reciprocated. No one would describe me as good-looking.

After she moved in, Freyja liked to stand in the doorway, directly below the lintel, and observe me as I watched matches in the windowless room that I'd created for the purpose. It was as plain as a monk's cell. I'd sit on a long leather sofa, looking at three games simultaneously on big televisions. We acquired a rescue cat, its fur as black as anthracite. Freyja christened it Otta. The cat would perch on one of the square arms of the sofa.

Its head would turn quickly from one screen to the other, like a spectator sitting beside the net at a tennis match.

I put a desk in the room. I would read and research compulsively, plotting tactics and committing thoughts and diagrams to paper. Afterwards, I'd clip the work into bulging black ring-binders for the other coaches. I had enough ring-binders to fill an entire wing of a library. They included analyses of teams I would never face, players I couldn't afford to buy and managers with whom I barely had contact.

'Of all this,' I said to Freyja, 'I'll probably only use 30 per cent. The problem is, you never know *which* 30 per cent.'

Finally, I realised she admired the thing about me that the women before her had found off-putting: my slavish work ethic. To Freyja, I'm sure, it reaffirmed the type of man I was, and also the better man I might become.

She'd been born in Moss, a Norwegian coastal town. Her mother taught modern languages; her Swedish father was a professor of chemistry. Football had never been a part of her academic household. She had fibbed in her application and again during her interview, feigning interest in the game only because she thought the variety in the job, however lowly, and the profile of the club would improve her future prospects.

She knew little about me, which was a good thing. We'd been seeing one another for three months when I took her to a hideaway on Södermöja, one of the islands that make up a vast archipelago in the Baltic Sea. They are pin-small; you won't find them on a standard globe. Södermöja is less than 30 miles east of Stockholm; the boat hardly sets sail before it docks again. A scattering of houses and cabins, mostly rust-coloured, are hidden behind broad trees, playing hide-and-seek with newcomers. Our cabin overlooked the water, which was as still and shiny as oil. The light didn't begin to drain from the day until 9 p.m. You could still read without a lamp two hours later. No one disturbed us.

Freyja wanted to know about my footballing life. The more gently she put a question, the more I revealed to her, willingly peeling away another bit of myself for her inspection. I did so, perfectly aware that another question was always waiting behind each answer I gave. Freyja began at the very end, asking: 'Why did you come here?'

'Because I had to,' I said. 'There was nowhere else for me to go. I couldn't find a club to take me on – certainly not my own, the place that was home.'

'You're still angry about that? Resentful too?'

'A little,' I said.

A week before, I'd received an invitation to attend the club's annual autumn get-together of ex-players and coaches. The old soldiers would talk about their old battles and their old scars, every story embellished a little since the last time I'd heard it. The occasion was always less grand than it seemed, held more out of habit than tradition. It was a piss-up, and a pissing contest too. A lot of beer would be spilt and wasted. A lot of boozy quarrels about who did what and when – and also who was better than whom – would sour it.

I'd taken the gilt-edged invitation out of its envelope and handed it to Freyja.

'You could go. You could take me,' she'd said, not grasping from my expression that it had fallen on the mat like bad news. The honest way to reply to an invitation you have no intention of accepting is to say simply: 'Cannot come – lie follows.' But no one wants to break protocol or be so bloody about it. I had already framed my lie around the usual excuse: a line or two about previous commitments. That was plausible and, not knowing whether or not it was true, people would have no choice but to believe me.

We were sitting outside the cabin, drinking white wine and looking at the water. One boat and then another drifted by, the occupants waving at us like friends.

'I don't want to go to that players' reunion,' I said. 'Even if I did, I wouldn't put you through it. There'll be someone there that I don't want to see.'

For half an hour I spoke about Frank Mallory. After I'd finished, Freyja said: 'You talk about him as though he's a maze of man. He isn't. He plays his little games and enjoys them too much. I don't know how you put up with all that for so long. You don't even know what you did to be treated so badly. This Frank? He is a control freak, a bully. He thinks of no one but himself. You know this, but don't admit it.'

She was right. I found myself mouthing a defence of Frank. Freyja leant over and took my hand. She poured more wine into our bulbous glasses and slid back into her chair. 'One thing astonishes me,' she said, very coolly. 'You say you don't want to see him. But, after all he's done, it seems as though you love him almost as much as you hate him. You still call him Frank. I don't understand that. I don't know how you can speak his name without spitting in anger. He threw you out, for God's sake. Now I think you're biding your time in the hope of going back – and you want to do that to win his approval again and to prove something to him.'

She was right again.

Of course I wanted to go home. Of course I wanted to prove something to Frank. I just saw no possibility of it happening.

The city was too thick with ghosts for me.

6

THE SWEDISH CUP FINAL was staged close to the anniversary – May 22 – of my Wembley goal, scored 13 years before. I'd taken charge only after the quarter-finals, played the previous October before winter set in, but when we took the cup – we beat AIK 3–1 in the final – no one in England saw me as a carpet-bagger. Fewer than 5,000 were inside Gothenburg's old Gamla Ullevi, a stadium named after a Nordic god. The minuscule crowd didn't matter; no one in England knew about that either. To them, I was someone who'd won a trophy. The details were irrelevant beside the gleam of the silverware.

I expected to hear from Frank Mallory at last, but he made no sign and sent no word. 'I told you, and I keep telling you,' said Freyja, 'you need to forget him. You don't need anything from him. Shut the past in a drawer. Don't open it again.'

I revived a team, essentially a bag of bones but energised by its unlikely triumph, that had been stuck in the nether regions of the table. The following year, well prepared, we came from a long way back – we were seventh after two months – to win the Allsvenskan, finishing four points ahead of Malmö. Still Frank said nothing. I accepted that he'd let me slip away, a memory lost.

Frank must have known that I'd built my team with the same bricks and mortar he used. Sweden's best players move elsewhere, naturally drawn by bigger crowds and bigger salaries. The first game I ever saw in Sweden was in Helsingborg. I followed the movement of a striker who flitted about the pitch. It was like watching small flashes of lightning. He was lean and streaky, only 5ft 7ins tall and 21 years old. Irrespective of how or where a pass was delivered, he pulled the ball down and dealt with it nonchalantly. At one point, zigzagging in from the touchline, he didn't so much run with the ball as dance with it. He scored two goals – curling in the first with the outside of his boot – and made another. The striker was Henrik Larsson. 'Why don't we try to sign him?' I'd asked Edvard Bildt. Bildt gave a tart reply, as though I was colossally stupid: 'Because we can't possibly afford him, and he won't be in Sweden two months from now.' He was right; off Larsson went to Feyenoord.

When I took over Bildt's side, needing to shore up the gaps in it, our conversation that afternoon hummed around in my head. I began looking for the next Larsson. I wanted a young team because I was a ridiculously young manager. I reshaped the squad I'd inherited, taking them from cup winners to champions through the kindness of others. Bobby Robson lent me a left-sided midfielder, Antonio Saramago, who slicked back his black hair with grease and worked as methodically as a plough horse. Kevin Keegan wanted me to toughen up the 18-year-old Reece Chapman. We were a preparatory school for his career at Newcastle. When Chapman came to us, ready to be blooded, he was only 5ft 5ins tall and had less meat on his bones than a whippet. With sherry and spinach, a breakfast I'd seen Frank inflict on others, we fattened him up a little. When he went back to St James' Park, he was an inch and a half taller and one and a half stones heavier. He found himself beside Ginola and Asprilla, but wasn't overawed, outshone or out of place. He read the game so well that, just like Robbie Clayton, he didn't have to tackle much.

Only two players in our side – our goalkeeper Flemming Vilfort and our captain Thomas Ekstrom – were closer to 30 than 20. Vilfort was huge. He had hands the size of washing-up bowls. He was also the most superstitious man I've ever met. I've known players who won't change their underwear for a month in case it ruins a winning streak, or who insist on being last out of the dressing room, afraid of the calamity that will befall them if that custom is broken. Some won't put their boots or shirt on until the bell rings, forcing them to go into the tunnel. In Frank's FA Cup-winning team, Stuart Kelly had the most peculiar quirk of all. He'd flick the ball up on his left foot and kick it with his right towards the light switch. If he managed to turn the light off, he was fine; if he didn't, he'd try again. It once took him 52 attempts.

Vilfort's multiple rituals bordered on obsessive–compulsive disorder. He'd wash and rewash his hands in litres of liquid soap. He'd bounce the ball off a wall and catch it cleanly 21 times in succession. And he'd take off his gloves and then put them back on again, also 21 times, before going onto the field. If he got distracted or miscounted, the whole slow process would start again from scratch. Vilfort had already broken almost every bone in his body: his nose (three times), four of his fingers, his collarbone and one of his arms. He was brave, for sure. He was reckless sometimes too. I indulged him because Frank taught me that every team needs a spine – goalkeeper, centre half, central midfield, centre forward. 'But you start with your goalkeeper,' he said. 'What's the point of scoring three goals, if your goalkeeper's such an arse that he lets in four? A bad goalkeeper means you're weak at the roots.'

Today there are databases covering every player and club. Football is a nerdy science. The modern analyst is like a cartographer, mapping the landscape of a match infinitesimally. He has an algorithm for everything. How many touches a player takes in a game. How many runs he makes – and how many yards he travels. How many corners he wins. How many times the ball bobbles off his shin and dribbles out for a throw-in.

Frank epitomised how it used to be. He wasn't able to spell the word 'algorithm'. He demanded simplicity, guts, unquestionable commitment. He believed the best players would always overcome their inferiors simply by getting the ball first and holding on to it. He hated blackboards. He was suspicious of bosses who liked the smell of chalk, preferring diagrams to language and theory to practice. He trusted his scouts, blokes such as my father who'd played the game and knew it from the inside.

As much as the minutiae fascinated me, both then and now, I decided simplicity would be our policy. I spoke in sentences that were as clean as bone. We played 4–4–2 or 3–4–3. We absorbed pressure and capitalised on our speed on the break, possessing it in abundance. I adopted the conventional approach, just as Frank did, because I wanted everything to be uncomplicated. I also wanted the team to play the way I could never play myself – with panache and flair. I remembered what Johann Cruyff had said to me. I didn't want to bore the arse off anyone who came to watch, winning matches attritionally by grinding teams to powder. I wanted to live up to his principles and example. 'The only clubs who hire negative managers are those who lack ambition,' he'd said.

How ironic that my career took off at the point at which Frank's began to plummet.

7

I THOUGHT FOOTBALL HAD LOST its capacity to surprise me. I was so used to the unexpected – cup upsets, players bought for fees three times higher than their actual worth – that I came to accept even ludicrous happenings as commonplace. The game was played in a world of its own making, and the normal rules of business, logic and common sense didn't apply.

'And this too shall pass' is a Persian adage that highlights the briefness of everything – including reputations and empires. I never thought it applied to Frank Mallory. He seemed indestructible.

In 1994 Frank won the League Cup again, beating his old club, Bolton, at Wembley. No one, other than the winners and losers, ever remembers a League Cup final. Only if you do your lap of honour in May's bright sunshine, rather than at the end of winter, does it stick in the memory. Frank claimed the result as evidence that 'old dogs' such as him were still relevant 'in a game of young pups'. Before the next home match, he went to the end of the ground where the most loyal and vocal of his supporters gathered. One of the club's silk scarves was wrapped around his neck; a second was tied around his wrist. He stood with his arms flung upwards, his fists balled in aggressive triumph.

Truly, I felt nothing at the sight of this. 'It's peculiar,' I admitted to Freyja. 'I'm not even envious of him. I really don't care.'

'That's good,' she said. 'You're over him.'

The following season, Frank only got as far as the second round of the UEFA Cup before Milan, with a goal from Baggio, tore his team down in the San Siro. I saw that tie. My seat, high up and far back, was directly behind the dug-outs. Frank chewed stick after stick of nicotine gum before spitting it out. He prowled, as though squeezed into a narrow cage, from one side of his technical area to the other. He punched the air, threw his head back in grief and shrieked instructions that no one could hear amid the din.

It's easy to identify something ending: you hear the crack as it breaks. Milan was Frank's last hurrah. Asked once what would constitute a crisis at his club, Uncle Charlie Bembridge had stroked his chin, as if in meditation, and replied: 'A crisis? Running out of claret.' Later on, the Cobbold brothers of Ipswich appropriated that quote and gave it a little twist, swapping white wine for claret.

The crisis for Uncle Charlie was actually running out of money. His financial excesses caught up with him. He had to make a choice between the club or his country house.

8

JACK J. MUNROE VI was into shipping, steel, oil, energy and mining.

Like Uncle Charlie Bembridge, he was shaped by early advantages. He didn't start with nothing and make a fortune. His ancestors, from Connecticut, got outrageously rich by smelting some of the hard weaponry that enabled the Union to defeat the Confederate army. Thus, the Civil War became a family victory. Unlike Uncle Charlie, who pretended to wrap his social conscience around civic pride, Munroe had a reputation for the total subjugation of suckers. He was 43 years old when he bought the club from Uncle Charlie. Munroe was ruthless. His sister Geraldine, who swept up after him, was even worse, a combination of Mary Tudor and Ma Baker.

Some wield power while denying possession of it. Munroe made great play of what he could do, but refused to talk publicly about it, giving no interviews to newspapers or TV. He revelled in his reputation for corporate takeovers. He'd rapaciously hunt down and devour those too frail to resist him. He also took gloating pleasure from ferociously going after whatever wasn't for sale. The impurity of his approach never seemed to bother him. Munroe was no philanthropist. He handed out money only as a honeyed bribe.

Uncle Charlie would wander through the club's double doors and punch in the key code that guarded the corridor outside Frank Mallory's office. Absent-minded, he'd write the code on the back of his hand in blue Biro. Munroe had a factotum press every button and hold every door open for him. He had a slight phobia of germs, expecting surfaces to be vigorously wiped before he touched them. The room Uncle Charlie used was boxy and unprepossessing. The office Munroe built for himself – even though, busy elsewhere, he seldom occupied it – shone like a gold bar.

Frank's policy towards owners and directors was: 'Flatter them. Butter them up thickly, like a slice of toast. Then, when they think everything is cosy, kick them in the bollocks. That's how you rule.' Munroe was Frank's screaming nightmare. He repelled flattery. He didn't stand still long enough to be kicked. Everything about him was orderly. It was said he owned 125 identical black suits, 125 identical blue suits and 300 white shirts with double cuffs.

When Munroe was in Britain, which wasn't often, his helicopter would land on the pitch and blow into the ground like an icy draught, disrupting everyone around him for half a day. Worse still, Frank couldn't talk to him about football. Munroe had only a vague grip of the offside rule and didn't know the difference between a direct and an indirect free kick. I doubt he'd have recognised Pelé even if the great man, wearing full Brazilian kit, had sat down beside him.

I saw Frank's first game of the 1996–97 season on TV. The sun blazed. Frank was tanned like a holiday-maker just back from a Mediterranean summer. Munroe sweated in one of his blue suits. His sister wore a dress of white cotton. They stood and waved to each corner of the ground, displaying the entitlement of monarchs taking a bow from a palace balcony. Uncle Charlie, now the club's titular president, stood up and clapped too, as though giving his public blessing to them.

The game, against Arsenal, was a terrible scrap. Dull. Untidy.

Settled by a lone, late goal in Frank's favour. The Arsenal side, including Seaman, Adams, Vieira and Wright, would soon be managed by an obscure, bespectacled Frenchman who resembled a professor of philosophy, and of whom almost no one had heard.

Afterwards Frank was asked: 'Can you win the title this season?'

'We've got half a chance,' he said, his tongue almost poking through his cheek. He knew the truth and was showing his contempt for the interviewer.

9

THE STUPIDEST SAYING IN the game is: 'A team is too good to go down.' Of course it isn't.

Over the next six months, I watched Frank Mallory struggle to breathe. By mid-October, he was seventh from bottom. By mid-November, he'd slipped two places further down. By New Year's Day, there was nowhere else for him to fall except into the Championship. Yes, there had been injuries. Yes, Jack Munroe had arrived too late to splash his fortune about in the summer transfer market. But Frank, who now had sufficient cash at his disposal, didn't know who to spend it on. He prevaricated, unable to decide which striker suited him or which midfielder could rebuild the ruin his season had become.

This seemed preposterous to me. I couldn't conceive how Frank had allowed it to happen. I wondered, like everyone else, whether he just expected a revival to occur naturally; that the law of averages would soon guarantee a spurt of results to save him. Nothing came except more defeats, the odd draw and bad headlines. The teams Frank managed always had a strong sense of 'we' and 'us', rather than 'I', about them. That ceased to be so. There was gossip of splits, factions, dissent. There were rumours, put around anonymously by the agents of players who wanted away, that Frank had lost the dressing room. You couldn't reason with him, they said.

There was speculation that Munroe, who didn't like him, had deliberately set up Frank to fail; that he wanted him out and could think of no other way to do it. The story caught alight. Love and respect are supposed to drain from a dying king, but heaping blame on Frank galvanised the ordinary supporter's backing for him. The jeers on match day were directed at the man who wasn't there. So were the home-made banners. 'YANK, GO HOME,' said one.

Even in the prison of his days, Frank was protected from the sort of criticism that would have consumed lesser figures. Football lives off the fanaticism it generates. Even Munroe, who I was convinced came into the game motivated only by the profit he could make from it, now understood that. The heritage of a club is made of many parts, but the supporters knew Frank's proprietorial claim was more convincing than a stranger's – a stranger, moreover, who didn't seem to understand them, their team or their city. Almost all of Frank's 20-odd years in charge of the club had been successful to one degree or another because of his idiosyncratic management. He carried on drawing goodwill from the well of his previous achievements.

Frank was phlegmatic about things until late January, acting as though the table had been printed upside down. Manchester United and Newcastle were duelling for the title. Frank was fighting for the club's life against Sunderland, Middlesbrough, Derby, Queen's Park Rangers, Coventry and Sheffield Wednesday.

Only after a hopeless midweek defeat at Middlesbrough did he act like someone in shock. An hour after the game finished, Frank wandered out of the tunnel, his face flushed. The pressure of the season seemed to have rounded his shoulders. He slowly followed the pitch markings, walking along the halfway line to the centre circle, as though he were a wire-walker aware of the huge drop below him. Then he stood in the centre circle and looked around the deserted ground, lost in his surroundings, for five minutes. Something inside him had uncoiled. In the press box the journalists, who still spoke to Frank in a supplicating tone, stopped writing their reports to stare at him. Jonjo Whelan had to come onto the pitch and shepherd Frank back to the dressing room.

Another story, a week later, made him look more eccentric still. Frank liked to take a bath at the club. The baths were wide and deep, and he'd shave his face as he soaked his body. One of the apprentices found him floating in the water, his eyes closed. The water was smeared bloody red. The apprentice fled, thinking he was dead, but Frank had only nicked his chin and neck with his razor. When the apprentice returned with help, Frank was sitting up and smoking a cigarette. 'Can't a man close his eyes in his own fucking bath?' he'd asked.

The cameras tracked Frank like prey during matches. You got to see him close up. Aware of how he'd been steadily shedding weight, I was still surprised at how far his eyes had been sucked into their sockets. The whites of those eyes were yellowish too, as though lightly poached. What I noticed most, however, were his hands. He had a habit of putting them over his face. How thin and creased his flesh had become. How withered and bony his fingers looked.

'He can't rouse the team because he can't rouse himself any more,' said Freyja. 'It's over for him, isn't it?'

'But how do you get rid of a legend?' I asked.

I O

THE START OF THE new Allsvenskan was only three weeks away. It was also the second anniversary of Freyja moving into my flat, the start of a marriage without a ring or any vows to complicate matters.

We marked our day quietly. Freyja gave me a map of Britain that had been hand-drawn at the end of the 19th century. 'Hang it in your TV room. The walls are still very boring,' she said. The present was wrapped in the sort of kitsch paper you'd buy for a football-mad child: row upon row of black-and-white-panelled balls against a garish green background. My card was football-themed too: a goalkeeper, unmistakably the writer Albert Camus, was leaning against his left-hand post. The joke was in the title of the book he was reading: *The Off-Sider*.

We went for a very early dinner. The restaurant's owner, a season-ticket holder, gave us a booth at the back and poured glasses of champagne as a greeting. I drank mine in gulps. Freyja sipped hers, finally tipping the rest of it into my glass.

'Are you as excited about this season as you were about the others?' she asked.

I wasn't. 'No one expected anything of me when I took

over. Now everyone expects everything. Whatever I do won't be enough.'

I believed the months to come would be my last in Sweden. I had another two years to run on a decent contract, which had been improved even after I signed it, but I couldn't achieve anything more at Östers, where slender resources would never take me where I wanted to go. We couldn't go far in Europe, and another title or the domestic cup, while satisfying, would only be repeating myself.

I had no idea where I'd go next; I just knew I had to go *somewhere* – even if that meant drifting for a while.

I knew I'd never forget Östers. I'd always be grateful to them too. I worried, though, about stagnating there. Everything was too nice, too comfortable, too friendly. There are people content to let their lives stall or who can't lift themselves out of the mud they get stuck in. I didn't want to be like Frank Mallory. He'd stayed in one place for so long that he'd become inert. He claimed to be dogmatically opposed to dogma, but with him everything always went the same way – his way. The city had long since become too small for him. He'd stayed because the very size of it allowed him to dominate.

I was forever thinking about the day after tomorrow. And I was always preparing myself for that one chance, an opportunity to grab at something bigger.

It was a mild evening. Freyja and I walked slowly through the city, taking a circuitous route back to the flat. 'Who'd have thought it?' she said. 'You came here as a stranger and met another stranger.'

I had two matches to watch. They were recordings of Degerfors, who we'd face on the opening day. Degerfors were no threat, but I prepared for them as though we were playing Juventus or Real Madrid in a Champions League tie. I went into the TV room and spooled through the first game, spinning it back and then forwards again. I was about to start on the second when the phone rang. It was nearly 10.30 p.m.

I heard Freyja's footsteps on the wooden floor of the hallway. I heard her ask who was calling. She knew I didn't like being disturbed. She'd take a message, leaving a note I'd find in an hour's time. The door clicked open.

'You'll want to take this call,' she said. 'I think you might be going home. If you still want that. . .'

I I

I WENT TO LONDON THE following afternoon. Jack Munroe had arranged a private jet. We met in his house of cream-washed Portland stone. It was in Kensington Palace Gardens, aka Billionaires' Boulevard.

The night before, Munroe had got to the point without pre-varicating.

'Frank Mallory is undergoing an operation tomorrow. You'll be able to guess what his trouble is, I'm sure. He can't finish the season. He wants you to finish it for him. I spoke to your club 15 minutes ago. They've agreed you can come to us on a kind of sabbatical. I'm paying very generous compensation for that. Believe me, I will make it worth your while too.'

I give the benefit of the doubt to those I don't know well; after all, they haven't yet deceived me. But when I met Munroe, who asked me to call him Jack, I thought immediately of a description I once read about someone unsavoury: 'He was the sort of man who, if he gave you the kiss of life, would count the breaths you owed him.'

From the outside, Munroe's house looked huge but penny-plain, shielded a little by the broad, leafy spread of trees and high iron railings. The tall concrete pillars flanking the gates were like graveyard memorials to a distinguished Victorian. On the inside, the atmosphere of privilege was all-pervading. The butler was waiting for me beneath the portico. His courtesy was so effusive, so exaggerated, that it slipped blatantly into condescension. He thought I belonged at the tradesman's entrance, wearing navy overalls. He turned on his polished heels and set off for his master's chandeliered study, always two brisk steps ahead of me. The walk there seemed to take five minutes.

Hung along one corridor after the next was Munroe's private collection of paintings: a Matisse, a couple of Degas, a Blue Period Picasso, one early Constable, three Hockneys and two Bacons. There was no theme or sequence to the arrangement of the pictures.

Munroe acquired paintings without seeing them. He was content to buy something purely because Gauguin or Turner had signed it. He had stored enough ancient and modern art and artefacts – sculpture, glass, china, Egyptian scarabs, Greek pottery – in bank vaults and hermetically sealed rooms around the world to have filled one of the world's great museums. He had a penchant, too, for historical documents, autographs, photographs and even clothes. He owned a stovepipe hat that Lincoln had worn, a silver cigar box that had once belonged to John F. Kennedy, a pair of Gandhi's gold-rimmed glasses. He did not collect any of these things because he needed them or took pride in possessing them. I learnt later that Munroe had a pathological fear of a second Wall Street crash and a world depression. If the financial markets imploded and his stocks and shares slid off the chart, Munroe's art would be his insurance policy. This attitude explained his parsimony too. While he would happily invest a million or two on his collection, I learnt that he would go through the household expenditure and complain about the amount of liquid soap being bought for the staff bathrooms, the cost of cleaning his carpets, the price of foodstuffs and the amount of food being wasted.

The rich truly are different from us.

The butler opened the double doors to the study, and Munroe rose from an ornately carved mahogany desk at the furthest end of the room. It was as though that movement had been choreographed, adding a theatrical element to the meeting. Four wide windows cast light that was as fresh as white linen, illuminating art deco statuettes, pieces of Meissen porcelain and an enormous leaping salmon carved out of glass. Munroe strode forward, his gait imposing, and then stopped, waiting for me to reach him. He adopted the power stance – legs apart, shoulders back – but didn't offer me his long, lean hand. After a few perfunctory, impersonal pleasantries, he gestured towards one of two identical high-backed chairs covered in dark-red velvet. The look he gave his watch was so conspicuous that I knew I wouldn't be in there for long.

We sat in front of a bookcase containing rare leather-bound first editions. I imagined that Munroe no more read his books than he noticed his paintings. He told me he was teetotal; the smell of alcohol revolted him, apparently. The butler, hovering discreetly around us, began pouring tea into china cups that carried Munroe's monogram and family crest. He liked his tea brewed at a certain temperature and for a particular length of time. The tea itself came from a specific plantation in Sri Lanka. On the table were copies of the *Financial Times* and the *Wall Street Journal*. The newspapers were crisp enough to have been ironed.

Munroe's hair was thin and combed back. Worry lines spread

like fine netting across his forehead. He had the blanched pallor of someone who stayed out of the sun, favouring instead the great indoors. He wore a black suit, too heavy for spring, a navy silk tie and one of those brilliant-white shirts. His cufflinks were silver. He also had on a pair of yellow braces. He was taller than I imagined, and he didn't so much sit down as fold himself into his chair.

He took a sip of tea, his little finger raised in the act, and gave me an insistent stare, compelling me to return it.

I learnt later that Munroe often gave answers that sounded like riddles, but he spoke very plainly in the beginning to me.

'You are here, Thom, so that I can offer you a lot of money over a short period of time. Nothing exceptional is expected from you to earn that money. I am bringing you in as palliative care. As I said to you last night, Frank is very ill . . .'

I saw Frank then as he had been in the boot room all those years ago, flipping his gold Dupont lighter from one palm to the other and smoking one cigarette after another.

Munroe wanted only this from me: the team, now beyond rescue, should disappear from the Premier League with as much brio as possible. I would then disappear as well, making way for a boss who was better qualified and with a higher profile, his skills more restorative than mine.

'I don't want to hurt your feelings, but I will get someone more experienced afterwards – *a name*. The club will need some starry glamour to show how serious I am about starting again and rebuilding when this awful season is over. In the meantime, do what you can and limit the damage. Hold on to what's good. Clear the way so that your successor can get rid of what isn't. Do it as quietly as you can, without too much fuss. If you can win the odd game or two, pacifying everyone in the cheap seats, and . . .'

That last instruction was incomplete, forever paused, as though a wholly different thought had submerged the original one. Munroe looked away from me, staring at something only he could see – probably the identity of the other manager he was already courting. When Munroe focused on me again, he became blunter still. He lifted his left hand from the armrest of the chair, the sun catching the ring on his wedding finger.

'Thom, let me be even more candid.'

A sentence beginning as superciliously as that is always the preface to an insult. You're also expected to accept that insult passively, on the basis that it is honestly expressed and well-intentioned.

'I want you because a mascot is more useful to me than an experienced manager at the moment. You're a club hero. You scored a goal that won a trophy. Everyone will be pleased to see you. The fans need someone who's known to them, someone who brings with him the comfort of old successes and is capable of spreading nostalgia about. You don't have to flaunt your allegiance ostentatiously with a club scarf or a badge stitched onto your coat. That will mean a lot. And you've won things in Sweden. You bring qualifications of a sort with you.'

What I had done so improbably 15 years earlier meant more to Munroe than anything I could feasibly do now. I understood that.

Munroe reached for his cup. He was about to drink from it again when he stopped. 'In case you're wondering, which I'm sure you are, this *wasn't* my idea. It was Frank's. He wants you back. You're *the one*, he says.'

'Why does Frank want me back?' I asked. 'He didn't speak to me when he let me go. He hasn't spoken to me since.'

Munroe took a breath. A direct appeal to my emotions was coming, a distress signal played on a violin.

'I know Frank once regarded you almost like a son, and that you regarded him almost as a father. At least, that is what am I told. By the way, I know all about your own father. Frank regrets the fact you and he "lost touch". He assures me you'll be prepared to overlook that. He says he knows you better than you know yourself. He also says he always knew you'd be successful somewhere. As I said, he regrets everything – very deeply. He'll tell you all this himself, of course. He's looking forward to seeing you again. But it's important to him that you say yes to all this first. After his operation, he will convalesce for a few weeks. We're going to get him as well as we can.'

Munroe began confessing to errors and fallibilities since his takeover. His admissions took me aback, until I realised the purpose of them.

'You're wondering why I got involved in all this. Everyone does. I got all romantic about the game – the thrill of a goal being scored, a save being made, the sight of the pitch on the first day of a new season. Hard to believe, isn't it? The club was acquired on a whim, to impress others and to satisfy a new infatuation. It appealed to an ego that I confess is, at times, overwhelming. Like a lot of businessmen before me, I convinced myself that owning a sports team was like owning a factory, a coalmine or an oil field – and also that I could run it like one. I now understand the game requires more careful study than I gave it. It's more complicated than I imagined. I underestimated the task. I neglected it when the shine wore off. I need to make amends for that. I don't fail at anything.'

I didn't know then what, if anything, was true in those shared confidences. His story sounded too pat, too nicely fairy-tale. It occurred to me even then that I was being given an invented version of events, peddled because it covered up motives that were neither professional nor altruistic.

I was right. Munroe had bought into a game about which he knew next to nothing because one of his industrial rivals in America had got himself a gridiron team, while another had invested in a baseball club. Not wanting to be outdone, he'd tried to get his hands on one of those shiny toys of his own.

He not only failed to find anything suitable, he also discovered that his businesses and character would face exhaustive vetting, which put him off. In good old England, however, the process of scrutiny – the questions of how you got your money and where it came from – was far less rigorous. Once you found a club and agreed on the price, you didn't have go around the track again to reach the finishing line. And there were almost no hurdles to jump. When his deal went through, Munroe had claimed: 'Buying this club was quicker than buying my last car.' Now he wanted to be seen as someone who had unexpectedly become besotted with football and genuinely cared for it.

Munroe spelt out what I would get in return for my acquiescence.

'The arrangement for you has more advantages than disadvantages. The disadvantages are that you lose the momentum you've built up in Sweden. If you go back, the supporters there will see you as a mercenary who left them for cash and all your good work unravels like poor stitching. The advantages are much greater. What I am giving you is the chance to catch the spotlight for a while. Make a go of this and you never can tell where it might lead. Not here. Not with us. But somewhere decent, perhaps . . . That's what Frank wants for you.'

Munroe had a habit of interlocking his fingers and cracking his knuckles, a belligerent punctuation between statements he clearly regarded as definitive. He did so then.

'Where I come from, we don't like or understand relegation in elite sport. I'd abolish it in the Premier League. Because we're "going down", I've taken the kind of abuse that I'm not used to receiving. The British newspapers aren't quite as polite or measured as those back home. Well, I'm going to stick it to them next season. I'm going to build a new team and get promoted. Then I'm going to build a new stadium. Everything will begin again. Five years from now . . . who knows? Think of yourself as the start of that whole process, Thom. I know you'll want to do this for Frank. To pay tribute. He'll provide help, if you need it. So will I. Whatever you want, just ask.'

His politeness, the trouble taken, was again for appearances' sake. Nor did some moral imperative drive the care that was being lavished on Frank. Where Frank was concerned, I knew Munroe had to be good – and his munificence had to be conspicuous and publicly witnessed.

With a man like him you can never rest easy, but I thought he couldn't do me much harm if I stayed out of his way. And opportunities like this do not wait. While Munroe was offering only a slim chance of something, I had nothing – or next to nothing – to lose from snatching at it. He hadn't realised that.

So I said yes to him.

'I'll make sure Frank knows you're with us. Thank you,' he replied.

Munroe rubbed his hands together and cracked his knuckles

again. He took an inelegant gulp of his tea, rattling the cup back onto the saucer. He got up, fiddling with his shirt cuffs, adjusting them fastidiously so an equal sliver of white was visible beneath each sleeve of his jacket.

'I am expected elsewhere.'

He pulled a white envelope from his inside jacket pocket. 'Your terms of employment,' he said, handing it to me. His smile, as sincere as he could make it, couldn't mask the air of weary distractedness that had fallen across his expression. Our deal had been done; he was moving on to another. We'd been together for 12 minutes. When I motioned to get up too, assuming we would depart together, Munroe shook his head and pressed his open palm downwards. It was as though he was instructing a dog to sit.

'Take your time. Don't rush. Drink the rest of your tea leisurely. Look around the room. Wander about the corridors, if you like. In fifteen minutes there'll be a car for you. The driver will take you wherever you want to go and wait for you, if necessary. I hear you've got a partner. Freyja? I hope she comes over with you. I'll arrange everything.'

With that, Munroe was gone. He didn't bother to shake my hand again. The double doors to the study opened. He had shouted no command and pushed no button to make that happen.

How 'yes' drops off the tongue more felicitously than 'no' ever does – even when you say it while shaking your head, the gremlins of doubt swimming around you. I had been bullishly eager to throw myself into a cause that everyone would say was catastrophically lost before I even joined it. I did it because of the nagging pull of *possibility*. I convinced myself that the best of me would make a difference, and also that something better than what I already had would come out of it.

I 2

IN THOSE FIRST, FEVERED days, when everything was done in a hurry, I felt like a trespasser at best and a house-breaker at worst. Frank Mallory's office was exactly as he'd left it. If there'd been a cigarette smouldering in the huge onyx ashtray he used, you'd have assumed Frank had just slipped out and would be back again in five minutes. Training shoes, some of them still in boxes, were heaped in one corner. On the coffee table was the mug, adorned with the club crest, from which he'd drunk for the past decade at least. There was a heap of private correspondence, some of it waiting to be opened.

I began to rearrange things on his enormous desk: paper-weights, a half-smoked packet of fags, old newspapers and magazines, a stack of vinyl records. Still on the turntable, which sat on a unit beside the desk, was his favourite jazz album, Dexter

Gordon's *Our Man in Paris*. He'd played it so often that anyone who came regularly into his office recognised the tenor sax, the tickling cymbals, the rapid grace of the piano. I put the record on, afraid of scratching it as I lowered the needle. When the opening bars began, I half expected Frank to appear in the doorway.

I poked about in the unlocked drawers. In the bottom one, beneath more newspapers, I found three black notebooks. I ought to have left them there, untouched, but curiosity overwhelmed discretion. I turned the pages slowly in case I left some tell-tale mark that would show I'd read them. The contents were revelatory. The notebooks were evidence of Frank's fan worship of Helenio Herrera, the coach born in Buenos Aires who won back-to-back European Cups with Inter Milan in the mid-1960s. Herrera, 'the Wizard', claimed to have invented *catenaccio*, but he only perfected it, moving a midfielder into the sweeper's role. He liked his full backs to attack and played what he called 'vertical football at great speed', with the aim of getting into the opposition's box with a maximum of three passes. Frank had copied out quotes from Herrera – among them 'He who doesn't give it all, gives nothing' – and his tactical plans and strategies; his analysis of training methods and player psychology; his ideas about three-day retreats, during which his teams would be completely isolated; his insistence that food ought to be wholesome and plain.

Herrera got to know his players by observing them minutely, but from a slight distance, the way you'd study a painting in a gallery. He would look at them until he saw a flaw. If he couldn't repair it, the player would be sold. A new signing didn't always know whether his coach meant what he said to him. Herrera expressed his humour laconically and with a dead-pan seriousness. Those who did not know him well, or were unable to tune in to his wavelength, were constantly confused.

He was also a tyrannical perfectionist, his standards sometimes impossibly high. He didn't so much manage as enslave. Dissent was sacrilege. Anyone, irrespective of reputation, was banished for the merest flicker of it. Inter's players were afraid of losing because of the basilisk stare, which was normally the prelude to a bastard of a bollocking that Herrera would inflict on them in the dressing room. He flogged players until their bones rattled. He could treat them with kindness one moment and disrespect the next. Herrera refused to tell one player that his father had died until he'd squeezed a performance out of him in a match. He tried to split another from his girlfriend, who was deemed unsuitable for him. Herrera even suggested the club hire someone to seduce her and end the relationship.

The notebooks Frank had so carefully assembled on Herrera included news cuttings, photographs and ticket stubs from 1960s Serie A matches. Clipped to the inside of one of the back covers, the paperclip rusty now, was another ticket: the 1964 European Cup final in Vienna, where Herrera's Inter had beaten Real Madrid.

What astonished me was this: I'd *never* heard Frank talk about Herrera. He'd never even mentioned his name. Here, though, was proof of how overwhelmingly Herrera had influenced him. It was like a schoolboy crush. Frank had used him as a role model. For some reason, rather than acknowledging his debt, he'd sought to cover it up, feigning indifference about 'bloody tactics'. Herrera had been at his zenith when Frank began coaching, so his worship of him must have started then. He'd seen himself as an English Herrera, copying his personality, his mannerisms, his approach.

He'd *become* Herrera.

13

THE WALLS OF THE office were crammed with framed photographs, arranged in chronological order. You could start at one end of the room and walk to the other, watching Frank age as he became successful. There were goals, team pictures, celebrations. One of the first dumb questions a journalist tossed at me was: 'The photos must be intimidating. Will you be taking them down?'

'No,' I said. 'I'm in most of them.'

Included in the small print of my deal with Jack Munroe was one stipulation: the club would pretend that Frank's illness was debilitating but not critical. I had to pretend that Frank would return, fit again, possibly before the season ended.

No one believed that.

In those days, you could still buy players until the end of March; the two transfer windows were not created for another five years. So I was prepared for the question: 'How many new players are coming in?'

'I'll sign whoever Frank wants me to sign,' I replied. 'It's his team, not mine.'

The truth is that I wasn't allowed to sign anyone. Jack Munroe wouldn't countenance it. I saw his point. 'The players we need won't come. The players we don't need, but might get, will only come if I stuff them with cash. It would be like wiping your butt with banknotes and then flushing them away,' he said.

On top of that, the arrangement Munroe had struck with Östers stopped me from taking anyone from there on loan. If it hadn't, I'd have signed Flemming Vilfort. I didn't rate the goalkeeper I'd inherited. Curtis Taylor was a 28-year-old who was still prone to making elementary mistakes. Brazilians have a saying about 'keepers like him: they call them '*mão de alface*', which translates as 'lettuce hands'. Taylor would flap limply at the ball. Whenever I saw him come off his line, I half closed my eyes, anticipating disaster. There had been a contributory factor to his shoddy form over the past few months: Taylor had discovered his wife had been cheating on him with another Premier League player, whom she'd met during a family holiday in Portugal the previous summer. Taylor had been blissfully ignorant of that. He found out only while waiting for a corner to be popped into the box. In a crude effort to distract him, one of the player's friends, who played for another club, told the cuckolded Taylor about the affair, sparing no detail. His confronted his wife, who subsequently left him, taking with her the children, most of the furniture and a considerable amount of money.

Taylor was not alone in suffering a failure of confidence. Most of the team didn't seem to believe we'd win another match. I'd played alongside only two of them: the captain Aaron Buchan, a little like Robbie Clayton in style and attitude; and Ross McClean, a winger capable of switching flanks, who was useful rather than industrious. Our star, the side's luxury item, was Stefan Fournier, a sublime Frenchman whom Frank had bought from Nantes. He passed the ball so accurately that he could have kicked it clean through a child's hoop from 75 yards. You don't play football at 100mph – except in your head. Quick thinking is as good as speed, and Fournier possessed that. He saw the Premier League as his shop window. He wanted to sell himself to Aimé Jacquet, the French coach, in time for the 1998 World Cup. It was Fournier's misfortune that the number 7 shirt he coveted already belonged to Didier Deschamps. For Jacquet, Fournier was like a spare piece in a jigsaw; he fitted nowhere. For me, he was our only hope. In the dressing room, I'd watch him play keepy-up indefinitely while sitting down. He would park himself on the bench beside his clothes and ask someone to chuck a ball at him. He would take it on his left boot and flick it onto his right, swapping it from one to the other until he became bored. Like a lot of players with an abundance of flair and a bohemian attitude towards exploiting it, Fournier was insouciant in terms of hard work. Frank used to say that 'talent without discipline is wasted' (I now know Helenio Herrera said that first). How Fournier had survived so much as a week with Frank was a compelling mystery to me. His shoulder-length blond hair was held back with an Alice band. Frank had loathed long hair. Before training, you'd find Fournier sitting in his car, shaving off the previous night's stubble while squinting into the rear-view mirror. He was perpetually late. For practice. For the team coach. 'Why,' I asked Jonjo Whelan, 'didn't Frank kick his arse out of here?' Jonjo shook his head. 'You've got to remember this, Cally: the Frank you knew isn't the same Frank who fucked up the season.'

If Jonjo had been a churchman, you'd have described him as someone who unselfishly gave a lifetime of service. He was so devout towards the club that I'd assumed he would always be part of it, but Jonjo had decided that his departure, clean and definite, ought to coincide with Frank's, a symmetry he thought fitting. Out of duty, and so I wouldn't stumble through those first weeks, he agreed to stay on until the season ended.

The first conversation I had with Jonjo began with his assessment of the team, but soon became dominated by Frank's struggle with himself. 'The team's in a mess because Frank was in a mess,' he said. 'Something was wrong from that first game. Frank couldn't focus. He had a bad cough, terrible shortness of breath. He wasn't able to climb the steps into the directors' box without stopping. Once, on the training ground, he got cramp and tripped up. Another time, his hand shook so much he couldn't hold his mug of tea. I don't know how he kept things together. On bad days, he couldn't get out of bed.'

Frank's problem child – and now mine – was Mikhail Blaga, a Bulgarian who'd been signed solely on the strength of the 'super goal' he'd once scored for Fortuna Düsseldorf. Blaga had been on the edge of the box when a cross came in. Hanging four feet in the air and practically horizontal, as if freed from the laws of gravity, he produced a volley that flew in just inside the angle of post and bar, the ball ripping off his boot. It won him the Bundesliga's Goal of the Season award. But his reputation had nothing else to feed on. In seven months, he'd scored only twice for us. One of those goals, against Blackburn, had bounced off his knee. 'He knew bugger all about it,' said Jonjo.

Blaga was a moody braggart with a peacock's strut, a man never happy unless he was unhappy and also being demonstrative about it. Convinced that any fault lay with the world rather than him, he believed the shortcomings of others were starving him of goals. I've never entirely trusted a player who constantly refers to himself in the third person or goes around kissing the badge of his shirt. Blaga's displays of illeism – 'Blaga was pleased with the way he played today' – were partly about self-importance and partly about self-delusion. As far as I'm concerned, only players possessing superior talent had the right to do that. The likes of Pelé, Maradona and Cruyff in the twentieth century and Ronaldo, Messi and Ibrahimović in the twenty-first. As for the badge-kissing, it is the kind of conspicuous virtue-signalling that makes me want to vomit. Blaga cared only about Blaga and his next transfer. The health of the team was immaterial. His agent was already touting him about like a work of art, ready to be shown off to whomever paid most money. He was all ambition and no loyalty.

I watched recordings of the goals Blaga had scored. He'd sprinted towards a corner flag after both of them, determined not to share his success with anyone else. He was a lazy cheat, the sort of striker who, after making a tame, ineffectual run, grimaces, shrugs and throws up his arms when the ball goes elsewhere. 'Frank had a word for people like Blaga,' said Jonjo. 'Shitbag.'

I asked Jonjo to explain why Frank had bought him. 'He didn't. Munroe did. Frank was just told he was coming here. Munroe knew someone, who knew someone else, and Blaga was "recommended" to him. Munroe was naïve enough to believe he'd got himself a proper striker. He said Blaga would score us 30 goals a season, like Shearer or Cole. You know, someone once said that to own a football club you had to be a multimillionaire, you had to love football and you had to be a fuckwit. Few people in the world are all three. Well, we found one of them. If you want to know why we're neck-deep in shit, it's because of players like Blaga and an owner like Munroe, who's also got the coldest eyes of any human being I've ever met.'

Jonjo told me one other thing about Blaga: 'He pretends not to understand English very well. Don't be fooled. He understands everything you say to him.'

I 4

JACK MUNROE GAVE ME what I asked for, which was the penthouse apartment in a hotel. It had a private lift, sparing me from small talk with inquisitive neighbours. The living room was minimally furnished: a black leather sofa, matching armchairs, a long teak dining table. The place had high ceilings, triple-glazed windows, whitewashed walls and oak floors on which a good deal of wax and polish had been used, the wood buffed to a shine. It was like living in a Hammershøi painting. The hotel sat on what was once described as the 'ugliest street in Europe', but the apartment overlooked the ragged walls of the castle on one side and the Council House dome on the other. When I couldn't sleep or awoke at dawn, I'd climb the short metal staircase from the balcony onto the roof terrace. Up there, stubby trees and shrubbery grew out of steel troughs and pots. As though I had scaled some fabulous peak, I'd look down and over the city, picking out its landmarks. If the weather was bright, I could make out the far-off floodlight pylons of the ground, which rose beside the fat curve of the river. Every night I'd hear the rattle of traffic, the clang of tram bells, the shouted conversations between those well lit up by drink. I'd see the burning stacks of office windows and rows of street lamps, still aglow like coals. Light pollution spread like hazy yellow smoke above the rooftops.

Munroe had guaranteed me a bonus, if we avoided relegation. I'm embarrassed to tell you how much, but the sum was extravagant enough to suggest he was sure it would never be paid.

We had 11 games in nine weeks and were 12 points adrift of safety. Our goal difference was minus 27. We hadn't won a match in three months. That coming Sunday, we were off to Old Trafford to face Keane and Beckham, Cantona and Giggs, Cole and Scholes. If we got around them, we'd have to stick the ball past Schmeichel. Manchester United were top of the table, a nose ahead of Arsenal and Liverpool. Newcastle, consoled by matches in hand, were chasing the three of them.

At Old Trafford, I'd have to walk along the touchline, my back to the Stretford End, and shake hands with Alex Ferguson. I'd have to smile and look as though I was up for the fight. I'd have to stand, head raised, through 90 minutes in which I knew we'd get sliced and diced whenever we didn't have possession. You get tired quicker when you have to play without the ball. I feared that we'd exhaust ourselves in less than half an hour. The odds of us conceding fewer than three goals were so long that you could have put a pound on us and paid off your mortgage if the impossible happened. That's a minor exaggeration – though not much of one.

There were teams who had found life after near death. Luton, who beat Manchester City on the last day of the 1983 season, sending David Pleat on an elated dad dance across the pitch. Coventry's clean sweep two years later: three wins on the spin, the unlikely hat-trick achieved against Everton, who were already champions. And Everton themselves, who climbed out of the grave in 1994 with a last-gasp goal in their final game. But every statistic was against us emulating them. The bleakest, the one which newspapers liked to quote, was that no team since the Premier League's formation had survived after living for so long in the bottom three.

Sometimes we forget that our game is psychological before it becomes physical. Self-doubt barely has to infiltrate the bloodstream before it takes hold, a poison without an antidote. And defeat brings no nourishment. We had lost so often over so many months that lassitude had overcome us. We could only ever summon enough energy to brace ourselves for the next blow. The players had lost faith in themselves and in one another. No one wanted to pass the ball in a tight space; they didn't trust the receiver to hold on to it. No one, apart from Stefan Fournier, was prepared to run with it either. Most of the players wanted the season to end, the ridicule to be over. I saw no point in having a tantrum and throwing teacups at the wall, or working them until their feet bled. I'd have to cajole and charm.

I watched my first training session in silence for 45 minutes. 'Let's do something different,' I said to Jonjo Whelan. I arranged a practice match. It was played across two pitches, laid side-by-side, rather than from goalmouth to goalmouth. I told everyone to take off their bibs and pile them up as makeshift posts. 'We're going to have a 14-a-side game,' I said. To play football well, you have to enjoy it. We hadn't enjoyed our work since the dog days of August. I wanted to recreate the kind of atmosphere all of us had known as boys, a kickabout in which we played until it got dark or someone shouted 'next goal wins.' There'd be no tactics. No formation. No half-time. No changing ends. No throw-ins. No whistle. 'Play any position you want. Pass the ball around. Shoot from anywhere. Do any trick you like,' I said.

It began to rain. No one noticed. Fournier scored one goal with a lovely low back-heel from fifteen yards. Aaron Buchan went between the bibs for ten minutes, pretending to be Lev Yashin. He dived for shots he could have taken two steps to gather. Our full backs, Davie Fuchs and Daniel Lejeune, played the whole match up front. There was competitive squabbling about whether or not a 'goal' might or might not have hit the bar or struck a post.

There was more competitive squabbling about the legitimacy of corners and free kicks, which were awarded through the sheer persistence of someone's argument. I watched the players slide around and get hideously muddy. An hour later – the score was 9–7 – I walked back along the embankment and into the ground with Jonjo Whelan.

'Some of this lot are smiling,' he said.

'Not Blaga . . .'

'Blaga never smiles.'

15

THE CLUB STILL USED the team bus I'd travelled in six years before. 'The King's Throne' was now mine. The Throne was a high-backed swivel chair, positioned directly behind the driver, belonging to Frank Mallory, who'd had it installed. No player dared plant his backside there. Sitting on it felt odder for me than making Frank's office my home.

I decided – against all convention – to travel to Manchester on the day of the game. Jonjo Whelan looked at me as though I'd suggested getting off the bus at Stockport and walking to Old Trafford, dragging the wicker hamper that held our kit behind us.

Jonjo was usually so phlegmatic. He had the unnatural ability to seem to be standing still while the world whirled about him. This decision, though, rankled with him. 'What if there's traffic? What if we're late?' he asked, his voice several octaves higher than normal. 'We won't be properly prepared.'

'We haven't been properly prepared for six months,' I said.

I'd spent only four days with the team, which wasn't long enough to develop some fabulous scheme to dumbfound United. I played the standard 4–3–3. The only player who complained was Mikhail Blaga, who sulked. He slid his gaze away from me whenever I attempted to make eye contact. I'd decided to pick Blaga because then he couldn't protest that I hadn't given him a chance. At that stage, I wasn't aware I had much of an alternative anyway.

In the dressing room, I stressed only the basics: 'Don't give away stupid fouls – you'll lose your rhythm. Don't give away the ball. You don't have to be graceful or beautiful. We do have to be effective. Scrounge a result for me.'

I'd arrived in Växjö not long after Sweden hosted the 1992 European Championships, the competition elevating the country's status in the game. As an ordinary fan, I'd been there when the Swedes beat England 2–1 in the Råsunda Stadium, the place where Gary Lineker's international career ended with his abrupt substitution. I was back in England nine months after the 1996 European Championships had almost, but not quite, brought football 'home', which would have rid us of the golden millstone of 1966 – a burden that subsequent generations of English footballers have had to carry.

Posterity has a way of winnowing out the inconsequential. I remember well the highlights of '96: Gazza's closely cropped, bleached-blond hair; Shearer's goals and raised-arm salute after scoring them; Pearce's penalty against Spain and the emotion that flooded out of him – that screaming, the muscles of his neck tightening, as he urged England to 'come on'. But, until I'd watched some of those games again recently, I'd forgotten the bagginess of everyone's shorts and shirts, the black boots, how plain and ancient Wembley looked, and also how the corporate advertising around the perimeter of the pitch was ubiquitously bland.

When Sweden reached the semi-finals in '92, it was a minor triumph. When England did likewise in '96, it was a gallant failure. The impact they made was nonetheless substantial. The game became more beloved and popular than ever. Everyone had colours to wear, a team to support, a Sky Sports subscription. You counted as a celebrity if you were a Premier League player or a manager.

I became aware of that in the build-up to Old Trafford.

We were the only team in the Premier League not to have a press officer. Frank Mallory wouldn't hear of it. Sitting in the press conference, I felt like a zoo animal alone in its cage. Behind me were sponsors' boards, wheeled in like stage scenery.

In front of me were TV cameras, microphones and electronic recorders belonging to reporters, most of whom I didn't know. I thought about Frank, who liked to give impromptu press briefings in the corridor outside his office, everyone forced into a semi-circle while he stood against a wall. I also thought about the press conferences in Sweden, which were often held in my office and on whatever spare chairs we could find and drag in. I'd learnt this much: responding with the stock phrase 'good question' – even when that question was absurd or ill-judged – gave you three seconds longer to mull over a proper reply. I also knew that you could, if you were clever enough, get away with giving an answer that was only partly related to the question. The trick was to hand the reporters your line before you got pushed into following theirs.

Asked again about Frank, relegation and the changes I expected to make, I replied by saying that I'd never played in a winning team at Old Trafford. I added, very quickly: 'As far as I'm concerned, there are only two types of manager: those who learn from Alex Ferguson and those who don't.'

I'd never spoken to Ferguson. He had, however, glared at me once in the tunnel at half-time and implied that I wasn't much more than a kicker. I'd been trying, unsuccessfully, to haul down Ryan Giggs ever since the match had started. That afternoon Giggs had played like sweet music. Few wingers had made me so feel vulnerable when they collected the ball on the halfway line.

You hear a lot of anecdotal stories, most of them from disgruntled ex-players, about how intimidating Ferguson could be. He didn't intimidate me. I'd been raised on Frank's insults. I was shaken only because I had wanted to impress him and seek his approval. Now, as a manager, I was seeking his approval again.

I was about to sit in the dug-out when Ferguson came down from his seat and offered me his hand. He put his other hand on my shoulder and leant in to whisper. 'Good luck – and I mean that. Character will get you through the next couple of months. I mean that too.'

Even now, I can't tell you definitively whether United were complacent, thinking we'd fold easily, or whether we summoned the unlikely, devil-may-care spirit of that practice match. We had a midfielder, George Cully, who could be a bit of a knucklehead. He got his retribution in first, believing it saved time. You had to ban him from making a tackle in training on a Friday; he was liable to take out one of our own with friendly fire. The game was just three minutes in when he took on Keane. His lunge was about as subtle as chucking a house brick through a window. I'd played against Keane during his first season in England. He was young and thin, but whenever he went into a 50/50 – or even a 60/40 in his opponent's favour – his eyes glinted like the blade of a hatchet. His accent, as heavy as peat, meant I didn't understand the sledging he meted out to me. The odd obscenity was the only thing I registered. If I kicked him once, he'd kick me twice.

Cully escaped with a yellow card only because his impetuous tackle had occurred so early on. The referee's leniency enraged the Stretford End. The more worked up United became in response to that, the more we slowed the match down. We passed the ball along the back four. Stefan Fournier put his foot on it in midfield. Even Blaga contributed. Only four days earlier, United had made Porto dizzy in the Champions League quarter-final, crushing them 4–0. Their fans expected us to be similarly crushed and became impatient when we weren't.

We reduced them to a whisper by going in front two minutes before half-time. Fournier funnelled the ball upfield. Blaga chested it down and shot. His drive struck Gary Neville on the shin, ricocheting to Cully, who toe-poked it in from six yards. The goal ran through the crowd like an electric shock. Cole and Cantona, Keane and Beckham, Giggs and Scholes looked at one another, displaying a kind of how-can-this-be-happening-to-us incomprehension. Schmeichel retrieved the ball from his net and hurled it upfield with his strongman's right arm, furious that Cully had deprived him of a clean sheet. The ball soared and dropped again like a military shell. I stole a crafty glance at Ferguson, hoping he didn't think I was gloating. He had sucked in his cheeks and his eyes were wide and glassy; he couldn't believe what we'd done any more than I could.

We spent most of the second half in full retreat. Giggs twanged the bar. Beckham hit a post. We hacked one volley and a header off our line after failing to clear corners. I looked at the clock, wishing time away.

There was a quarter of an hour to go. Then ten minutes. Then only two. I prepared myself for the worst, thinking a point would be progress.

Our second goal was flukier than the first. I'd substituted Blaga to shore up midfield. He'd peeled off his shirt and slung it over his shoulder before dashing into the dressing room, ignoring Jonjo Whelan, who had gestured him towards the bench. United's attack broke down. A pass from Beckham dribbled into the hands of Curtis Taylor, who booted it 60 yards. I was livid with him. I was still cursing Taylor – he ought to have thrown the ball safely out to the flanks – when his kick slid off the head of Pallister, who misjudged it, the ball squirting towards Blaga's replacement, Karl Hooper. He squared it to Cully, now one-on-one with Schmeichel. No one beats Schmeichel in those situations. The ball at the player's feet is suddenly the size of a marble. The goal seems to shrink. Schmeichel seems to grow. I waited for Cully to trip and fluff his chance, the ball ballooning into the Dane's hands. Instead, Cully took it around him, the way George Best once took the ball around Benfica's Henrique at Wembley, and side-footed it into the open net.

Jonjo thrust his face towards mine. 'Fuck me,' he said. 'We've won.'

Everyone in football management knows failure of one sort

or another awaits them in the end, which makes it less of a profession and more of a brotherhood. But Ferguson and Frank Mallory seldom spoke after 1985. They treated each another with cold civility. The fault was Frank's. He'd always wanted to be manager of Scotland. When Jock Stein died, after a heart attack on the touchline at Ninian Park, Frank expected the Scottish FA to ask him to take over. In his eyes, he was the 'only choice'. Except he wasn't. The SFA appointed Ferguson, who'd been Stein's number two. Ferguson steered Scotland through the World Cup qualifiers and then to the finals in Mexico the following summer. Frank forgave neither him nor the SFA. He ignored the fact, or thought it irrelevant, that by then Ferguson had won so much at Aberdeen, wrestling trophies away from Celtic and Rangers, that his superiority over Frank was indisputable. Aberdeen got used to open-top-bus parades, and silver polish appeared in the club accounts under 'major expenditure'. Ferguson came to United with three Scottish league titles, four Scottish Cups, a Scottish League Cup and a European Cup Winners' Cup.

Frank didn't accept his own shortcomings because he didn't believe they existed. It never occurred him that the Scottish FA might not want someone so mouthy and controversial to represent them. He saw Ferguson as a usurper and still regarded him as a whippersnapper. His antipathy towards him, while transparent, was never publicly acknowledged. As I was now being promoted as Frank's prodigy, the anointed one, I worried about how Ferguson would react to me in defeat. He left his seat at the front of the stand, tugging at the collar of his black coat. As he came towards me, he said: 'You deserved it. Come and have a drink, if you like.'

In his office, Ferguson poured me a glass of one of his favourite red wines, Domaine de la Romanée-Conti. 'You've had a good day,' he said. 'Not only by spoiling mine either. None of the teams above you got a scrap of anything. No matter what anyone says, you can stay up. Your team believed in themselves today.'

You get a lot of free advice as a manager. Most of it is useless. The advice Ferguson gave was gold bullion. He was so successful for so long that people's impressions of him became fixed solidly. You assumed he'd always been accustomed to playing for high stakes. You forgot he had to begin quietly in a backwater. Ferguson talked to me about his start in management at East Stirlingshire, a part-time post that brought him £40 a week and a transfer kitty of £2,000. The bottle of wine we were drinking had probably cost more than that. He spoke about St Mirren, his next club, where the average crowd barely broke 1,100. At Aberdeen, aged 36, he wasn't much older than some of his team. Three things Ferguson said stuck with me that season. The first was: 'You can't lead by following.' The second: 'Once you bid farewell to discipline, you say goodbye to success.'

The third? Well, it came in useful ten days later.

Ferguson's words burnt with his great understanding of the game, and I was grateful for all of them. In half an hour, he had condensed the principles of management into bullet points on my behalf. He did it despite choking back his disappointment. The defeat could have spun Ferguson's season the wrong way around, but he was still willing to share what he knew and get back only small talk in return. At the end of our conversation, he went into a cabinet and brought out another bottle of wine. 'Take this,' he said. 'Save it for one of those days when you've got even more to celebrate . . . or when you wonder why you came into management at all. There'll be a lot of those.'

The wine had made me a little light-headed. I so nearly told Ferguson I thought he'd win the title and that I'd avoid the drop. But I was only absolutely certain about the first of those predictions, so I merely thanked him for his generosity.

A general election was imminent, about to be called by a beleaguered government with no hope of being returned to power. I'd taken almost no notice of it, but posters and billboards had already been put up everywhere in preparation, and the overwhelming majority of them were as red as our shirts. On the way home from Old Trafford, the world so rosy now, I took them as a sign, a portent of our future success.

I lifted the unopened bottle out of my bag and held it like a winner's medal. I didn't regard myself as an imposter any longer. I had won my first match. I had arrived in the Premier League.

16

Our win at old Trafford coincided with two things: an unusually warm spring and the appearance of the Hale–Bopp comet, which for weeks on end turned all of us into astronomers. The memory of seeing the comet, a wondrous spit of heat and light and dust, has never left me. And so, whenever I think back to that time, it looms over every event that still seems to matter.

Those of a darkly superstitious nature see the appearance of a comet as a bad omen. For them, it's a harbinger of doom and calamity. For me, it seemed providential that night.

I saw Freyja for the first time in a week. She'd arrived at the apartment two hours before I got back. 'I won't go to the match,' she'd told me, sounding like the partner of a boxer who didn't want to see her man mauled to near-death in the ring.

When I arrived, I gave her the bottle of wine Alex Ferguson had given me. She cradled it in her hands while examining the etching of the sombre bearded man on the label. 'Is he the patron saint of wine?' she asked.

'Not a clue,' I said, 'but I'm already thinking of Ferguson as the patron saint of novice Premier League managers.'

I told her what Ferguson had said about drinking that wine. 'We can open it now,' I said. 'We can celebrate the fact that you're here.'

'Save it,' she said. 'Let's go onto the roof terrace. I'd like to see the comet. Make some coffee instead.'

It was the first night I properly took in the comet, brightly resplendent against the smooth inkiness of the sky. Hale–Bopp blazed into view on the north-western horizon. It had seemed to appear instantly and from nowhere – as if bursting through a black hole. The bulbous head was luminously white, its long tail tapering into a tip as sharp as a bodkin. Once we began looking at Hale–Bopp we couldn't stop. The comet was travelling at a terrific, burning lick – 100,000mph – but its speed was imperceptible to us. It was wider than a county and 122 million miles from us, but the thing seemed quite small in the vastness around it and very close to the earth. Hale–Bopp drew our eye to the extent that even the moon could not compete for attention against it. The stars seemed dimmer than before too, far less interesting, even in the gorgeous point pattern of their constellations.

We finished our coffee. 'Let me open that wine,' I said again. 'I really do want to celebrate – and I want to celebrate with you. I've just won. At Old Trafford.'

Freyja took my hand instead. 'Better not,' she said. 'I can't drink wine. I'm pregnant.'

PART FOUR

LOOK ON MY WORKS
AND BE AMAZED

THE INVITATION SPECIFIED 12.30 P.M. Turning up late, even by a minute, would neither be forgiven nor forgotten. If Frank Mallory abhorred anything, apart from dissent, it was unpunctuality. He regarded it as disrespectful. Frank had a way of meting out retribution for that. Anyone late by ten minutes would be kept waiting for an hour. Anyone late by more than a quarter of an hour wouldn't get an audience with him at all.

After convalescing for three weeks, Frank had written the card to me himself, a few lines in ragged ballpoint, his address embossed in red letters along the top. 'Let's have a conversation,' he had said.

He lived in beautiful isolation on the periphery of a village. It was in another county, an hour and a half's drive from the city. The house was a former vicarage, built near the end of the 1870s. Frank had added two wings to the property and also extended it at the back, using glass as well as stone. He had gradually acquired the farmland around the house, buying five acres at a time. The ridges and furrows of the countryside that belonged to him rolled off into the far distance, guaranteeing him privacy and quiet.

Like Helenio Herrera – or probably because of him – Frank could be aloof. He gave the impression of being semi-detached, even from his coaches or the few who might have claimed the right to call him a friend. I was like that too; perhaps that's why we'd got along for so long.

I'd been at his house only once before. A couple of months after we'd won the FA Cup, the new season very close, Frank had surprised everyone by throwing a party there. You could barely glimpse the property from the road because of the chestnut trees. Only its five chimneys and the top edge of its high, red-tiled roof were visible from the gate. The driveway – red too – was about a quarter of a mile long and plumb-straight, until you got to the turning circle in front of the door. I imagined I'd wandered into one of those wing-collar Victorian dramas and that a coach and horses was about to wheel past me. Wisteria grew up and around the sash windows and below the eves; I wished I'd seen it bloom in late spring.

Frank and his wife Martha met everyone on the front steps. The ornamentation around the doorway – sawtooth and nail-head carvings – was peculiarly different from the rest of the architecture. It was as though a stonemason had sculpted it a couple of hundred years earlier, waiting for the house to be added later. The grounds were a feast. There were four rose gardens, a couple of ponds that you could have swum in and a wildflower meadow full of harebell and corncockle, cat's ear and ox-eye daisies. There was even a ha-ha, the stone imported from the Yorkshire Dales.

White canvas marquees were pitched on the wide, formal lawns, beside Frank's orchards, which were already full of ripening fruit. Waitresses in black dresses and white aprons and waiters in tuxedos carried drinks on pewter trays. On a wooden stage, where a jazz band played, stood the Cup. Its silver lid glinted in the mid-July light. You'd have thought Frank owned the trophy. Once our civic parade was over – a tour that took us from our ground to the balcony of the Council House – he'd taken it home with him and refused to give it back. He let the thing out of his sight only with a grudging reluctance, and on the strict proviso that it was quickly returned to him.

We were all there, except for Robbie Clayton, who was about to undergo a second operation to rectify the mistakes of the first.

At some point during that hot afternoon, Arend van het Hoff and I stole into the coolness of the house. If Frank discovered us, we planned to say that we were sheltering from the sun. We moved tentatively through the rooms, searching for the Frank we didn't know. In the heart of the house, where even the inner walls were two feet thick, the sound of the jazz band wasn't much more than a murmur.

All the furniture was square, sturdy and made of the darkest mahogany. On a wide bookcase we found shelf after shelf devoted to gardening. There were prints of formal gardens, mostly the work of Capability Brown: Blenheim Palace, Compton Verney, Sherborne and Stowe. They hung from brass hooks, the wire deliberately visible.

'This is how he escapes,' I said. 'Constructing his own Eden.'

Van het Hoff pressed his face so close to the prints that his breath misted the glass: He said: 'Frank's a closed-off bugger, isn't he? You ever heard him talk about gardening? I haven't. Not once. I've never seen this house before either. Why now?'

'We've made him prouder than he's ever felt,' was the only explanation I could think of.

We heard footsteps and crept behind a door to avoid whoever was coming. We were like two boys playing hide-and-seek. Davie Collins appeared, a glass of beer in his hand. 'Caught you,' he said, grinning manically, as if he might blackmail us about it. 'You'd better come back. Frank's about to make a speech.' On the way out, he asked me: 'Hey, how do you think Frank afforded this? Where's all the money come from?'

The speech, done off the cuff, was unremarkable. The memorable aspect of it was Frank's body language. He kept glancing at the Cup. 'He thinks someone's going to steal it,' said van het Hoff. Occasionally, Frank reached out and touched one of the handles gently, every non-verbal cue a sign of how much love he felt for it. 'Bloody hell,' van het Hoff said, nodding his head towards Martha, who stood next to Frank in a red and white summer dress. 'Frank's going to ask her to present the trophy to him, like the Queen. He's going to do a lap of honour around the garden.' At the end of the speech, Frank kissed Martha on the cheek, picked up the Cup and lifted it shoulder-high, rather shyly. In response to the applause, he turned too sharply. The lid fell off, landed on its edge and rolled off the stage, Martha chasing after it.

The comedy of that scene came back to me now as I pulled up in front of the house. Martha was thinner and greyer now.

I looked at my watch. I was twenty minutes early.

2

EVERYONE INVOLVED IN IT thinks the Premier League is the most rigorous league in Europe. You could accuse us of being biased, but that claim is unarguable. None but the finest and the fittest survive nine and a half months of that competition. They don't come back, year after year, and go through it all again solely for the money, even though the very best soon get rich enough for three lifetimes. Vanity and pride drive them. They don't want to be accused of scoring their goals or picking up their medals in leagues where, for five months, you hardly need to get a sweat on.

You have to be Superman to play and succeed in the Premier League. You never get a week off. The fixture list hurls games at you like knives. In La Liga, Barcelona and Real Madrid can showboat against teams at the rump end of the table, conserving their energy for the next *El Clásico*. In Serie A, the likes of Genoa and Bologna aren't going to plant a dent in Juventus's defence, unless Juventus muck about. In the Bundesliga, which Bayern Munich control like a monarchy, the word 'contest' too frequently doesn't match its dictionary definition. Here, *any* team – even one that hasn't earned a point for six weeks – can bite a lump out of your arse. You want to know why English clubs haven't dominated the Champions League? You want to know why England haven't won another World Cup? Because the Premier League pummels you to a pulp. By mid-May you're done in, exhausted. Pulling your socks off or on almost takes too much effort.

Four days after beating Manchester United, we'd faced Wimbledon – awkward, physically rumbustious and unworried about relegation. Our home attendances had been low, sometimes embarrassingly so. Some season-ticket holders had stopped coming; others had returned their tickets, ripped up or cut in half.

Winning at Old Trafford had a galvanising effect on our morale, and also on the whole city. I felt it as I walked through the Market Square. Expectations became disproportionally high. One fan had a letter published in *The Post*. A few weeks before, disgusted after another defeat, he'd chucked his season ticket onto the pitch like litter. A steward had retrieved it and chased after him. He had handed the ticket back and said: 'I have to watch this rubbish whether I like it or not. You're not getting away from it that easily.' The fan wrote: 'After what we did at Old Trafford, I want to thank that steward. He was an angel in disguise. Anything's possible for us now.'

We didn't quite get a full house, but there were queues because some supporters arrived late, thinking they'd stroll in. Before kick-off, I had to come onto the field and take a bow, which I did just long enough not to betray how much I disliked it. There was a great stir among the crowd. Everyone thought that beating United gave us immunity against a side as modest as Wimbledon.

I'd wallowed in 72 hours of extraordinary serenity. I'd taken Freyja to the art gallery in the castle. Every night, the sky unblemished, we'd gone onto the roof and followed Hale–Bopp, the comet more compelling still as the days passed. Every morning those newspapers that had originally ridiculed my arrival were now demanding I got the job full-time, incredulous that a deal hadn't been done already.

I knew this blissful honeymoon would soon be history, but it might have lasted longer than it did if Mikhail Blaga hadn't miskicked in the 10th minute. No one had tracked Blaga's short diagonal run to the near post; Wimbledon were ball-watching. All Blaga had to do was swing his boot at the cross. You could hear the intake of breath from 30,000 people, just waiting to release it again with a long shout of 'Goal', like a Brazilian commentator. Blaga leant too far back, snatching at the opening instead of waiting for it to come to him. The ball took off, rocketing over the bar. Blaga landed on his back and lay there, contemplating the floodlights.

There are players capable of rivalling Ronaldo or Messi in training. From Monday to Friday, you gawp at their mastery. They can do *anything* at will. But on match day, under the pressure of scrutiny, their game falls apart, and so do they. Blaga was that sort of player. He was still picking himself up when Wimbledon got the ball back and booted it upfield like something launched from a bazooka. Ekoku got to it first. He nudged a pass on to his partner, Holdsworth, who took one touch to control the ball and a second to steer it in from 14 yards. His low, side-footed drive bobbled in off a post. Blaga was still trotting out of Wimbledon's box. After that, we never looked like scoring. Blaga didn't summon another shot.

TV focuses on managers so much that you'd think the game was all about us rather than the players. The manager's response to what's just happened seems to be as important as the action itself. At the end of the game, Sky stitched together a three-minute compilation of me, most of it in grisly close-up. I've only ever been able to sit through the film once. I looked like a madman plagued by visions. The camera caught me gurning my face into the sort of tortured expression that you'd find on a cathedral gargoyle.

I was grateful that Sky didn't repeat the exercise during our next game, our third in a week. I'd been coaching and tweaking our tactics as we bumped along. Most of that coaching had to be done, out of necessity, on the pitch or in the dressing room. We didn't have time to polish up our set-pieces on the training ground. I don't want to use it as an excuse, but I was striving to revive players who, brittle after seven months of disappointment, might not survive another setback.

Sometimes the fixture computer is a cruel bastard of a machine. It sent us next to art deco Highbury, which was Arsenal's home then. Tradition dictated that visiting managers addressed the bronze bust of Herbert Chapman, which was placed in the marble entrance hall. It was supposed to bring you luck. It didn't work for me. That opening-day loss Frank Mallory had inflicted on them was Arsenal's motivation. Under Arsène Wenger, they were a vastly different team now. Ian Wright and Dennis Bergkamp operated in perfect synchrony, like the blades of a pair of shears. They slashed us into strips, and we lost 4–0. Three of the goals flooded in during the last twenty minutes, but only the type of character who'd find something positive to say after a nuclear explosion would have been consoled by that.

Freyja had gone back to Sweden that morning. Even the thought of travelling made her nauseous. 'You'll be home in seven weeks,' she'd said. 'It's better for the baby if I don't shuttle back and forth. OK, we'll be a thousand miles apart, but we'll look at the comet at the same time every night.'

When I got back from Highbury, the apartment seemed empty without her, the rooms more cavernous. She'd left a bottle of red wine and a glass on the dining table. Her note said: 'Sorry. Not quite up to Fergie's vintage.'

I can't explain it satisfactorily, but Hale–Bopp briefly brought a sense of perspective that night. Like nature, the comet reminded me that there were things that were so much bigger than myself – bigger, indeed, than the roll of a ball and a pair of bad results.

The following morning, I made the mistake of looking at the newspapers. I'd gone from sainted saviour to shattered no-hoper. Gossip is meant to be spread, otherwise what is the use of it? Over the next few days, I found only rumours, dressed up speciously as fact, about the managers likely to replace me. They were the usual suspects, a peripatetic troupe – names with whom you'll be very familiar – who wander from one club to another, failure lucrative for them. I ought not to have read those stories or taken them to heart so much.

But I knew that Frank would have memorised every word.

3

'H E'S LOOKING FORWARD TO seeing you,' said Martha, leading me through the hallway like a tourist guide. She stopped in front of one colour photograph and stood back so I could admire it. The photo had been taken in the tunnel at Wembley. I'd turned the FA Cup upside down so I could wear it like a hat. Frank was embracing me. 'You're so young in this,' she said, looking first at the photo and then at me, as though checking she'd let the right guest into her house.

The dimensions of the place seemed a little smaller to me than before, but I remembered the acute right turn and the short corridor that took us into the sitting room. We passed a grandfather clock; I remembered that too.

Frank Mallory sat on a velvet sofa that was the colour of a cornfield. Newspapers, the back pages visible, were scattered at his feet. His right elbow was propped on an arm of the sofa. He was smoking a cigarette that I guessed had been lit only seconds before. Six feet away stood an oxygen tank and a mask. At his feet, stretched out and half dozing, lay a large, dark-brown dog, which looked like an Alsatian crossed with a wolf. Its ears were long and pointed, the paws the size of saucers. Its tail occasionally slapped against the base of the sofa.

Frank was watching a recording of *Match of the Day* – specifically, our game at Highbury. He'd hit the pause button in the 70th minute, a split second before Arsenal's second goal and the beginning of our collapse. On the screen Ian Wright was a blur, leaning forward on the half-turn. He was 25 yards out, about to run on to a ball from Patrick Vieira. No one had closed Vieira down. The closest defender to Wright was 12ft away, an Atlantic Ocean of space for a striker so lethal. Our centre backs were too far apart. Frank looked at me and pressed play. Wright followed the pass, letting it go beyond him, before catching up with the ball and smashing in his shot. He did so without breaking his stride.

I'd assumed Frank and I would spar gently before any solid blows were struck. The first words he said to me were: 'Who the fuck allowed that to happen?' He pointed his cigarette at the screen, a flick of ash spilling onto the carpet. 'You know you conceded that goal from your own throw-in near *their* corner flag? I'll wind the game back if you don't believe me. Talk about sloppy. You gave Arsenal the ball. Then you didn't pick up Wright. Then didn't check Vieira. Then your centre halves got fucking cross-eyed wondering where Bergkamp had gone. Why wasn't someone near enough to haul Wright down? And as for your striker . . . If Blaga parked himself on the bog to squeeze one out, he'd still end up shitting on the floor. At least I wasn't responsible for buying him. You can't blame me for that.'

A stranger witnessing this, ignorant of our history, would never have guessed that 2,145 days had passed since we'd last spoken. They'd have thought Frank and I had seen one another only yesterday and were picking up the loose threads of an unfinished argument, which I was losing.

French doors opened up onto the garden. The wide, well-raked borders were starting to come to life in rainbow colours. The lawn, which was being watered with sprinklers, was a soft spring green cut into gorgeous stripes. The trees had begun to bud and swell. A breeze, of which Frank seemed unaware, wafted against the curtains. I heard, rising above his criticisms, the song of a blackbird.

Knowing Frank, he'd been going over the highlights of the game for an hour or more, settling on the most embarrassing segment. He lifted the cigarette to his mouth and took a long drag.

'Should you be smoking?' I asked. If Frank had a heart attack, he'd still want to light up in the ambulance taking him to the hospital.

'There doesn't seem to be any point in not smoking,' he replied. 'My lungs are like your defence: fucking shot.'

Frank was the same in some ways and not in others. The eyes were very cloudy. The face was an antique map of creases. The collar of his shirt, gaping open, sat loosely around his neck. The ridged veins on the back of his hand were Prussian blue. Only the voice, much more vigorous than the body, reminded me of the Frank I'd last seen. But when he spoke, his Adam's apple bobbed prominently in his scrawny throat, the skin saggy around it.

The dog sat up and stretched. 'Vulcan,' said Frank, 'this is Thom Callaghan. You can eat him later.' The dog turned its head from Frank to me, as though assessing whether I'd be hors d'oeuvre or main course. 'Vulcan's a gentle sort, but he doesn't look it. He's very useful for persuading people not to come over for a chat or ask for an autograph.'

Frank patted the dog. The animal's expression seemed to soften into one of kindly pity, as if my fragile plight was graver than its own.

'You've got some job ahead of you. But I've examined the table and also your fixtures and everybody else's too. It's unlikely that you can get out of this, but not impossible. Your first week to ten days was always going to be a shit-show. You're already three points better off than you ought to be. You lost the last two games because winning at Old Trafford took so much out of you. I'll tell you this: I'm kicking every fucking ball with you.'

Weakened by the effort of another short speech – he began coughing – Frank stubbed out his cigarette in an ashtray that already contained half a dozen butts. A short vine of smoke twisted into the foggy air. He took a blue-spotted handkerchief out of his pocket and wiped his mouth with it. The dog whined in sympathy with him.

Only a few weeks before, Frank had been the whole club. He was the turnstiles and the floodlights. He was the seats in the stand. He was the grass on the pitch. The club's supporters, the men and women who did ordinary jobs while waiting for the weekend to come, recognised something of themselves in him. They all felt he understood them. *They would barely recognise him now*, I thought.

Everything Frank had considered solid had suddenly turned to air. When he walked me into the dining room, the dog trotting ahead of him, his heart seemed too heavy for his chest. He was bent forward, as though leaning into a strong wind, and using a cane, the metal tip of which went tap-tap against the wooden floor of the hallway. I was afraid he would fall. Martha registered the alarm on my face. 'He's improving,' she said, so quietly that her husband couldn't hear her.

4

FRANK MALLORY DREW A kind of perverse pleasure from reading the ghosted autobiographies of other managers. He mocked the contents, gloating at what he saw as the predictable plot of a rival's rise and fall.

'You know how a lot of those books start? What's nearly always on the very first page?' he'd ask. 'It's about getting the sack – and about how the poor sap never saw it coming.'

You couldn't stop him from elaborating.

'The manager describes how the chairman blindsided him. Called him in, casual like, and gave him the heave in one quick sentence. Then it's all about the wrangle over what he's owed and what compensation his contract promised him. Next, he'll tell you how afterwards he drove home, rehearsing what he'd say to his wife, the kids, the dog. He wails about the injustice of it all . . . about how he needed just another fortnight to turn things around . . . about how it shouldn't have happened. He'll tell you how it made him physically retch . . . how he couldn't take it in . . . how depressed he got. Well, fuck me. It's as if he didn't imagine the sack could ever happen to him. Not after the things he's won. Not after the sacrifices he's made. Not after the team or teams he's built and the players he's discovered. You read it and think: "This guy, stupid bastard, thought he was immortal. Everyone gets the chop." I'll never write an autobiography. You only expose what an idiot you've been.'

Frank would reel off the managers he thought had either been naïve, thinking of themselves as unsackable, or had botched their departures. How winning a World Cup didn't protect Alf Ramsey. How Matt Busby ought to have quit as soon as he left Wembley on the night Manchester United lifted the European Cup. How

Don Revie was wrong to say goodbye to Leeds United and take over as England manager.

'At least Bill Shankly went of his own accord – even though he spent every year left to him regretting that decision. No one grabbed him by the collar and booted his arse out of the door.'

No one had booted Frank out either, but I saw that the days to come would be dreary for him without football. Already his routine had narrowed, filled with the trivial and the mundane. Ramsey, Busby and Revie had gone on to other things. Shankly was beloved like a saint. What was left for Frank?

We sat down for lunch at a circular table, which was laid as though we were dining in a high-end restaurant. The linen tablecloth was thick and shining white. The cutlery was heavy in my hand. Martha had picked a small bunch of wildflowers and arranged them in a slender vase. Frank had pushed the dog into the garden and began glancing up from his plate, watching it bound about. He found eating difficult. His knife slipped against the plate because his grip was so weak. The dog came back in, and Frank began feeding it pieces of chicken like treats.

I felt sorrow rather than resentment towards Frank. It dawned on me – but only belatedly – that he'd stored up and spent all his energy on that little show in the lounge. He'd gone greyer. His lids had drooped over his eyes. His face had the pinched appearance of someone unable to get warm. I had an urge to fetch him a blanket. He was no longer the man who'd once have put your balls in a sandwich for daring to disagree with him.

Frank and I were trying to restore the easy familiarity, the natural rapport, we once had, but it was awkward because neither of us knew what to say to the other. With good intent, I thought we'd move forward if, at first, we went back. Memory Lane was the safest route to take because everything there was exactly as we'd left it. I told Frank that Martha had showed me the photograph of the two of us together after the Cup final. Frank said Wembley constituted his 'favourite moment' in his 'favourite season'. That team was his 'favourite' too, he added. He'd admitted none of that before, never wanting to favour one side above the other.

Frank remembered making us drink all that alcohol on the eve of the final . . . the sight of Robbie Clayton being carried into the hotel foyer . . . throwing the TV cameras out of the hotel because he didn't want Spurs to know Robbie was crocked . . . his team talk, which he recited verbatim, as though it was May 1982 again and we were twenty minutes from kick-off.

He told me something I didn't know. Nat Lofthouse had paid him a visit on Cup final morning, arriving unannounced before breakfast. By then, Frank had stopped resenting his friend because he'd long since surpassed him in achievement. The two of them hid in Frank's room for a quarter of an hour. Lofthouse had come on a well-meaning mission. He'd told

Frank to ignore the critics, the bookmakers and anyone else who said he couldn't possibly win the Cup. 'But all he succeeded in doing was to give me awful flashbacks. I saw myself on crutches, hobbling up that tunnel 24 years earlier with broken ligaments and a broken heart. Then, later on, I saw Robbie and I thought: *Fuck. It's happening again. It's someone else's turn.* That's why I couldn't look at the poor lad.'

Frank began coughing. He took a sip of water, wetting his throat. The break allowed him to change the subject.

'I felt sorry for the people watching the final at home. We bored them shitless.' Frank said his mind always flicked first to the TV replays of my goal because he's seen them so often. 'I see them and it feels as though I'm sitting in the stand, a fan like anyone else, rather than on the bench. Mind you, I couldn't believe you'd scored. You hit that ball harder than Bobby Charlton.' He reached across and laid his hand on my forearm, squeezing it as best he could. 'We had a good team. It played together, didn't it?'

I agreed, my untruth simply a wish to please him.

Frank said he used to deliberately wind up Davie Collins, whom he thought played better in a sour temper. Before the big games, including the Cup final, he'd tell the hotel to wake him up at the wrong time, deliver the wrong newspaper and bring him tea instead of coffee. He'd tell Jonjo Whelan to lose Collins' bag or 'forget' to tell him about a team meeting so he'd have to rush into it. 'By the time he got to a ground, he'd be mad enough to bite the head off a chicken,' said Frank. 'I preferred him like that. He was a miserable fucker anyway'.

With each story, I gave a smile of understanding, but I knew Frank was misremembering some things, making others too significant and inventing a few more. He spoke of finding a remedy for Jimmy Bradley's laziness. 'I sent him on a run in the fog. I knew he'd get so far and then sit on a tree stump. I knew which tree stump. I got Jonjo to hide nearby and scare the shit out of him.' I doubted the veracity of that story; Bradley hadn't been lazy.

Frank was fulsome about Nick Carson's bravery; how he'd take cortisone daily because wear and tear and tackling had reduced his knees to rusty hinges. 'He was never pain-free – and he never complained about that.' He remembered how Tommy Smith, at Liverpool, once knocked out one of my back teeth with a stray elbow – and how, a season later, Robbie knocked out one of Smith's in the same way. That story was true, but only up to a point. Robbie had blacked Smith's eye so badly that he seemed to be wearing a patch over it.

In those days, a footballer could never be anonymous when driving about the city. Though you were grateful for a sponsored car, your name was plastered across the doors. When you picked it up, you always had your photograph taken on the garage forecourt, holding the keys aloft or shaking hands with the dealer. According to Frank, Alec Taylor was too image-conscious to accept a Skoda because he considered the brand, fairly new then, grossly beneath him. 'He wanted a BMW. Stuart Kelly got it instead. Every day he gave Taylor a lift to the ground.' Frank had mixed up Stuart Kelly with Ned.

The huge discrepancy between what Frank assured me had happened and what I knew to be the case was most glaring when it came to Robbie. While he lamented losing touch with him, Frank claimed not to know why. 'Have you seen or heard from him? He comes to fewer player reunions than you do.'

I told him what I knew, which wasn't much.

Frank said: 'I tried. I was the only one who knew, absolutely, how Robbie felt. I went to his home. I offered him anything he wanted. I got the FA's approval and arranged a winner's medal for him. I persuaded Manchester United to play in his benefit game. I don't understand why he put so much distance between himself and the rest of us and chose to be an outsider. He could have come to any match, any time. I'd have given him anything too.'

Frank's words were so warm with feeling that I knew he had wholeheartedly convinced himself of all that. He always did. Contradicting him would get me nowhere. He constructed narratives that satisfied his needs, his ego. It was part self-protection, part self-promotion. He imagined everyone believed them – even those who were there and knew better.

Martha left the table twice, returning on each occasion to find Frank going on, unstoppably, putting his spin on everything. 'Stop all that talk about the past,' she said. 'Tell him about the present.'

Frank shifted in his chair. 'I imagine Jack Munroe hasn't spared you much of his time since you got here?' he asked.

I hadn't spoken to Munroe since our minor slump began. 'I like it that way,' I reassured Frank. 'You always told me that you don't make friends in football boardrooms. Not real ones.' Frank had actually said that the ideal boardroom comprised only five directors. One dead. One dying. One deaf and dumb. One in Costa Rica. One to sign the cheques.

'Munroe climbs on ladders made out of other people's bodies,' spat Frank. 'If it's any consolation, which it probably isn't, he knows he made a mistake buying the club. He'll slink away soon enough. But I'm going to get him to spend some more of his money before that happens. Being sick has its advantages. He doesn't want to piss me off because he'll also piss off the fans. I can get anything I want out of him at the moment. And I've decided that what I want is a banquet in my honour for the Cup-winning squad, so we can celebrate the 15th anniversary of our triumph. We didn't celebrate the 10th anniversary, so I think we deserve it. It'll be the reunion of all reunions. I'll give him all the hearts and flowers crap. I'll tell him it's a kind of farewell for me, the final time I'll see all of you in the same room. For effect, I might even break down and cry. Munroe won't be able to say no. Not to me. If he does, I'll make him out to be even more of a villain than he is now.'

Frank paused and looked at me defiantly. 'Munroe thinks I'm

going to die. He thinks I'm going to save him a lot of inconvenience and expense. But I'm going to carry on living to spite the fucker. He motivates my every breath.'

He pressed both palms against the table and lifted himself up from his chair. He went across to a bureau, which sat in an alcove next to an Adam fireplace, and rummaged through the pigeon-holes. Out came a newspaper clipping. It was from *The Pink*.

'Let's go into the garden. There's some lovely cherry trees there. We'll sit under one of them.'

5

THE WIND HAD DROPPED and the early-afternoon sun was warming the grass. The surface of the biggest pond was so still that the water seemed solid enough to walk on. I looked around, remembering where the makeshift stage had been all those years before. I saw the red and white bunting again, the FA Cup on its pedestal, the thick knots of happy people.

Frank, walking slowly, began to talk. 'When I was a boy, we lived in a back-to-back. The front door opened directly onto the street, which was the only place we could kick a ball. I promised myself that if I ever got rich, I'd have a garden bigger than a royal park. Well, here it is . . .' He looked around, like Wren in St Paul's Cathedral, as if to say: 'Look at my works and be amazed,' and then he gestured towards the horizon. The news clipping flapped in his hand. He folded it, as best he could, and slipped it into the top pocket of his shirt.

'Are you about to read that to me?' I asked. Frank looked at the clipping and attempted, very awkwardly and without success, to straighten out the paper. 'Only after I've explained something first . . .'

We sat on a slatted wooden bench. Around us were two dozen cherry trees, each with buds that were ready to burst. 'You know why the Japanese love cherry blossom?'

I did not.

'It reminds them every spring of how brief and how beautiful life is. The blossom comes out in a pink froth and goes again before you know it, blown away and scattered.'

The house was a long way off. Frank had chosen a secluded spot, as though wary of eavesdroppers.

'My sources tell me you're about to be a father?'

I knew who those 'sources' were: I'd told only Jonjo Whelan about the baby.

'About five months from now,' I said.

'We wanted children, Martha and me. I'd have liked a daughter. We should have adopted, but I was away such a lot. I was father to lot of hairy-arsed footballers instead.'

Some are afraid of silence, especially in company. I'd learnt that silence, used strategically, can persuade others to talk. Frank was visibly nervous. I added to his discomfort by widening my eyes and fixing my gaze on him.

He began: 'You're into the game's history, Cally. You'll know who Helenio Herrera is. I bet you've studied him the way I once did. I was a disciple of Herrera's — at least from afar. He used to compile notebooks. I began to compile some of my own. I bought them from the same shop in Milan where Herrera bought his. I wrote down everything he said. I looked for those notebooks this morning. Can't find them now.'

In my mind's eye, I saw not only the notebooks, which I'd taken to my apartment, but also Frank's handwriting on the narrow-lined pages.

'Herrera was a top manager in the late '50s and early '60s. Champion of Europe. We had something in common: he'd been a defender when a knee injury, exactly like mine, finished his career. I went abroad to watch his teams play, first in Spain and then in Italy, but I kept that as quiet as possible. Some managers disliked Herrera intensely. Bill Shankly was one. Jock Stein was another. I didn't like Herrera's motivational messages, the "your desire for success must be greater than your fear of failure" kind of bollocks. He stuck slogans like that on walls. I didn't like the way he gave his players herbal tea and aspirins. Or that he shut them away in a hotel for days. He could be desperately cynical.

I didn't like that either. Herrera wanted to win irrespective of how it looked – or what it took. So he got mired in all sorts of allegations. Bribing officials. Match fixing. Even doping. What I did like about him was the way he understood his players. He was into psychology at a far deeper level than anyone here. He knew how each player thought and what they felt. He was aware that you can't treat them all the same way. One player, a lad called Suárez, became convinced that if some wine got spilt during a team meal, he'd score in the next game, so Herrera would knock over someone's glass to make him feel more confident. Tactically, I thought he was a genius. Also, he didn't give a fuck about what anyone thought of him. I think he liked being disliked.'

Frank produced a packet of cigarettes and lit one. He was still using his Dupont lighter. He blew smoke upwards and through the branches of the cherry tree.

'I met Herrera a few times. He was like a bull. You didn't want to say or do the wrong thing in case he charged you. He's the only man I never dared smoke in front of. Cigarettes disgusted him. He was a health fanatic. He didn't even like to drink too much water. Every morning he did yoga, while telling himself he was "strong" and "beautiful". Can you imagine me doing yoga, with a fag in the corner of my mouth?'

Frank reached for the newspaper clipping. With it in one hand and his cigarette in the other, he said: 'I asked Herrera how to survive as a manager. "Trophies," he said at first, which was a joke. Then he told me: "There is always a body count associated with success. The real secret is to constantly protect yourself, always be on your guard and always beware of who is coming up behind you. There can only be one Caesar at a club. If you have rivals, you have to be ruthless and root them out. You must rid yourself of any threat before it becomes established and gets rid of you. Don't be sentimental. Don't be nostalgic.'"

Frank solemnly handed me the clipping from *The Pink*. It was the interview I'd given about my ambition to become a manager. He had circled the last paragraph:

Callaghan speaks and acts like a manager. He has done so almost ever since he became a player, steeped in the club he has no wish to leave. Perhaps he never will. By the time Mallory retires, Callaghan could emerge as the candidate to replace him. He could, like Kenny Dalglish at Liverpool, move from the dressing room into the manager's office.

It was a moment of complete understanding. I leant back and began to laugh, looking at the sky through the latticework of branches. I vaguely remembered the words and how indifferent, even nonsensical, the reporter's conclusion had seemed to me at the time. I was flattered, of course, but I took none of it seriously. Had Frank been so insecure – paranoid, even – that a few throwaway lines in a Saturday-night football paper had brought about my banishment?

Apparently, he had.

'I thought you'd asked him to write that. I thought you were chasing my job. Not then, but one day, and perhaps before I was ready to give it up. From then on you were . . .'

Frank didn't finish the sentence. He drew his right forefinger across his throat. 'I thought you wanted it too much. I thought you were too presumptuous, too cocky, too disrespectful. I apologise. It was ridiculous. I knew that very quickly but, somehow, telling you became impossible. It would have embarrassed me. I didn't know what to do – and so I did nothing and made it worse. I've always followed your career. I even came to Sweden to watch one of your matches. I planned to see you afterwards, to make amends. I didn't know what to say, how to explain myself without sounding weak or like a prick. Everything had gone too far by then. I wanted to make it up to you. When I knew I was ill, when it became clear I would have to quit, I knew I could do this one thing for you, and also for myself. Salve my conscience. I gave you the keys of my kingdom – a smaller one than it used to be, admittedly.'

I wanted an answer to one question. 'I wrote a lot of job applications. I got nowhere. Were you to blame for that, Frank?'

He threw away his cigarette and fumbled for another, lighting it quickly.

'How would it have looked for me if you'd gone somewhere else and been successful? I'd already told the board that I didn't think you were ready to become a coach.'

A cabbage white butterfly fluttered by. Frank instinctively reached out and tried to grab it. He was horrified when he actually did. He opened his hand again, watching the butterfly flap its wings, as if testing them, before flying off.

'That wasn't supposed to happen,' he said.

An hour later, Frank insisted on seeing me off. When I looked back, he was standing, a matchstick figure, in the dark frame of the front door. It occurred to me that Frank had got the life he'd wanted – the house, the garden, the reputation – but he'd paid too highly for the privilege.

That night, speaking to Freyja on the phone, she asked why I wasn't angry and how I could possibly forgive him.

'Because everything worked out,' I said. 'I came to Sweden. I met you.'

6

YOU HAVE TO CHOOSE carefully the battlefields on which you try to prove a point. Mine came a week after I sat beside Frank Mallory in his garden. It was at Villa Park, my lucky ground. When I made my debut there, the pitch had been so smooth you could have played croquet on it. For our FA Cup semi-final, hard and shorn of grass, it had looked like a thread-bare carpet. The ball had been difficult to pin down because it had bobbled so capriciously.

The surface for our Monday-night game against Aston Villa wasn't fit for anything. The weather had turned as our bus headed along the motorway. It began to drizzle. Within half an hour the clouds had thickened, leeching away the late-afternoon light, before the rain started to come down in tin buckets. Through the murk, I saw only my reflection staring palely back at me in the window next to my seat.

The floodlights were on full beam when I squelched from the touchline to the centre circle, the heels of my shoes sinking into mud. The rain had stopped by then, but the damage was already done. Villa's ground staff were forking the pitch with such fero-cious effort, especially around the goalmouths, that you'd have thought buried treasure lay beneath it. Water dripped from the roof of every stand and even off both crossbars. If Sky hadn't been televising the match live, I doubt it would have gone ahead.

That morning I'd experienced the prickings of sheer panic. Suffering isn't relieved by sharing it, so I said nothing. Not even to Freyja.

None of the teams now above us – Middlesbrough, Derby, Coventry and Sunderland – had managed to win over the weekend. Coventry, however, had drawn 1–1 at West Ham. Upton Park was the kind of ground where the crowd seemed to press against your back, making it unbearably claustrophobic for the opposition. Once West Ham went ahead, early in the second half, I didn't envisage Coventry recovering. I stole away from the game five minutes before the end. Their equaliser, after a scramble in the six-yard box, came in the 93rd minute.

That goal made Sunday purgatorial for me. I couldn't stop looking at the table. The gap between where we were – second from bottom – to where we needed to be looked so wide and so precipitously steep that I went into the bathroom and retched over the sink. You must always pretend to be what you aren't, so the next morning I put on my best suit, a dark navy one, and wore it with a confidence I didn't possess. Villa were pushing for Europe. A draw was the best we could hope for. A draw, however, wouldn't be enough.

I did what Frank Mallory had always done: I took along two young players who had shown sufficient promise in the reserve or youth team to warrant being there. Their job was to act like waiters, fetching and carrying and mopping up for everyone else, including me. Only someone who had a realistic chance of making his debut on some future Saturday got the invitation. His name would be scribbled on the team sheet, below the substitutes, under the heading 'ALSO TRAVELLING'. We would pack his kit in the hamper and tell him to bring his favourite pair of boots 'just in case'. The idea, drenched in common sense, was to acclimatise him for his own big day, however far off that might be. To let him mooch around the dressing room, sit on the back row of the benches, hear the banter close up and in all its expletive splendour and have the piss royally ripped out of him. Frank claimed you could tell a lot about a person's character, their maturity and general nous, from the way they carried out mundane chores. 'These lads dream with their eyes open,' he'd say. He'd watch them meticulously, mentally dishing out gold stars or black marks.

The 'boys' were the last on the bus, anxiously glancing about for the seats that hadn't been taken. I knew how they felt. I'd once done the same thing. They parked themselves down very self-consciously, afraid of being tricked, and fidgeted a lot, waiting for some shouted instruction. I had done that too. In fact, one of the first things Frank ever said to me was: 'What the fuck are you doing on my bus, Callaghan?' He'd prodded me on the breastbone. Of course, he knew perfectly well why I was there. Frank alone had ordained it.

I took a 17-year-old left-sided midfielder. A month later, he wrenched and tore his ligaments so badly that the potential he undoubtedly had went unfulfilled; he'd spend half a dozen years wandering about the lower leagues. The other player was a striker, not quite 19. He was squarely built and still putting on beef and inches. I'd watched him a week earlier, spending a damp Sunday morning on a barren touchline. What he accomplished seemed at first merely about strength, until you saw the shrewdness behind it.

Early on he dipped into his marker and gave him the merest flick with his shoulder. The defender went down in a slapstick dive, as though a patch of ice had appeared beneath him. The striker then took an arcing clearance on his broad thigh and turned with the ball more adroitly than you would expect of someone of his bulk. What constitutes classical style is subjective; you're either transfixed by someone or you aren't. He had a show-off swagger. He constantly sought out the hot spots on the pitch like a narcissist searching for a mirror. He went on to make one goal, steering a low cross into the box off his instep, and scored another. He also did something quite naturally: like Jimmy Greaves, he knew when to stand still.

This was Jason Deane.

Often the small stories, waiting to be prised out, tell you more about someone than the big sweep of their lives. Say what you like about Frank, pillory him for being a bully or madly eccentric, he nonetheless knew, almost infallibly, who could and who couldn't play. So when the club's slip-ups turned into a nose-dive, I couldn't understand why Frank hadn't identified Deane as a possible alternative source of goals.

I asked Jonjo Whelan: 'Why haven't I seen or heard about this lad before?'

Jonjo's personality was one of conciliation and great sensitivity. He was the ideal foil whenever Frank's temper took a riotous turn, exploding like a box of rockets. Jonjo would afterwards seek out whomever Frank had beaten up and apply balm to the bruising. He'd explain what Frank had *meant* to say to him. But he'd been unable to do that with Deane.

I discovered Frank had tried to send him out on loan. Each deal fell through. 'Right now, the kid could be at Rochdale. Or Walsall. Or Scunthorpe. Hacking about at the foot of the Football League,' said Jonjo.

At the start of the season, Frank had gone to a youth game that Deane had dominated. He'd scored two goals in the first half and another two in the second. Towards the end of the match, the opposition woebegone after such a whipping, he broke free from the halfway line and sped on alone towards the box. He drew and went around the goalkeeper, who tried to cut him down at the ankles with a scythe-like swish of his trailing leg. Deane was about to score again when he noticed his fellow striker, who hadn't got a goal, lurking about the penalty spot. He rolled the ball back, giving him a present.

'Frank went lunatic-crazy,' said Jonjo. 'He had him substituted. In the dressing room, in front of everyone, he stood nose-to-nose with him. The kid was bloody petrified. No one knew where to look, and most were too frightened to move. Frank told him he was a soft fucker. Said he'd never be a centre forward if he gave goals away like that. Said he'd never given away any goal – not for anyone. "You've got to be selfish," he kept saying to him. Frank worked himself into a fever. His eyes were popping, his face went maroon. He ordered the kid to close his eyes. Frank put the flat of his hand against his chest and just pushed him hard, slamming his back against a wall. He slid right down it. "You really are a pushover. You're not playing for me again," he said. The boy's form went to pieces. I'd see him avoid Frank. He'd go around a corner or hesitate in a doorway, afraid to cross his path. If Frank watched a game he was in, the kid would curl up and make himself smaller. He'd disappear. It was as if he'd found a hole and dropped himself into it. I tried to tell Frank: "You've got to put this right. He doesn't deserve it." He took no notice. The kid only came out of hiding after Frank left.'

7

OUR BUS WAS MID-JOURNEY to Villa Park when I looked down the aisle. I saw Jason Deane leaning across a table, clearing away a clutter of plastic cups and soaking up the spillage with thick napkins. He pushed the trash carefully into a plastic bag, the action done with the utmost seriousness. If he made a mistake, mishandling something, he was appalled with himself. I liked above all his conscientiousness, his willingness to do things before being asked. He went from table to table, soliciting tasks rather than avoiding them.

I called him down to the front of the bus. Frank Mallory, always prying, wanted to know everything about everyone's background, his inquisitiveness like an interrogation. To understand a river you had to track it back to its source, he would say. To understand a man you had to look into his lineage and the way in which he had been brought up. I asked Deane about his parents. He had never met his father. 'I don't even have a photograph of him. He left my mum when he found out she was pregnant with me.' His mother was a ward sister now. She'd come to London in the mid-1970s, from Idi Amin's Uganda, and moved northwards when a position in a new hospital came up. She married another man. It was complicated, said Deane, but his stepfather had left them as well. Deane had two younger half-brothers and a younger half-sister.

He was diffident, taking a stuttering step backwards after every answer he gave. When, finally, I asked about his exam results at school, he stiffened in response. He turned sideways a little, his gaze sliding bashfully away from me. It turned out that Deane had enough A-levels to have gone to medical school, which is what his mother wanted him to do until the club's inducements persuaded her otherwise. 'She said I could give football a go for a couple of years. If it didn't work out, I'd go back to studying.' Revealing this, almost whispering the news, he half shut his eyes and his chin gradually sank towards his chest. Jonjo told Deane to go back to his seat. If it's true that we live our most real and interesting life under the cover of secrecy, then I had been pathetically slow on the uptake. Deane had prevaricated about his achievements in case proclaiming them meant he wouldn't fit in where he most wanted to belong. He feared the dressing room would regard him as boastful. 'He doesn't let on about those qualifications,' said Jonjo.

As I watched Deane hurry off, I said on impulse: 'Go and tell him to get changed tonight. I'm sticking him on the bench.'

Jonjo's eyes were probing in their contemplation of me. 'You can't be serious,' he said.

8

THERE'S ALWAYS SOMEONE WHO throws statistics at you, someone who plays every game on paper. The areas in which a striker scores his goals. The phases in which he gets them. Too much information can clutter your thoughts. You end up ignoring the basics. That's the mistake I made against Aston Villa.

Frank Mallory would always tell me that football was 'the simplest game ever invented' and only 'idiots and charlatans' complicated it. Often, he'd say: 'You receive the ball. You pass the ball. If you can't pass, then you can't play.' I momentarily forgot that lesson.

I became over-concerned with the form of Dwight Yorke. Already, Yorke had scored 13 times in the league, including a hat-trick in a game in which he finished on the losing side. His stats consumed me. I watched all his goals and looked at all the bar and pie charts that revealed how he scored them and from where. But Yorke wasn't our problem. He had an off night. The player we couldn't handle was Savo Milošević, a Serbian who was over 6ft tall.

The ball got stuck in the muddy patches or slowed down as soon as someone hit a low pass into one of the puddles. Villa were still superior to us. Only the conditions helped us to contain them. By half-time, we ought to have been so far behind that we could never have clawed our way back again; being 3–0 or even 4–0 ahead wouldn't have flattered Villa. Milošević had torn holes in us. He was too strong, too big, too tough. He hit the bar and a post and had a shot from 10 yards booted off the line.

There I was – yet again – prowling around my technical area, yelling and gesticulating as madly as Lear on his heath. I looked more animated in that tiny space than Jürgen Klopp does today. We couldn't hold the ball. Only Stefan Fournier, who had art in his feet, gave us any respite. He was dragging possession into the corner flags, trying to fritter away time as early as the fifteenth minute.

Despite the rain, there were nearly 30,000 in Villa Park – 99.9 per cent of whom wore claret and blue, mocking us for being so absurdly lucky.

Usually, you're either too far from the action or you get so caught up in the game that you don't always hear what's being said on the field. But, with half-time looming, Andy Townsend, Villa's captain, shouted: 'This lot's about to crumble,' which (though he never knew it) was an act of mind-reading; I'd said the same thing to Jonjo Whelan less than a minute before. By then, I was counting the micro-seconds to the break and silently praying to whichever saint was responsible for protecting teams under pressure. We needed to reorganise, take a breath, gather ourselves.

When the blessed relief of half-time came, I walked along the touchline and back into the dressing room, determined to be radical. 'If I don't do something big now, I may as well resign,' I said to Jonjo. 'We're going to get a beating we'll never recover from. The season will be over.'

Who'd been our worst player? Of course, it was Mikhail Blaga. I tapped Jason Deane on the shoulder. 'Stay out here for five minutes. Get loosened up properly.'

Helenio Herrera reverted to a sweeper system to save himself. He'd arrived at Inter in 1960. By 1962, the club had given him an ultimatum: he had 'one more season' to bring them a trophy. Nine months later, Herrera won Serie A. His decision to make the switch was retrospectively hailed as masterful and inspired rather than desperate. My gamble was pure desperation. I went across to Fournier: 'Play as sweeper. Lock us up at the back. What we lose in midfield, we'll gain in defence.'

As sanguine as ever, Fournier neither protested nor questioned me. 'No problem,' he said, only telling me afterwards that he'd never played there before. I could have kissed him.

Jonjo looked at me as though I had just scaled the summit of insanity. He did so again after I told Blaga: 'You're coming off because you're a fucking disgrace.' What came to mind then was the third slice of advice that Alex Ferguson had given me as we drank wine together at Old Trafford. It was: 'The most important thing is control. The minute a player threatens your control, you have to get rid of him.'

Blaga hadn't tracked back. He hadn't chased into the corners to support Fournier. He'd lolloped from one position to the next and then stood there, hands on hips. His features were habitually grim. His shoulders had a weary slump about them. He was wholly uninterested and without conviction. Blaga also lacked one thing I couldn't teach any player: courage. Someone either possesses it or he doesn't. Those who do are priceless. Those who don't – the players who close their eyes in tackles or when heading the ball – aren't worth a light. They'll always let you down and, as Ferguson stressed, you have to clear them out. Two things were obvious to me from the beginning, probably even from my first day. Blaga thought I was a country bumpkin. He resented me. He was a late entrant into the world of maturity. He was also a wastrel whose petulance grew out of his misplaced belief that he was never in the wrong.

That's what he believed now.

Blaga began to rage about 'the shit Swedish League' and my lack of qualifications to manage him. 'You scored a goal in a Cup final a century ago. You think that gives you the right to coach me. Fuck off. Fuck yourself. You're no one.' He took off his right boot and hurled it against the facing wall, smearing the paint with mud. He grabbed the front of his shirt and ripped it. 'Fuck you,' he said again. 'I play for this club no longer.'

What I did next was calculated. I had prepared for it. Blaga was my height. I'd picked up and thrown down much taller men than him. I took two strides and grabbed him by the throat with my left hand and balled my right into a fist. 'You're right about one thing: you won't play for this club again. You won't even get back on the team bus tonight. Make your own way home. To Bulgaria, if possible.'

He was expecting to be punched; he even shut his eyes to ready himself for the blow. I hooked my right foot around his left leg instead. He fell onto the tiled floor, landing on his back. I'd held his throat so tightly that my finger marks were visible on his flesh. 'I'm about to go out for the second half. If you're still here when I come back, I'll rip off your flesh the way you ripped off your shirt. Pick up the boot you've thrown, get changed and get out. You're the most overrated player I've ever worked with.'

Not once did I shout. Not once did anyone attempt to come between us. Blaga always did a lot of talking, but I'm not sure the other players understood him; they certainly didn't warm to him. There was absolute silence. Jonjo would say later – exaggerating, I'm sure – that my face went volcano-red but that my voice was low and calm. I wasn't disturbed – then or afterwards – by that display of emotion.

I took pleasure from the discomfort I caused Blaga. Getting rid of him was like purging our system of a poison. My only regret? I should have done it a fortnight earlier.

9

FRANK MALLORY HAD REFUSED to reinvent himself. He'd got stuck tactically somewhere in the 1980s, allowing the game to roll on and refine itself without him. As a new manager in the Premier League, I had one advantage: I was a surprise package. My rivals didn't know what I could do – or what I *might* do, even from one match to the next.

Looking at our formation, and also at the sight of a novice

teenager up front, Aston Villa thought I'd thrown in a towel from all four corners.

The worst thing is to ask someone to do a job you think is beyond them, but I knew Stefan Fournier would be a graceful and effective sweeper. The whole pitch was now in front of him. And I had a hunch – don't ask me why – that Jason Deane would do *something*. I gave him the most elementary instructions. Don't dribble with the ball for the sake of it; you'll only get us in trouble. Don't try to be clever; concentrate on what you do best. Don't listen to the sledging; words aren't tackles.

When Deane was standing on the touchline, waiting to go on, I heard some of the crowd behind me ask one another: 'Who's this?' I turned and saw others taking the rolled-up match programme out of their coat pockets and scanning through it, looking for a brief line about what he'd done and where he'd come from. Of course, the programme didn't even list him. No one but us knew he existed.

Unlikely twists occur so frequently in football. Unpredictable results. Outrageous tilts in fortune and enormous changes in the closing minutes of a match. These are the bizarre concurrences that fiction must always avoid to remain credible. But football is real life, in which anything can happen.

The Villa defence barely seemed to notice Deane, his arrival making no impression on them. The danger he posed seemed so minimal. Within a minute, he got his first touch of the ball in the Premier League, mucking up a 40-yard clearance by miscontrolling it dreadfully. He fell over, coming down with a hard slap into the mud. Gareth Southgate picked up the ball and strolled beyond him. Jonjo Whelan sighed and laid his hands against his forehead.

To relieve the pressure, we thumped everything long to Deane, who was already looking lonely in his isolation. Things didn't get better for him. Trying to take an awkward pass, his legs wobbled and the ball bounced off his knee. Again, Southgate was available to collect it. The crowd spared Deane none of their derision. 'Has he played before?' one of them bellowed from behind my dug-out. 'Who's this fucking joker?' shouted another.

In the dressing room, after Deane had warmed up, I'd asked Fournier to speak to him. 'Tell him not to try too hard. Tell him not to get dispirited. And, above all, tell him to say calm.' The Frenchman had walked out of the tunnel with Deane, draping a hand across his shoulder. Now, as he struggled, Deane looked down the pitch at Fournier, who communicated with him in hand signals, a hastily invented semaphore.

We showed a willing that I didn't know we had in us. We fell back deep into our own half, absorbing punchy attacks. Villa, who had begun with aspirations of elegance, got slowly dragged down to our level, hacking at the ball indiscriminately when it needed to be passed sensibly. Fournier frustrated them; he always seemed to know where Savo Milošević would go, blocking the runs that had cleaved us apart in the first half.

It began to rain again. The game was going so well for us that I didn't notice, even though it plastered my hair to my scalp and soaked the long coat I was wearing. I'd resigned myself to taking the point that, before the match, I'd decided would be almost worthless to us. So had Villa's supporters. With five minutes to go, there were rows upon rows of empty seats. Those who were bored had left to get an early bus, taking the disillusioned with them. No one thought the stalemate could be broken.

But just then, we somehow counter-attacked in a mad sprint, the move beginning with a pass Fournier hit from our penalty spot to the right flank. Villa, who had pushed too many bodies forward, had to back-pedal. Ross McClean was in a lot of muddy space, with only Deane ahead of him. The ball, struck by McClean first time, came in speculatively at thigh height. It was the poorest of crosses. The break we got was that Villa, forced to defend at last, did so lamely. By now Deane was in five square yards of his own. The nearest man to him – Southgate, I think – clearly believed that any ambitious attempt at a shot would spoon into the Holte End. With a short, lithe leap, Deane got over what didn't qualify even as a half-chance and wrapped his bottle-green left boot around it. The volley, hit from 16 yards, thumped into the bottom corner. The goal was a delicious thing, an exhibition of improvisation as well as technique. A few seasons later, watching Sweden in a World Cup qualifier, I saw Zlatan Ibrahimović smash one in just like it – identical pose and poise, identical distance, identical placement.

I gave the thumbs-up in Deane's direction and nodded at Jonjo. He was on his feet, staring skywards and slamming his fist furiously against the air. He looked as though he was pounding on some huge invisible door.

Deane's effervescence had given us the shock of life. My concern was to get everyone focused again. I've always said that managers deserve neither the amount of the credit nor the amount of criticism given to them. Sometimes we're just lucky or unlucky. 'Don't let them back into it,' I kept shouting. 'Hold the line.' No one paid the slightest attention. Not even Fournier. I shouted louder, as though I was trying to get a message to someone half a mile away. I could feel the great beat of my heart.

Rather than funnelling back and hunkering down, letting Villa come to us, we surged forward, the giddy momentum of the goal carrying us adventurously on. In the 93rd minute, still revealing more dash than discipline, we won a corner, our first of the match. I expected us to take it short and hug the flag. Instead, we lobbed it in gently. The Villa goalkeeper, a deputy for Mark Bosnich, thought the take would be easy and consequently stretched too far for it, spilling the catch off the tips of his fingers. In the scrum to reclaim possession, Deane – on the half-turn – back-heeled the ball in from close range. The 'keeper tried to paw at the ball with his big, gloved hand before it crossed the line.

The linesman's eyes were the only piece of goal-line technology available to us back then. He awarded the goal. As though wanting to distract everyone from his own mistake, the 'keeper quickly hauled himself off the floor and began to chase the referee, accusing him of missing a blatant push. Mud stuck to him everywhere, even caking his face; he looked as though he had been buried and then dug up again.

In the dressing room, amid the smell of sweat and soap, I watched Deane flop onto the bench. He pulled off his boots and his shirt. Through the steam, billowing in drifts from the showers, I saw him holding the shirt, his head bowed over it. He began to trace the outline of the badge with his fingers.

'Take it home and give it to your mum,' I said. 'Tell her I'm sorry she wasn't here.'

Frank Mallory had once refused to give the match ball to someone who had scored a hat-trick. Provocatively, he announced his reasons in public: 'He can have the ball when he learns how to play with it.' As if wanting to make up for his lack of belief in Deane, Jonjo disappeared into the officials' room. He cajoled the referee into giving him the ball – a break with convention. He returned holding it aloft in the palm of his right hand. The leather was still sticky. He presented it with neither ceremony nor words. The act itself was enough. He simply dropped the ball into Deane's canvas bag. Deane zipped up the bag quickly, afraid someone might steal his souvenir from him.

In our teens, most of us pretend to be older than we are; he did so only on the pitch.

I O

Each fresh start had previously led us into a dead end, but I sensed immediately we were halfway to somewhere at last and that the win over Aston Villa was startling enough to be transformative.

So it proved.

We beat Manchester City. We beat Sheffield Wednesday too. One player, unknown and previously cast off, had changed us completely. He'd appeared almost as miraculously as Hale–Bopp. When journalists asked me where he came from, I replied: 'He arrived on the tail of that comet.'

Jason Deane was a non-stop revelation and fascinating for the newspapers, who were grateful for someone new to write about. In that period, which was so sweet for us, the papers couldn't believe we had – in embryo – a superstar who lived at home with his mother, didn't have a girlfriend, couldn't drive a car and spoke softly in coherent sentences. He caught the bus from 'down the road' and walked into the ground with a small rucksack slung over his shoulder.

I'll always owe a debt to Stefan Fournier. At our first training session after Villa Park, I barely recognised him. He'd gone to a barber and had asked him to shave off his long hair. When I asked him why, he ran his hand across his scalp and explained: 'You'll want me to stay as sweeper. A new position demands a new me.'

He was wearing a blue T-shirt with white lettering. 'Don't Worry,' it proclaimed. 'I'm Here to Save You.'

Fournier's sacrifice, a great one for him, demonstrated his commitment to us.

In ancient Rome, slaves had the task of whispering the message 'Remember you are mortal' into the ears of army generals who, after winning a titanic battle, were in danger of forgetting that fact. It was a risky business. Many generals didn't want a pin stuck into the balloon of their egos, and some slaves didn't survive. To protect Deane from himself and also from hangers-on, Fournier reminded him after every match: 'Without football, you're just like anyone else.' Deane didn't resent that.

He began to dress differently, his clothes becoming more expensive. He acquired a girlfriend, her hair peroxide blonde. He also acquired an agent and began to do small bits of promotional work, such as opening a store or a snooker club. The game attracts unsuitable hangers-on, people you'd usually walk 50 miles in your bare feet to avoid – the spivs, the spongers, the chancers. All of them want to leach off you and give nothing in return. Deane side-stepped them in the same way he side-stepped central defenders who wanted to clog him. He was nonchalant even when two different men claimed to be his father. They hadn't read the newspapers properly: they both believed his mother was dead.

I like to think my attitude is always laid back and grown up. I don't care that much what a player does, providing I know about his little schemes in advance; providing he doesn't take his social life onto the pitch with him; providing the police are never involved.

Deane behaved himself. Our winning spree continued because of him.

Against Coventry, he stopped a pass with his left foot, re-adjusted his body position, took a step and flicked the ball – yes, *flicked* it – into the top corner. Against West Ham, he under-scored his credentials as a poacher. From inside the six-yard box he side-footed in one goal and headed in another. On the last Saturday of April, at Liverpool, he hit *that* shot: the one from 20 yards, struck on the run, that went past David James before the goalkeeper or the Kop saw it take off. Deane had so much energy that he carried on running and collected the ball himself, tucking it under his arm and dropping it onto the centre circle.

We'd have won that game if Curtis Taylor – only 20 min-utes from the end – hadn't dived over a scuffed shot from Stan Collymore. It was as bad a mistake as Gary Sprake's. Trying to clear a ball at the same end thirty years before, Sprake had thrown it into his net instead.

We clung on so hard to the draw that our fingernails bled. In a pantomime finish, Taylor was so nervous that he began punching everything – including balls he could have caught.

Our unexpected successes, home and away, inflicted chronic suffering on Middlesbrough, Sunderland and Derby. Winning at Anfield would have put us out of their reach; a point meant we still needed two draws from our last two matches to avoid relegation. Southampton awaited us next. Our final game, at home, was against Middlesbrough, who had reached the FA Cup final, despite their disastrous form in the league. Even with a match in hand, there was no possible escape for them. Certain to be relegated at least a week before the season ended, the theory was that Middlesbrough would be too preoccupied with dreamy thoughts of Wembley to bother us.

Everyone assumed we'd clear the first hurdle at Southampton, which would make the second irrelevant anyway. They also wanted to know about my future.

I was due back in Sweden in mid-May. I was repeatedly asked: 'Are you going or staying?'

I didn't know. I was waiting for Jack Munroe to tell me.

PART FIVE

A GRAND OLD TEAM
TO PLAY FOR

FRANK MALLORY AND I settled into a pattern. I went to see him once a week, mostly on a Monday afternoon. If the weather was warm enough, we'd sit on the bench beneath the cherry trees. If it wasn't, I'd wheel two armchairs in front of the French doors and we'd look across the garden, noting the changes in it since my last visit. His dog would lie in the gap between us, a pink tongue lolling from its mouth like a strip of bacon. I noted the changes in Frank too. The way he lost colour, as though anaemic. The way his clothes hung more loosely than before over the thinning frame of his body. How his eyes, like dull stones, sank deeper into his face. The number of times he paused when speaking, punctuating a sentence with a cough that seemed to come from the rawest of throats. Out of habit, and also for comfort, Frank carried a packet of cigarettes with him, but he smoked fewer of them and stubbed some out before they'd burnt a quarter of the way down. Sometimes he even took a cigarette from the packet without lighting it, twirling it between his fingers.

On one of our walks to the bottom of the garden, Frank tripped, couldn't recover his balance and fell down a minor slope. His fall was cushioned by a patch of high grass in which more wildflowers were beginning to appear. Watching us from an upstairs window, Martha came running out of the house. We picked him up together. His ribs were visible beneath his white linen shirt. Frank, though badly winded, was only concerned about whether his cigarettes, which were tucked into a pocket, had been squashed beneath his weight. When we got him to a bench, he groped for my hand.

Accustomed to one another again, the awkwardness of our first meeting had been forgotten. We never referred to it again. We followed an agenda, which was set by Frank. He'd start by declaring an opinion, which I was expected to accept as an inarguable statement of fact. This was usually some snappy criticism of another manager: Ferguson, Dalglish, Venables, Hoddle, Wenger – anyone, indeed, who in the previous seven days had done something he didn't like or expressed a view contrary to his own. I let him blow it out of his system.

We'd replough the furrows of the previous weekend's match. Frank would tell me what he thought I'd done right and, chiefly, where I'd made mistakes. One player ought to have come off earlier. Another ought not to have been picked at all. We had to sharpen up defensively at set pieces. We had to move the ball quicker or slower through midfield, or hold on to it more assuredly at the back. Despite our upsurge in form, the list of my deficiencies never seemed to shrink.

'It's for your own good,' he'd say. 'I'm not picking on you. I'm not saying any of these things out of envy. I'm trying to make you a better coach, a better manager. You're a beginner, really. At this level, anyway. I don't want you to make a balls-up of this. I've got my reputation to think of.'

With a groaning reluctance, Frank conceded he'd been wrong about Jason Deane. He had no choice. 'If I hadn't been ill, it would have been different. I'd have seen the boy had talent. I don't suppose he'll ever forgive me. When he writes his life story, I'll be the villain in it. He can say what he likes. I won't be here by then.'

On my fourth visit I handed over the notebooks he'd compiled on Helenio Herrera. I said I'd found them in a filing cabinet while looking for something else. Frank set aside his cigarette, resting it on the arm of the bench, and began turning the pages. His fingers were stiff. His nails needed clipping. It was like watching someone who, after discovering an old photo album, doesn't quite recognise himself and can't identify some of the people looking back at him from a different century. 'I wrote all this and drew these diagrams?' he asked, as though not believing it. 'I haven't looked at them for so long . . . I really had forgotten.' When he finally closed the notebooks, caressing the covers as he did so, I wondered whether he'd ever open them again.

'Herrera's still alive,' Frank said, turning his face towards mine. 'He's in his 80s. I have no idea whether he follows the game any more, or whether he's able to. I'd like to think so. I'd like to think he knows what you're doing and is impressed. Perhaps I could write a letter to him.'

Frank announced his latest news with a yelp of triumph.

'Munroe's agreed,' he said.

'Agreed to what?'

'To the banquet. Well, he's calling it a dinner. He's paying for the lot – even each player's hotel bill. You can all drink as much as you like.'

I had never imagined Jack Munroe would support Frank's idea of holding a banquet to celebrate the anniversary of winning the FA Cup. Why would it interest him? What, after the initial blush of publicity, would he get out of it? Wouldn't celebrating our glorious past only spotlight our present struggle? Even if Munroe did agree to fund anything, I was sure it would only be a glorified version of the annual players' reunion.

I was wrong.

'It's going to be a red carpet event,' said Frank, proudly.

Munroe had booked the Great Room in Willoughby Hall, a 16th-century pile of Ancaster stone. A hundred years before, it had been crammed with butlers and footmen, cooks and parlour maids, grooms and gardeners. The hall was set in 300 acres of parkland. Herds of deer roamed between the trees, the lakes, the ornamental ponds and an assortment of follies. It was another of those landmarks that I could see from the roof terrace of my apartment. Only five miles away, built on a hill, each of the hall's four towers had pepper-pot turrets. With a pair of binoculars, I could even pick out its cornices, pilasters, niches and balustrades. As a boy, I'd once tried to count the hall's leaded windows, giving up when I reached 130. Whoever came to wash them must have been the county's richest window cleaner.

'The boat's being pushed out just for us,' said Frank, gloating. 'Of course, Uncle Charlie Bembridge tried to cash in. Offered to host the thing at his place so he could show off. Munroe said no. That's a fucking punch in the chops for Uncle Charlie.'

The event was open to corporate sponsors, advertisers, executive-box holders and even fans – if the price of the ticket didn't deter them. ITV's commentator, Brian Moore, a friend of Frank's, had agreed to host it. The best commentators know when to stay silent, letting the viewer fit his own words around the pictures. It was Moore who described my goal at Wembley, like this:

'The ball's flying everywhere . . . Spurs can't clear it . . . OH, CALLAGHAN! . . . THOM CALLAGHAN . . . He might have won the Cup for Frank Mallory with less than FOUR minutes to go . . . and what have Tottenham got left now?'

On paper, this seems neither memorable nor poetic; there's no 'They think it's all over' beat to the words. But trust me (or search YouTube if you don't), the pitch of, and the inflections in, Moore's voice made each phrase soar beside the images on the screen: that frantic clattering around in the box . . . the ball breaking to me . . . my shot as it tore through the air . . . the sprint I made towards the corner flag . . . Frank rising from the scarlet leather benches, his arms aloft . . . our crowd madly delirious, swaying in red and white waves and flinging around scarves and banners and torn-up programmes . . . the Spurs players dragging themselves upfield for the kick-off . . . a flash of the scoreboard, confirming our lead.

'You won't have to make a speech, but you will have to be interviewed on stage,' said Frank. 'Everybody will. We're all part of the entertainment. Don't worry, the questions will be softer than a baby's arse. We're there to celebrate, not to grill you like the Inquisition. You only have to tell them what it felt like to score the goal.'

Munroe had promised to fit us all out with club suits, almost identical to the ones we wore at Wembley.

'He's slipped the FA a few quid as well,' said Frank. 'He's made sure the Cup will be on the top table, shiny and gleaming and with our ribbons tied to the handles. He's also invited the referee and persuaded him to bring the match ball with him too. Munroe knows how to organise a party. Or somebody who works for him does.'

I smiled, doing so in slow motion because I had a horror of the whole shebang.

'When is this banquet taking place?' I asked.

If the date was mid-June, I could find multiple reasons to be nowhere near it. I'd record a message in advance. It would begin insincerely with the words: 'Sorry I can't be with you tonight . . .'

'May the eighth,' said Frank.

'What the fuck, Frank? That's in the middle our last two games. Only 72 hours before the season's final Sunday.'

'I hadn't thought of it like that,' he said.

'You want me to go to a jamboree when all my thoughts need to be on a game that could decide whether or not we're in the Premier League next season? Why did you agree to that? Why did no one ask me? What the fuck would you have said if the club had arranged a dinner three days before the Cup final – and done it behind your back?'

Frank looked away from me. 'You have a point. But it's done now. It can't be undone.'

'When did Munroe tell you all this?'

'Two days ago.'

On my way back into the city, it occurred to me that Frank had colluded with Munroe to wreck my chances of staying up. I couldn't decide whether the banquet was an act of sabotage or bloody selfishness.

2

JACK MUNROE SEEMED TO be everywhere all at once. Toronto. Abu Dhabi. Reykjavik. Berlin. Wellington. Beijing. New York. Buenos Aires. If you'd plotted his route on a world map, using pins and coloured string, you'd have seen no logical pattern in it. The thing would have looked like a game of cat's cradle that had gone horribly awry. He turned up in one place and then appeared in another without any apparent effort. It was a joke that didn't quite come off, but I used to say, only privately, that Munroe possessed a magic door that he carried about with the rest of his luggage. He merely had to step through it to go from one city to another – even when a continent separated them. The only place the door didn't bring him was into my office.

As far as the club was concerned, Munroe became the man who wasn't there. This was a bonus for me: he didn't interfere. It was also unsettling: he didn't seem to care either. Frank Mallory believed Munroe was 'fed up with the lot of you'. I convinced myself of something else. I thought our unlikely resurgence – and my part in it – had spoilt the plan Munroe had made. I was sure he'd chosen my successor, drawn up the contracts and possibly already got most of the paperwork signed and stored in a safe. But I was making it more difficult for him to justify getting rid of me. I also began to think that I might not belong anywhere after this was all over. Östers were coping without me – playing well, winning matches. I wouldn't necessarily be welcomed back joyously there. And I wouldn't be needed here. I didn't like to admit that – even to myself.

'Too far-fetched,' said Frank, during one of our Monday get-togethers. 'As usual, you're overcomplicating everything. Why wouldn't Östers want you back? You're a Premier League manager now. Whatever happens, your credit is high. As for that shitbag Munroe, I'd say he's fallen out of love with football, but I doubt he ever felt much for it in the first place.'

Munroe had watched us win at West Ham. He'd arrived a quarter of an hour late and vanished ten minutes early. The thing is, I'd known nothing about it until he was long gone from Upton Park.

The post-match press conference is always the trickiest to navigate. Adrenalin is still rushing around your body and looking for somewhere to go. Your mind is dealing with a windmill-whirl of different thoughts. You're still kicking every ball, making every tackle, cursing each mistake and wondering – even if you've won – whether you could have done better. You can snap at a question or answer the follow-up too honestly for your own good. I did that sometimes, embarrassing myself. We'd beaten West Ham, but I was still irritable and a little on edge.

'What do think your owner made of that?' I was asked.

'I don't know. You'll have find him to ask him. He's in Mumbai, I think.'

'Not today. He was here. Sitting in the directors' box. You didn't know? He didn't speak to you? He didn't come into the dressing room?'

'I haven't spoken to him for six weeks. He doesn't ring me. If he needs something, he gets someone else to pass on a message. That's the way we do business.'

'He must be pleased with what you're doing? The results you're getting? Even tonight, when you didn't play that well?'

'No idea. I've never had that kind of conversation with him.'
'Isn't that odd?'

'Puzzling, but it doesn't matter. Not to me. Not to the team either. None of us know him. Some of the players wouldn't recognise Mr Munroe if he asked them for an autograph. But he owns the club. He can stroll in and stroll out again whenever he likes.'

'And he'll appoint whomever he likes as the next manager? You're not expecting to get the job? Even if you stay up?'

'I'm not expecting anything. If he ever had my phone number here, I think he's misplaced it.'

The *Daily Mail* printed that exchange word for word. It appeared as a sidebar next to the story about Munroe's surprise appearance and the deductions that could be drawn from it. Munroe was photographed sitting in the directors' box. His expression was as dour as one of those carvings on Easter Island.

The story, like every other, was flavoured with a lot of sympathy for me. Munroe was portrayed as a bad guy with a stony heart who lacked common courtesy. I was the heroic underdog, battling on while being belittled. Neither of us came out of it well.

At one o'clock the following morning, the phone rang. I was sure the worst had happened: Freyja had lost the baby.

'Mr Callaghan?' said a man with a Midwest American accent.

'Yes?'

'I have a message for you from Mr Munroe. He just wants you to know that he hasn't misplaced your number. Sorry to have disturbed you at this hour.'

3

IT WOULD HAVE BEEN a bloody stupid thing to have done, but I had the crazy notion nonetheless of making some sort of statement. If we won at Southampton, I'd make a French exit. I'd quietly clear out the small number of possessions I'd accumulated in Frank Mallory's office. I'd do it the day before our last game, which I'd watch from the directors' box. Jonjo Whelan could take over. He'd pick the team, decide the tactics and occupy the dug-out alone. It would be his day, not mine. When the whistle went, I'd slip out of my seat and leave without a word. There'd be little left to say anyway.

Our game at The Dell was staged on a Monday night.

The general election had taken place only four days before, the result historic because the win – for the red team – wasn't so much a landslide as an avalanche. The country, which felt cleaner afterwards, was in an ebullient mood, a party atmosphere everywhere. The football didn't live up to that. I knew, after only ten minutes, that neither of us would score. It was a 90-minute scuffle. We were like two boxers who, afraid of taking a punch, didn't want to escape from the clinches. Already thinking of a holiday on some sandy beach, Southampton seemed very relaxed about the outcome. We were pent-up, trying hard not to lose even when the match was there to be grasped.

Like other grounds of the same vintage, The Dell was eventually reduced to rubble, its acres levelled smooth for a housing estate. Back then, the pitch was so close to the stands that, as a player, you heard every cough and spit and fart from the crowd. I always thought it would take only the gentlest push from someone at the back of the West Stand to send those at the front onto the touchline. I never liked going there because of the advantage Southampton got from the architecture could be overwhelming when their supporters were particularly vocal. You could sense from them when the tide of a match was about to shift, subtly and incrementally.

At half-time, I said to the players: 'You're shitting yourselves.

I know you don't want to go into our last match needing to win, but we can get what we need here and then forget about Middlesbrough. You can go on the piss tonight and drink till Sunday morning as far as I care. I might do it myself. Southampton aren't that bothered. Be braver. Push on. Pin them back.'

Any shot of enthusiasm my words gave them didn't survive beyond the first minute of the second half. Southampton won a free kick on the right flank. It was angled in from 35 yards. Aaron Buchan left it for Stefan Fournier. Fournier left it for everyone else. The ball fell to Matt Le Tissier. I half turned away, waiting to hear confirmation of what I knew would happen. But Le Tissier, unaccountably, lifted his drive over the bar and into the Archers Road End.

'Our luck's in,' said Jonjo.

We sank back into our shell. No other clear chance fell to anyone. The saves both goalkeepers made came from long-range efforts. Only something outrageous would have broken the deadlock. An own goal. The daftest of mistakes. The sort of sublime slice of skill that had, thus far, been lacking from the match. During the last twenty minutes, a very fine rain washed over us. It was the first rain I could remember, in an inordinately dry spring, since that biblical deluge at Villa Park.

'We didn't turn up,' I said to Jonjo.

'Give them two days off. They're done in,' he said. 'Mentally, we're in the knacker's yard.'

Jonjo was being kind. I'd lost my focus as much as the players had. I blamed it on the banquet. Not because I'd taken any part in arranging it, but because I didn't want to go. We'd all kick up dust from the past that no one wanted disturbed. I'd have willingly given up the lavish bonus I was due from Jack Munroe to avoid the thing.

On the way to Southampton, I'd looked down the bus. Jason Deane had been scurrying about, still serving coffee to everyone, as though his goals were insufficient to make him part of the team. Fuchs, Hooper and Cully had been playing cards, each baiting the other. I remembered that Frank had once banned poker, 13-card brag and pontoon because too much money regularly changed hands. At one stage Ned Kelly owed Jimmy Bradley so much cash that Bradley wouldn't pass the ball to him until a cheque had cleared. Kelly was a compulsive gambler. Frank ended up confiscating his wages and giving him £40 per day pocket money. It prevented Kelly from losing a week's salary in less than two hours at the local bookmaker's.

Taylor and Fournier had been singing 'Wonderwall' very badly, making up the lyrics as they went along. Time had stopped and wound backwards for me. They had been sitting where Robbie Clayton and I used to sit: on the port side of the penultimate row of the bus. I had seen myself as I was almost two decades earlier. Skinny, pale, very blond. Wearing my club suit, which didn't quite fit across the chest, and my red and white striped club tie, the Windsor knot loose and chunky. I could feel the collar of my shirt chafing the back of my neck. In my kit, I looked even more like a waif; a gust of wind could have blown me out of my boots.

Robbie was fanatical about David Bowie. He was a human jukebox, belting out any Bowie song you liked. Because of him, the soundtrack to one entire season was Bowie's 'Modern Love', the song played so often that I came to attach it to all the other seasons too. We'd shout the chorus, a raucous and discordant choir about never waving 'bye-bye'.

The words and the music came back to me, piped into my head in quadraphonic sound. I hummed along. I saw the faces of the team that had won the Cup. The two Kellys, Bradley, Ramsey and van het Hoff. I saw Frank, who would be shaking his head at Jonjo and saying what he always said about 'Modern Love': 'I'm going to ban that fucking song.'

Soon we were about to come together again, the boys of May gathered incongruously and in haste. For eight hours or so we'd observe all the rites and pleasantries of the occasion. It'd be a grand old team to play for again. We'd strike our poses. We'd smile for the camera. We'd back-slap everyone and look glad to see them. The minor feuds and the petty resentments would be put aside, untraceable behind a façade of kindly warmth. A stranger would never be able to guess who didn't care for whom. Who'd fallen out. Who'd once been snubbed or ignored and had never forgotten. Who still counted those stored-up grievances, some of them 10 or 20 years old. Who believed himself to be better than the rest. We'd line up to shake hands with Frank, laughing on cue when we did so. We'd behave reasonably well in the company of those who didn't know us, who thought – or wanted to believe – that 90 minutes at Wembley had forged a fellowship for life between us.

There was one thing we wouldn't do: we wouldn't talk about the reason we were all there and the urgency behind the summons. We'd pretend Frank was fine. We'd celebrate the way we had once done, during that fine hour when champagne had made us the greatest of mates.

Frank had asked me in his garden: 'You are looking forward to all this, aren't you? You scored the bloody goal. You have to enjoy it. You will enjoy it, won't you?'

'Can't wait,' I'd said.

4

I GOT UP UNUSUALLY EARLY on the day of the banquet. I went onto the roof terrace, watching the city as it came to life. I looked at our floodlights and at the river, each obscured by a thin blanket of haze, and then at the towers of Willoughby Hall, which were visible above the lime trees that ran along the avenue towards the building. We were approaching the thick end of spring. The morning was already sticky with heat. I took my suit out of the wardrobe and draped it on the bed in the spare room. Beside it, I laid out a white shirt and a tie. The tie, a bit naff, had been designed especially for the event. A shock of red silk. A silver print of the FA Cup. The date of our win beneath it.

I liked the silence of those hours. I didn't often listen to the radio or watch TV during them. That morning was different. The previous afternoon, I'd given an interview to the BBC about the banquet. A camera crew had come to the ground and filmed me in the car park for 20 minutes, faffing about with the lights and the sound. The cameraman had wanted the club crest, splashed across the back of the main stand, to appear in the shot. I switched on the TV, eager to know how much of the interview had survived in the cutting room.

I was the lead story.

Not, however, because of the banquet. The presenter was holding a copy of the late edition of the *Daily Mirror*. He turned the back page towards the camera. The headline read:

SOLD DOWN THE RIVER:
Munroe sells club before relegation decider

The main illustration, beside one head shot of me and another of Munroe, showed an aerial view of the ground, the river twisting into the distance.

With a few tweaks, the same story appeared in the *Sun*, the *Mail* and the *Express*. The gist of it was this. Jack Munroe had originally planned to stay in football, primarily to save face rather than to protect his investment. When our form perked up, the threat of relegation receding, he'd snatched at the chance to bail out instead. He'd found a consortium in the Far East that wanted to buy us, and the deal was about to be finalised. Munroe would get slightly more for the club than he'd paid for it – but only if, as everyone expected, we stayed up. The consortium wanted one of three managers: George Graham, who'd moved to Leeds only the previous September; Fabio Capello, ready to depart Real Madrid after a falling-out; or Carlo Ancelotti, about to finish as runner-up in Serie A with Parma.

I didn't think Graham would abandon Elland Road, or that Capello and Ancelotti could be tempted here. But if the job didn't go to any of them, it would belong to someone else. There'd be a new boss next season, and it wouldn't be me.

According to the BBC, the story had been leaked from the Far East; Munroe hadn't wanted anyone to know about it until after Sunday. I didn't believe that. My phone went even before the item finished.

'That fucker Munroe knows how to shit on a party,' said Jonjo Whelan.

5

To BREAK OUR ROUTINE, I occasionally held light training sessions on the pitch, much to the chagrin of the groundsman. He'd stand near one of the corner flags and mutter his complaints as soon as the first divot appeared. That morning I sent the team onto the pitch. I closed off the inside of the ground to the media, a posse of whom had camped around the spot where I'd spoken to the BBC the previous day. I went in by the back door to avoid them.

When I took the job, I'd asked the players to call me 'Cally' rather than 'boss'. The informality seemed appropriate; I didn't think I'd be there long enough to build a relationship with anyone. I got changed and came out of the tunnel to find the squad arranged in a line along the touchline, as if waiting for someone to strike up the national anthem.

Aaron Buchan spoke: 'Boss, no matter what happens on Sunday, and whatever happens afterwards, all of us want you to know how grateful we are for what you've done. If someone buys us out, we'll ask for you to stay. If necessary, we're prepared to go on strike to make that happen. We're all agreed.' He began to clap. A second or two later, George Cully, standing next to him, began to clap too. Applause rippled down the line, echoing around the empty ground for a full minute.

When the clapping stopped, I said: 'Don't concern yourself with anything that may, or may not, be going on off the pitch. Especially not this week. We've come a very long way in a very short period of time. Let's not fuck the thing up now. If you do, I'll never forgive you. Don't get distracted. Don't get involved in the politics. And don't stand there when you should be working.'

The players, perhaps expecting something more from me, obediently began to jog away. I shouted after them:

'I forgot to add one thing. Thank you.'

Nothing more needed to be said then. Slightly less than half the pitch – the part in which we worked – was cast in sun, our narrow shadows criss-crossing it. We trained as well as I'd ever seen us. We were clear-eyed, eager and pumped up; Jack Munroe had seen to that. You'd have thought we were only a month into a fresh season. Passes were played at speed. Shots zoomed into the net from every conceivable angle. Defensive headers travelled 40-odd yards.

Jonjo Whelan and I stood in the centre circle, the players running around us. 'I wish Middlesbrough were coming here tonight,' I said. 'In this mood, we'd rip them up. They'd go into the Cup final in pieces. We'd be three up by half-time.'

Jonjo never acknowledged his considerable role in the trans-formation of a team that only two and a bit months ago had no chance of survival. 'You've done this,' he said. 'The side Frank left and the one you've remade? I don't recognise them. They don't recognise themselves.'

I wandered off towards the tunnel side of the pitch. I have no idea why, but something made me look along the length of the main stand. A figure sat alone in the back row.

It was Robbie Clayton.

He stood up and half-heartedly raised a hand. It was as though he hadn't wanted to be discovered. He walked down the steps, carrying a brown holdall, before climbing over the perimeter wall to reach me. He did so clumsily, his legs and his back stiff-looking. We embraced one another on the cinder track.

'How did you get in? And why didn't you tell me you were coming?' I asked.

A ball scooted off the pitch. Robbie trapped it with his right foot and side-footed it 30 yards along the grass. It was like one of those passes, played from the halfway line, that he'd routinely struck for Davie Collins in the late 1970s and early '80s. Robbie, though despising Collins, knew the forward runs he'd make well enough to have found him in the dark.

'I knocked on the ticket-office window. I told them I was here to see you,' Robbie said. 'I originally went down to the embank-ment. I thought you'd be training there. Then I walked along the river and saw all the company you've got milling around the car park. No one recognised me. I strolled straight through the middle of them.' He opened up his holdall, which bulged with newspapers. 'I bought these to pass the time on the train. Bad luck for you. You don't deserve it.'

We went down the tunnel together, turning left and pushing open the frosted glass of the double doors that took us into the directors' corridor. Robbie hardly looked at the photographs on the walls – even those of himself. He contemplated them only briefly and without comment. He even showed lukewarm interest in the oak honours board that listed all the club's captains, his name embossed on it in gold.

When we reached what I still considered to be Frank Mallory's office, Robbie seemed a little reluctant to step inside. He was clutching his holdall against his chest. I had to invite him in. He looked around as though he hadn't seen the office before.

I said: 'I wasn't sure you'd come to the banquet. If I'd still been in Sweden, I doubt I'd have come myself. I'll tell you the truth: I'm not looking forward to it. What are you drinking?'

Robbie asked for neat gin. I gave him a double in a heavy, grand glass. He nursed it in both hands, his holdall now between his feet.

'I wasn't sure I'd get away,' he said. 'Believe it or not, we're pretty busy, even in spring. Early holiday-makers, people taking caravans, trippers who come for a night or two just for the sea.'

Robbie sniffed his gin and then took a sip of it. 'We've just refurbished the pub. But Beth — you know what she's like — insisted I come. "You've got to go," she said. "It'll look very weird if you don't." You know, I haven't been to the city for five years. This is my first time inside the ground for seven years. Four of the lads I haven't spoken to in a decade. I haven't spoken to Frank for even longer than that. I haven't seen you since . . . How long is it? Beth sends her love, of course. She's always liked you.'

He took a second sip of gin, letting it lie for a while on his tongue before swallowing. I wanted to avoid talking about Beth.

'I understand why you don't fancy it, Cally. The thing must be a pain in the arse for you. Holding it this week, I mean. Having to do interviews about the past, when the present is the only thing on your mind. Why didn't your fuckwit owner wait until Sunday was over? The fans won't forgive him if you lose. Sorry, I shouldn't even bring up the possibility of that. You'll win. You're going to be the hero for a second time.'

I laughed. 'A hero who gets the heave-ho, obviously.'

Robbie was 51 but seemed six or seven years older to me. There were deep wrinkles on his face. His hair, grey at the temples, was combed forward in an attempt to hide places where the growth was patchy. My father said that you should always look at a stranger from the toes up. 'You can learn a lot from someone's shoes,' he'd insist. He based his opinion on first-hand evidence. A friend, pretending to be prosperous, had once visited him wearing a suit so new and so smartly cut that it could have come from the tailor's that morning. 'His clothes told one story. His shoes told another,' my father said. 'The toes were scuffed. The leather was battered to bits.'

Robbie was wearing a well-pressed black suit and a dark-blue shirt. His shoes had barely a mark on them. I remembered all the ironing he used to do, the brushing-down of his clothes and the way he hung them in the wardrobe. His appearance, the way others saw him and thought about him, was as important as ever to Robbie. It was a matter of pride and self-respect. I admired him for that.

'I came early this morning,' he said. 'I took my suit to the hotel and then had a walk around some of the old haunts. The Council House needs a bloody good clean. The Market Square has too much litter in it. Some of the shops I remember are gone. That's the way of things. Everything disappears, doesn't it?'

I asked why he hadn't brought Beth. I feared I might be the reason and that Robbie was about to say: 'I know all about the two of you. She told me. Now I'm going to knock you half dead, you disloyal bastard.'

Instead, he said: 'Refused to sit through a lot of football talk. Said she'd had enough of all that when I played. Told me not to drink too much.'

You remember people as you first met them, which is why you're surprised when they change simply by becoming older.

In our early days, I'd considered Robbie as father-like. Now, watching him as he watched me, he seemed astonished. To Robbie, and also to the rest of the FA Cup-winning team, I'd always be 21 years old. No matter what I did. Irrespective of who I became. However much time passed. The fact I was the manager now would be incomprehensible to them. I read it in Robbie's expression. He couldn't conceive how different things were – and how different I was. Nor could he comprehend that 20-odd years on from the day we first met, the balance of power had switched from him to me. He was weighing up those years and the distance that now stood between us. He was looking at an entirely different Thom Callaghan from the one he knew. Making Robbie uncomfortable was the last thing I wanted. I ought to have said, but didn't: 'I'm the same person you've always known. You're my friend. You always will be.'

There was a tentative rap on the door, which swung ajar. Jason Deane stood beneath the lintel. 'I wanted to ask about getting some more tickets for Sunday. If it's a bad time, I'll come back,' he said.

Deane had been a toddler when we'd won the Cup. Like the media outside, he didn't recognise Robbie. 'Come and meet someone I admire,' I said. 'Robbie was captain when I played here. He took care of me. Look at the photos on the wall. He's in more of them than anyone else.' I sounded like Frank Mallory talking about George Raynor.

Robbie rose from his chair, straightened himself and swapped his glass of gin into his left hand so he could offer his right to Deane, who asked: 'You're here for the banquet? You're a member of the Cup-winning team?'

'A member of sorts,' said Robbie. 'I got close to Wembley, but not close enough. That's a long time ago, and I've forgotten all about it. You realise as you get older that some things that mattered at the time aren't that important later on. Not very, anyway. People ask me about the final and expect me to be gloomy about it. I'm not gloomy. I'm absolutely fine.'

Deane was perplexed. He didn't know Robbie's back story. Our Cup final win hadn't been part of either his upbringing or his education.

'I can't wait to see everybody again tonight,' added Robbie.

It wasn't the fact he said it so wistfully that took me aback. Robbie had been talking for the sheer pleasure of talking and because Deane was a captive audience. He clung on to Deane's hand. When he finally let it go, Deane took a step backwards and folded both hands behind his back.

'I've never seen the match,' he admitted. 'Apart from the boss's goal.'

'Do you want to win the FA Cup?' Robbie asked him

'I want to win the Champions League.'

'Don't blame you, son. You'll earn more money doing that.

The money will be more useful to you in life than the medal. I played for 15 years and won a few medals. I wish I'd earned more money.'

Deane looked Robbie over. 'You were a centre half?'

'I was. Not quick, but astute. Or at least I like to think so. I've seen you on TV. You're a handful. Nippy too. You'd have beaten me in a sprint, for sure, but I'd have known where you were going before you knew yourself. I'd have been waiting for you. I'd have kicked you so hard that you wouldn't have come back.'

Deane's sideways glance was a plea for help. 'He's not joking,' I said. 'He was a tough bloke. The toughest, in fact. You needed shin pads made of titanium to play against him. Some of the players he tackled are still learning how to walk again.'

Robbie threw back his shoulders. 'Don't believe him. He's a bullshitter.'

I promised Deane the tickets he wanted. 'The whole family is coming,' he said. He left us, pleased to escape, with the words: 'See you both tonight.'

I poured Robbie another double gin, which he hadn't asked for. With a sigh of fatigue, he sat back down. 'I didn't know your lot were coming as well. I thought it was just the old bastards.'

'They're not drinking and they're leaving as soon as the speeches are over. I'm not sure what they'll make of it, but we might motivate them for Sunday's match. Or perhaps they'll just get jealous. We did have the best of it, didn't we?'

Robbie stared into his gin.

'Sometimes,' he said.

6

A BUS IN RED AND white livery stood in the club's car park, waiting to take us to Willoughby Hall. The words 'FA Cup Winners' had been stencilled on both flanks.

The team, widely scattered around the country in the decade and a half since that Wembley triumph, arrived in twos and threes for the pre-reception, which took place in the chairman's room. We hugged one another with elaborate fuss. We posed for photographs. We gave TV and radio interviews for the local stations. We signed programmes and books and banners for the thousand or so fans who had gathered behind a metal barrier to see us off. Some of them had brought their young children, not even born when we won the Cup, or their teenagers, who didn't remember the match but had heard bedtime stories about it.

Jack Munroe had fulfilled his promise to provide everyone with a suit, but the tailor he chose to make them must have been a novice. None of our suits quite fitted. Mine was a little tight across the shoulders. Others wore jackets that were a shade too long or too short in the tail. The bottom of Ned Kelly's trousers bunched around the laces of his shoes. When he hitched the trousers up, the belt sat around his navel, accentuating the barrel shape of his belly.

Since we were identically dressed, I couldn't tell who was or wasn't prosperous. The conclusions I made were drawn from the wives and girlfriends, most of whom chose to wear a red dress. Clustered together, they looked like a field of poppies.

Time had done its work on us.

John Slater's jacket flapped around the kind of paunch that only beer and junk food could have given him. He was dragging his stomach around like a heavy sack.

Sean Ramsey was practically bald, the fine strands of his hair combed back to reveal a high forehead.

Alec Taylor's hair, shaved close to his scalp, stood up in firm bristles. The knuckles of his right hand were slightly enlarged, a telltale sign of early arthritis.

Jimmy Bradley's swollen cheeks were blotchy, the colour of weak port.

Moritz Bleibtrau wore a pair of gold-framed aviator glasses, the magnification of which gave him bug-like eyes.

Arend van het Hoff had shed an appreciable amount of weight and moved cumbersomely, the consequence of three operations on his right knee.

On account of his sugar consumption, Sweets Wharton had dental implants of blinding whiteness. His mouth had shrunk around them.

Only Stuart Kelly and Nat Carson hadn't changed. Skelly was still slim, his face a glossy pink. Carson had recently broken his nose, but he'd never had good looks to lose in the first place.

Some players don't want anything to do with the game once their careers end. Apart from me, just two of the Cup team were still receiving a pay packet from football. You'd have easily picked us out in a line-up because our skin was rougher on account of the hours we spent outdoors and in all weather.

Van het Hoff was managing a lower-league team in Belgium. 'It's only part-time pressure,' he explained. He was content to saunter through his days. The things he did in them added up to nothing substantial, but he didn't mind because he never looked much beyond the end of any week. That irked me a little; I knew where his talent could have taken him.

Wharton was the obverse of van het Hoff. He had always aimed high, but the scale of his ambition had carried him no further than coaching lowly youth teams, chiefly in Leagues One and Two. The latest of them was Rotherham's. 'I was going to get you pissed tonight and ask for a job here next season,' he said. 'Then I read the papers this morning.'

All the 'boys' tried to say something consoling to me – even if it was buried a little beneath black humour or an insult. They approached me like mourners offering comfort to the bereaved at a wake.

Robbie Clayton arrived. He put his hand on my shoulder and asked, as though worried about my state of mind: 'You still OK?' He'd spent the afternoon walking around the city for a second time. 'I signed an autograph,' he said. 'Someone actually recognised me. Beth won't believe that.'

We drank warm, cheap wine, which was plentiful but disgusting. The alcohol made everyone talk at once, the commotion non-stop. Only Robbie, his back to the door, waited for company rather than seeking it out, and he listened more than he spoke. He kept looking at me, as if needing reassurance about his bearings. He moved from the space he'd claimed as his own only to avoid Davie Collins, who came into the room fashionably late and then bellowed: 'Your captain is here.'

With his arms outstretched, Collins expected us all to rush towards him. We didn't. He was dressed slightly differently, in a red waistcoat and matching red silk scarf. A red rose was pinned to the lapel of his jacket. 'Where's Frank?' he asked, pulling back his shirt cuff to make an ostentatious show of checking the time. A Rolex glinted on his wrist.

'We're waiting for Frank,' said Wharton. 'Have a drink, shut the fuck up and don't pretend you care about the rest of us.'

I was standing directly in Collins' line of sight. He came over and shook hands. It was not a gesture of friendship. He tried to crush my fingers. He pushed his face into mine, his breath stinking of red wine. 'You've done well for yourself. Shame you won't be here next season. That's why I got out of football. No security. You'll be buggering off back to Sweden, I suppose.'

I didn't ask about his life because I knew he'd tell me about it soon enough. He did so while winking at me.

'As for me . . . never better. Top of the pile, as ever. Do my bit too. Help out some of the lads here with the odd job or some cash in hand. We're all mates, aren't we? Always will be. Whether we like it or not.'

Collins as a philanthropist? I couldn't imagine it. Collins as a 'mate'? I couldn't imagine that either. If he gave money away, it was for the purpose of forcing someone to be grateful to him. That was the thing about Collins: he dug his nails into people. In football, he was so overbearing that even the recipients of some of his good advice had found it unpalatable. He'd since gone into what he called 'reclamation and restoration'; everyone else called it scrap metal. He'd become very wealthy. He opened his wallet to display pictures of the houses he owned, the vintage cars he collected.

A woman appeared at his shoulder. She looked younger than Freyja. 'This is Suzanne. Mrs Collins the Third,' he said. She was a shock of piled-up blonde hair, in a low-cut crimson dress and a pair of high heels as tall as library steps. She wore a diamond necklace and a matching bracelet the size of a manacle. I was relieved that she didn't attempt to hug me. Collins looped an arm around her slender waist, as though roping her to him.

'That young lad you've got up front, Jason Deane. Not bad,' said Collins. 'Quick enough. Decent on the turn. Finishes well. I hope you've told him that he isn't as good as I was.'

I replied, unsmilingly: 'In 18 months, he'll be better than you ever were. You were a decent player, but you didn't have what he's got, which is the kind of talent that gets you noticed wherever you go. He'll get more goals, earn more money and win more medals than all of us here put together.'

Collins twisted his mouth in distaste. He was about say something pithy in his own defence when Frank Mallory made his entrance. Martha walked on one side of him, Uncle Charlie Bembridge on the other. Those who hadn't seen Frank since his illness took a while to realise it was him. He startled them like a ghost. He held his stick with bony hands. His flesh was the colour of old ivory. The effort of placing one foot in front of the other made his eyes bulge.

Sean Ramsey shouted at him. 'Hey, Frank. We did win the Cup, didn't we? I don't want to watch the replay of the game tonight and find out that Spurs equalised.'

Frank pointed at me with his stick. 'I can see the goal-scorer from here.'

'What's your team talk tonight, Frank?' asked Stuart Kelly.

'The simplest one I've ever given. Drink as much of Jack

Munroe's booze as your system can take. Don't waste it now. The chance won't come again.'

If Frank hadn't ordered us onto the bus, we'd have stayed there for the whole night and forgotten about Willoughby Hall. I helped Martha lift him into the front seat. 'The doctor says I'm going to get a little worse before I get a little better. It's the medication,' he said.

We serenaded him with Bowie's 'Modern Love'.

'Not that fucking thing again,' he said.

7

EACH OF WILLOUGHBY HALL'S turrets flew a club flag and every window was festooned with bright red lights. This made it look as though the building was ablaze. Silk bunting had been trailed between the lime trees. The trees stood, like a guard of honour, from the front gates to the 17 stone steps that lead to the entrance. Red and white scarves also decorated the bell-metal barrels of a dozen hulking cannons, positioned behind a long parapet.

Some of the crowd that had seen us off from the club car park had travelled on to the hall. I reckon about 3,000 people were there. 'It's like a film premiere,' said Moritz Bleibtrau, taking off his glasses and wiping them with a cloth. Bleibtrau had never been inside the hall before. He looked in silent fascination at the ceiling. A frieze of saints lined the plaster dome.

The hall had become a museum of natural history. Taxidermy had preserved the big game on show, as well as birds, foxes, ferrets and the kind of fish that had eyes like saucers. A polar bear on its hind legs, claws raised in attack, was encased in glass. 'This lad would be useful at corners,' said Bleibtrau.

The Great Hall was 100 feet long and 50 feet wide. Balloons hung from its hammerbeam roof. Blown-up photographs of the FA Cup final, identical to those in Frank Mallory's hallway, had been fixed to the walls. TV screens showed the edited highlights of the game on a loop. I glanced across at one of them. The team was about to walk out of the Wembley tunnel. Frank was smoothing down his tie and fastening the middle button of his jacket. He glanced behind him, checking we were all there. Davie Collins was bouncing a ball against the wall, which seemed to irritate Frank. Collins stopped, spun the ball on his right index finger instead and casually chewed gum. He spat it out as soon as the signal came to start walking.

I was third from the back, jogging on the spot. A guest, whom I didn't know, asked me: 'Does it seem long ago?'

'Even longer than you can imagine,' I said.

It had taken me a quarter of an hour to reach the Great Hall.

I couldn't break away from those who had wanted to relive the occasion.

Jeff Astle had claimed the winner for West Bromwich Albion in the 1968 Cup final. His goal zipped into the top corner, the shot struck from almost the same spot on the pitch as mine. Six months after our final, I ran into him at a black-tie dinner in Birmingham.

'The official attendance on the day we won the Cup was 100,000,' he'd said to me. 'But I've met 150,000 people who've insisted: "I was directly behind your shot when it hit the net." You're going to meet a lot fans who'll say the same thing to you'.

I didn't believe him, but Astle was right.

I was always dealing with people who'd seen my goal better than I had. I came to regard each conversation as a tax that had to be paid on my good fortune. Astle had given me a set of instructions on how to handle things: 'Smile, agree with them and say thank you. Even if they're wrong. Even if you want to run away. Take a second or so. Be nice.'

So I offered banalities, flattery and pallid lies:

'I bet you do remember the goal as well as me . . . that's marvellous to hear . . . You had the perfect view then? . . . It's odd, but I've met a few people who've said the same thing . . . No, I don't watch the goal back very often . . . Yes, I'd love to relive that day again.'

There was always one person who would ask: 'Did you mishit the shot?' I'd play along:

'Can't be sure. I think the ball came off the top of my boot. No idea how it travelled so fast through the air.'

Myths become indisputable when everyone stops challenging them. There were people who thought I *had* mishit the shot and would never be convinced otherwise.

I was eager to get into the Great Hall as soon as possible and without being noticed. The organisers, wanting the other guests to see us, had arranged the team on one long table at the far end of the room. The stage was off to our left. I was keen to find out who would be sitting where. I knew Frank Mallory would occupy the centre of the table, close enough to touch the FA Cup and the match ball, which were prominently displayed together. I was immediately to Frank's right. Beside me was Davie Collins. Robbie Clayton had been shoved at the opposite end.

I wasn't prepared to accept that.

With a discreet movement, as deft as a magician's sleight of hand, I palmed Collins' place card and slipped it into my pocket. Next, I walked over to Robbie's chair and swopped the cards.

I'd been observing Collins ever since our arrival. He was determined to strike the dominant note of the night, behaving as though the event belonged solely to him. He was pouring tall tales of his successes into the nearest ear. Any ear would do, it seemed. Mrs Collins was fuelling him with champagne.

He never found out what I'd done. When the team was clapped in, ready for dinner to be served, I watched Collins take the seat

I'd given him. He stared forlornly, along the row of faces, at Frank, Robbie and me. I raised my glass towards him and smiled, very broadly.

I was halfway through the main course when I heard an enormous roar. I looked round as the diners rose to their feet. Applause began. Someone yelled: 'Get in.' Someone else said: 'What a beauty!' On every TV screen I was running towards the corner flag and then flopping onto the pitch in a starfish shape. The sound was turned up, allowing everyone to hear the last line of Brian Moore's commentary: 'and what have Tottenham got left now?'

'Bugger all,' said Jimmy Bradley. 'They're done for. We've just won the Cup'.

A minute or two later, after our celebrations on the pitch were over, the goal was replayed in slow motion and from three different angles. 'You won't believe this,' said Robbie, leaning across to make himself heard, 'but I've never seen the game all the way through. I was on the operating table when it was played, and I couldn't bring myself to watch the highlights that night, or the following afternoon either. I didn't switch the TV on in case I caught even a few seconds of it.'

I said to Robbie: 'Don't go home tomorrow. Stay for another few days. Come to Sunday's game. I'll take you into the dressing room.'

'That's thoughtful,' said Robbie. 'I'm not sure I can, but I'll let you know. I'll talk it over with Beth.'

Shortly before the speeches began, I checked my watch and contemplated the long hours that still remained. The present team were split between the two tables directly in front of us. I watched Jason Deane. He'd spoken to Collins but had shunned Frank. He even sat with his back to the top table to avoid making eye contact with him.

What must Deane have thought of us? We were all old enough to be his father. Some of us were old enough to be his grandfather. At the time, he surely felt that his youth would always protect him from getting to be as old as we were. Someone of Deane's age is either baffled by the generations before him or he idealises them. It was clear to me that Deane was still making up his mind. I'm not sure he knew why the club was making a fuss about a competition that was already losing its lustre beside the bigger prizes.

8

IT WAS 9.30 P.M. BEFORE Brian Moore climbed onto the stage and began the formal part of the evening.

Each of us was presented with a commemorative gold coin made by the company that had designed and cast the FA Cup shortly before the Great War. The coin, pressed into a red leather box, was stamped with an etching of the Cup and the date and venue of the banquet.

The interviews that followed dragged on. Uncle Charlie Bembridge bored everyone while babbling on, at vast length, about his conversations with the Duke of Kent, who had presented the Cup that day. Flushed with his own importance, Davie Collins, already glassy-eyed, paid tribute to himself. It was a lot of wind and piss. 'I was even responsible for the assist for the winning goal,' he insisted.

'Bollocks,' said Sweets Wharton.

Frank Mallory spoke dispassionately about his health. You'd have thought he was shaking off a mild cold. When Moore asked him: 'Did Thom Callaghan's goal surprise you?' Frank replied: 'Surprise me? It fucking astonished me. He didn't even score in training.'

Like the headline performer at a variety show, I was held back until the end. When my turn finally came, I could offer nothing original or enlightening about either the match or my goal because every anecdote and titbit had been repeated so often. There was nothing to add to the historical record unless I made it up on the spot. I was aware anyway that I wasn't there only to discuss the final, but also the here and now. The audience hankered after revelations far more than reminiscences. I made them wait. Annoyed that Robbie Clayton was the only player who hadn't been asked to speak, I paid him a tribute I hadn't prepared. It ended with the line: 'Without his advice early on in my career, I wouldn't have got close to a Cup final.' Moore said it was gracious of me to acknowledge my 'friend' in that way. It was a kindly remark, but it made me feel ashamed because I knew I ought to have asked for Robbie's forgiveness too.

Then, as I knew he would, Moore got to the point: 'This is a night of both celebration and commemoration, but what about Sunday? Can you tell everyone what you think of Jack Munroe's decision to sell the club? And where will you be next season?'

I took the deepest of breaths. The answer I gave perplexed everyone at first because no one knew where it was leading or what purpose it could possibly serve. I told them how, as a boy, I'd come to Willoughby Hall. How my father had bought a guidebook for me. How one story in the book stood out. 'It's about the wall that surrounds this hall,' I said. 'You probably don't know that it was originally six and a half feet high.'

On the day the wall was completed, the owner had walked his wife through the grounds. He saw a man, his head and shoulders clearly visible, peering at them from above the brickwork. Offended by the invasion of privacy, he ordered his builders to add another two feet to the height of the wall. 'The thing he didn't know was this,' I said: 'the man he'd seen was a giant, the chief attraction in a circus passing through the city.'

There was near silence in the room. I heard only the faint rattle of china and cutlery, a few coughs, the scrape of a chair against the wooden floor. Moore gave me an anxious look, afraid I'd drunk too much and was about to make an exhibition of myself. 'And?' his eyes seemed to be saying.

I turned away from Moore and addressed the audience directly. 'I don't know whether that story is true, but I've always wanted to believe it. It tells me not to reach a conclusion without possessing all the facts. I thought about the story again today, obviously because I was coming here tonight, but also because I see a parallel between the original owner of the Hall and Jack Munroe. The owner didn't have to rebuild his wall. He just didn't know it. He was too hasty, too ignorant, too gung-ho. Well, I have a message for Mr Munroe. He doesn't have to sell this club. He's being hasty and ignorant and gung-ho too.'

I wanted to say that I was constructing a team that would last. That I would manage it better than anyone else because the players were already mine, rather than Frank's, and because my blood ran through the club. That what I needed were three players – a goalkeeper, a central midfielder and a winger. But I couldn't go into those details – not when those I wanted to purge from the side were sitting in front of me and would all play on Sunday.

I could, however, tell Munroe what I thought about him. If I caused upset or offence, it didn't matter.

'Mr Munroe seems to have had enough of us – and enough of me. I think he's wrong. I don't understand his decision, but I have to confess that I don't understand Mr Munroe because I don't know him. For whatever reason, he hasn't given me that chance. The chance he has given me, I'm grateful for. I don't think I've let him down.

'But Sunday's match isn't about me. That sounds corny and very predictable, I know. I'm not saying it to dodge the question. The club matters. I don't. It was going for more than a hundred years before I played for it. It'll go on for a hundred years after I leave it.

'No, I'm not expecting to stay after this weekend. Really, I never did. I am expecting us to stay up, though. We'll get the point we need. Whoever comes in won't inherit a Championship team.

'I know everything finds its way back to Mr Munroe eventually. He'll hear what I've said to him tonight.

'I hope he listens.'

Somewhere, a switch was flicked. A glare of light from above illuminated the whole stage. Balloons began to drop from the ceiling. Music blared, drowning even the applause. People left their seats, wanting to shake my hand.

Something occurred to me only then.

Since Frank occupied the centre of that long table, and because every one of us sat either to his left or right, the scene resembled the Last Supper.

9

MY SHOES BEGAN TO pinch my feet. My neck sweated against my shirt collar. I wanted to loosen my tie or take it off altogether, but I'd have looked slovenly or half dressed. Not wanting to get tipsy, and because I was nervous about my interview with Brian Moore, I'd barely touched Jack Munroe's champagne. I'd drunk apple juice, which was pale enough to look like champagne during the toasts. Now I swallowed two glasses of wine almost straight away and asked for a third. I hoped it would take away the weariness I felt. Oddly, it didn't. Even in my tired state, I knew everyone else – apart from Frank Mallory and Robbie Clayton – was half cut or on the way there.

You'd have thought Prohibition was coming and we had to drink as much as we could before it arrived. Davie Collins had supped a great deal but didn't seem to be drunk. On the other hand, Sean Ramsey was wobbling like a novice stilt walker, the two Kellys gamely propping him up. Jimmy Bradley was slurring his words a little, while Sweets Wharton had reached the point at which another glass of anything and he'd keel over. Moritz Bleibtrau and Arend van het Hoff, both multilingual, were involved in a game I'd heard them play regularly. Bleibtrau was talking in faultless French, van het Hoff in faultless Spanish. They understood one other perfectly. Nat Carson was speaking to a diner who had only wanted his menu card signed. The diner didn't seem to understand him at all.

For the next three-quarters of an hour, the team drank on while the waiters cleared up the other tables. No one came to claim the FA Cup or the match ball. Anyone could have sneaked up and stolen them, and I doubt we'd have noticed. The Cup, brilliantly polished at the start of the night, was smeared by fingermarks. It had been picked up and put down again numerous times and sometimes paraded about. John Slater and Alec Taylor began to search the plinth to make certain the club's name had been correctly engraved on it. I examined the ball. The leather was still smooth. The maker's name was stamped prominently across one panel, the ink black and vivid. You'd have thought no one had ever kicked it.

I was holding the ball, spinning it in my hand like a globe, when Collins snatched it away.

'Give that fucker here,' he said. 'I know what we're going to do. We're going to have a kickabout. Slater, bring the trophy as well.'

Nothing that followed made any sense. With the ball in his possession, Collins marched off, and the rest of us followed him submissively, unsure where we were going or what would happen when we got there. He took us along a corridor that led us down many others. It was like being shoved into a maze without a map. Every turn, every cul-de-sac resembled the one before. Collins tried all the doors we passed. Some didn't open; others took us into empty rooms and even cupboards. In one room, a sash window gave us a glimpse of parkland, where we saw the silhouette of a herd of deer. Collins tried to lift the window, thinking we'd escape through it the way a burglar might. It refused to budge. Eventually, after twice twisting back on ourselves, we came to a fire door. Collins pulled down on the handle without caring whether or not it was alarmed. We spilt out onto the rear patio. I realised we were very close to the point from which we'd started; Collins had walked us in a circle. I looked up at the first floor. I saw Frank. He was about to take a puff on a cigarette. Jonjo Whelan and Brian Moore were standing next to him.

The back of Willoughby Hall was plainer than the front, but the stonework shone in blocks of harsh yellow. Spotlights, shining from squat boxes, were positioned in front of a low wall. Their glow fell across a strip of parkland about fifty feet wide.

'Here's our floodlit pitch,' said Collins. 'Just watch out for deer shit.' He kicked the ball high into the air and chased after it, wanting to reclaim the thing before anyone else. In the middle distance stood a bank of trees. Their tops were silvery, as though a coating of frost lay across them. The land beyond vanished into the darkness.

'What the fuck is that small streak of light?' asked Collins, looking into the sky. He pointed at the Hale–Bopp comet.

'It's a shooting star or an asteroid or something like that,' said Slater, placing the Cup carefully on the wall.

Satisfied with that answer, Collins shrugged in response. 'Who cares?' he said.

Wharton, who'd lit a Churchill cigar, blew out six blue smoke rings, each one wider than the one before. He laid the cigar, still burning, beside the Cup. Without being asked, we began to unknot our ties and peel off our jackets, shivering a little. The temperature had dropped, the cold prickling our skin.

'Let's see how much skill you've still got,' said Collins, holding the ball against his chest as though he owned it. He threw it to Bleibtrau. 'Who's going to put on a show?'

Taylor dug a heel into the over-long grass. He began to moan. 'It's hardly Wembley.'

'Don't let the ball touch the ground,' said Bleibtrau, who flicked it up and began a game of head tennis with van het Hoff. It was as fluent as the conversation between them had been. I should have made an excuse and sloped off, but I didn't, suppressing my resistance to Collins' will for the same reason I'd agreed to go to the banquet. I was anxious to prove that being a manager hadn't changed me and, most of all, I didn't want to strike a snooty pose or do anything that would suggest I thought of myself as superior to any of them. I let Collins boss us all about.

Every act, every word of his was intended to strengthen the authority he felt he had over us. He gathered up the jackets and made goalposts out of them. Each of us tried to outdo the others with keepy-ups, back-heels and tricks. We threw insults at those who failed. We said: 'Watch this' when the ball came to us. We pretended not to care when we made a mistake and let ourselves down. Sometimes we had to retrieve the ball out of the distant bushes. If we'd done all this in a public park, during daylight hours, we'd have looked ridiculous, out-of-shape men pretending to be lean young boys. More than half of us didn't jog or exercise or work out in a gym. Slater flagged quickly. So did Taylor. Ned Kelly dragged his genial bulk around in a semi-trot. When Ramsey misjudged a shot from van het Hoff and took the ball in the stomach – 'I didn't see it,' he complained – you heard the gurgling his gut made, all the alcohol sloshing around inside him. His face turned acid green. 'I'm going to throw up,' he said. He did – everywhere. Soaked in perspiration, he sat on the wall, his head bowed. He was sick twice more. I thought he was going to reach over and use the Cup as a slop bucket.

'We need a new goalkeeper,' said Collins. 'Who's up for it?'

No one volunteered.

I was five yards from Collins. He searched for Robbie Clayton, before addressing him with snarling hostility. 'It's your turn, Alice. Get between the sticks. You didn't play in the final anyway. I'm not even sure why you're here. You're just a player who fell down a rabbit hole and saw your career fucking disappear. We won the thing without you. With me as captain. Just be grateful that you got a medal for a battle you didn't fight in. Go in goal. It's the only place for you.'

I don't know whether I'm crediting him with a shrewdness he didn't possess, but it didn't seem to me as though Collins was making the most of an unexpected chance. This was a premeditated scheme, designed to humiliate Robbie. None of us had ever called him Alice before. Collins' mockery was calculated score-settling, designed to demean. He took a thrill of pleasure from it. He spat out his resentment of Robbie, which no doubt had begun on the day he'd come to us from Liverpool.

'I'll go in goal,' I said.

'You can't,' said Collins, now ready to hurl abuse at me too. 'We're going to recreate your winner at Wembley. It's the reason we're all here. It's why we've got the ball and the Cup. To relive old times. Don't you understand? You're brighter than this lot. That's what Frank always told me, but perhaps you aren't that fucking clever after all.'

Collins began to position us. He was like the director of a play, arranging his actors. 'Stand where you were when the corner was taken. Bradley, get out there and prepare to bang it over. I'll go on the penalty spot. Where's the ball? Who's got the ball?'

Ignored now, after refusing to respond to Collins' provocation, Robbie began to walk back into the hall, a light shining on his broad back.

'Fuck you,' I said to Collins. 'I'm not playing your game

any more than he is. You've no right to embarrass him like that. He did more for this club than you ever did. You're a disgrace. You've ruined the night.'

Collins turned away and spat on the ground. 'You know I don't like you, Callaghan? Never have, never will. You were – and still are – a teacher's pet who's too fucking up himself. The rest of us? We're shit on your shoe. Whenever I see it, even on TV, I always want to smash your face in. Fuck off and join your mate on the sidelines. Do something useful: get some more drinks in for us. We'll come in as soon as we've done this for old times' sake. Tell you what: I'll take your place. I'll score the goal for you. You were lucky anyway. You happened to be in the right spot. You didn't deserve any glory for that.'

Taylor nudged the ball towards Collins. I propelled myself at him. As Collins got the ball under control, ready to sweep it over to Slater, I leapt into a tackle, taking the ball away. My momentum took me through Collins, who fell in a clatter. I felt an extraordinary sense of triumph.

I got up before he did. A row of headlines danced in front of my eyes:

DISGRACE: KNEES-UP TURNS INTO PUNCH-UP

FIGHT AT THE 'CUP FINAL':

WEMBLEY HEROES BRAWL AFTER BANQUET

It was no way to prepare for Sunday. If I threw a punch or took one, my last, thin chance of staying on for next season would be gone. But I didn't care. Collins staggered to his feet and came at me. He slipped and fell over again. He complained that I'd 'fucked up' his left knee. I bent forward, ready to grab him by the scruff of his shirt. That's when I heard Jonjo Whelan's voice. He was standing on the patio, summoning me towards him. He was shouting something about Frank.

As I turned to go, Collins said: 'You're going to lose on Sunday. I'll enjoy that, you fucker.'

10

FRANK MALLORY HAD BEEN reminiscing about FA Cup final day. His admirers had gathered in a semi-circle in front of him. Someone had offered him a cigar. He'd taken his Dupont lighter out of his pocket. His eyes had begun to film over, and he'd dropped both the lighter and the cigar. He'd stuck out a hand, trying to steady himself against a small table on which a blue and white vase stood. His arms weren't strong enough to support his body and he'd tipped the table over. The vase had fallen onto the wooden floor, breaking into five clean pieces and dozens of smaller ones that no glue could fix. Frank had gasped for breath and then fainted. One of the waiters had run to get water, another to telephone for an ambulance. A third had found a doctor among the guests.

By the time I got to him, Frank had been unconscious for a couple of minutes, but he was finally coming around and trying to talk. Martha was cradling his head on her thighs. When a stretcher arrived, the doctor, a saturnine-looking man, drew Martha to the opposite side of the room so their conversation wouldn't be overheard. Martha was dabbing her eyes with a small handkerchief.

The doctor came back, telling me: 'Don't worry. I think he'll be fine. We'll let the hospital take care of him for a day or so. I can't be certain, but Mrs Mallory has told me about his recent medical history, which I'm sure you know, and also his symptoms. Fatigue, cramps, numbness. Difficulty with his breathing now and then. It's not a stroke, not even a minor one. I *think* it's as simple as potassium deficiency. The hospital will sort that out.'

The doctor looked at me. 'You know,' he said, 'I was right behind your shot at Wembley. Saw it sail in.'

At 1 a.m., I was sitting in the hospital corridor with Martha. We were drinking machine coffee and blinking against the harshness of the light. My jacket was still lying on parkland outside Willoughby Hall; my trousers were grass-stained. At 2 a.m., a doctor arrived to tell us that Frank was 'not in danger'. In the circumstances, he added, 'the patient is in robust shape'.

After Martha was told she could see Frank, she asked whether I would go with her. On a drip and attached to a heart monitor, Frank had been given a room of his own. The bed had been made around his body. His thin arms lay across the top sheet. I had a flashback of my father, pinned to his own mattress. Frank's skin was as pale as magnolia, making the small broken veins across his cheeks look redder. His face came alive briefly when he saw us. He tried to pull himself up, but couldn't do it and let his head drop lightly back onto two pillows. Martha sat beside him and held his hand. I found a plastic bucket seat and dragged it across the floor. Frank spoke only a few words – 'I've had better nights out,' he said – and blew a kiss to Martha, which she pretended to catch. He then closed his eyes and fell asleep. It seemed in that moment that Frank was attached to only three of life's corners and that his grip might be about to slide away from the fourth. We left the room on tiptoe.

I'd once believed Frank might become the first person never to die, that even cancer wouldn't kill him. Now I remembered something my father used to tell me: 'There are no great men. Only men.'

It was nearly 3 a.m. when I got back to the apartment. There was a parcel waiting for me outside the front door. Inside was a bottle of red wine, a gift from Alex Ferguson. The hand-written card read: 'One game to go. Stay focused. Forget the owner.'

I was exhausted. It was as though all the marrow had been

drained from my bones. But I was also wide awake. As soon as I closed my eyes everything swirled before me: the banquet, what I'd said in my interview with Brian Moore, stealing the Cup and the match ball, Davie Collins' attempt to shame Robbie Clayton, Frank's illness, Sunday's match. I slipped into bed and tried to force myself to sleep. It didn't work. I got up and went onto the roof terrace. There was now cloud where the comet ought to have been. I went back to bed. Still I couldn't sleep. I got up again, remembering to unplug the land-line and turn off my mobile, a perk few of us owned then.

That dispute with Collins would be back-page news. Even if no other player broke rank to talk about it, I knew Collins would give his version of events to someone sympathetic to his cause. He'd wait before doing it – probably until the weekend – so the story wouldn't shrink to a few paragraphs beside the news that Frank had been admitted to hospital. Looking for a fresh angle, the Sunday papers would pay generously for what Collins had to say.

I don't know when I fell asleep. I do know that I had an anxiety dream about the Cup final. It was played on parkland identical to Willoughby Hall's. The 'goals' were beech trees; Frank was sitting in one of them. The crowd was packed into makeshift stands. The pitch, full of deer, was so wide that I couldn't send a pass from one touchline to the next. When I should have scored, the ball got stuck in the grass. I couldn't get near to it.

Then I heard a bell, constantly being rung, and the

thump-thump of someone banging on a door. It was my door. The sun lay across me in a great slice of light. I'd forgotten to close the blinds. The bell rang again. I got up and looked at myself in the mirror, straightening my hair as best I could. I splashed some water onto my face and slipped my bare feet into a pair of trainers.

It was 10.30 a.m.

Jonjo Whelan was leaning against the frame of the door. 'You're not answering the phone. I've been trying to ring you for two hours.'

You always know when it's bad news, a clutch to the heart. Not only from the look on someone's face, but also because of the abysmal silence, only a second or so long, that prefaces what you're about to hear. Whoever is bringing the news, and however much they've prepared themselves to say what needs saying, they still hesitate in the hope that you might divine what that news is. They want you to save them from the ordeal of delivering it.

'It's Robbie Clayton,' said Jonjo.

I I

I'VE ALWAYS SPOKEN UP whenever someone trashes football's place in life's great scheme. I have a ready-made reply to naysayers who grumpily complain the game doesn't matter a jot and think – in a world of war and disease, famine and financial meltdown – that no one intelligent ought to get frivolously carried away by a winning goal.

I knew they were wrong.

In that sweetest of all seasons for me, I'd seen with my own startled eyes irrefutable evidence of the good that football can do, the transformation it wrought and the escape it provided from humdrum, ordinary days.

Winning the FA Cup remade my city. Before, the place had been dowdy and downcast. Afterwards, it had a noticeable pulse. The thump of life was there. You'd walk through the streets and see bright shocks of red and white everywhere. Scarves were worn like a badge of honour, declaring new-found pride. In those days, too, you couldn't go a hundred yards without hearing a newspaper-seller shouting about some story Frank Mallory had concocted to generate publicity: a raking swipe at another manager or the name of a player he planned to sign for huge money. In the beery warmth of the pubs, especially those around the Market Square, you'd find team pictures and individual portraits, plastic pennants, cotton banners and silk flags. They'd be tacked to Artex-covered walls, which were stained with nicotine, or hung in big wooden frames, displayed more prominently than a picture of the Queen. Well after last orders were called on a Saturday night, those who got chucked out would flail and stumble through the pub doors, meeting the cold night air with a terrace song or chant.

Aside from scoring the goal, my most distinctive memory of Cup final weekend was the homecoming, our open-top bus decked out like a holiday charabanc. It had taken three hours to travel the two and a half miles to the Council House. On the bridge the crowd had been at least 30 deep; I'd wondered how it hadn't buckled. Staring along the empty banks of the river, I'd seen the broken reflection of the ground in the water. At the Victorian railway station, the sandy-red stone had glowed in the sun as though lit from within. Fans had shinned up lamp posts, clinging to them with both arms like sailors embracing a ship's mast. Women had dangled out of windows, blowing air kisses and flinging flowers at us.

The swell of the crowd in the Market Square had knocked me into a daze. I hadn't known there were so many people in the city who cared. From the Council House balcony, gripping the rail next to one of the Doric columns, I'd stared down and across that fantastic scene. For a second or two I hadn't been able to find the breath to speak. The swaying fans had pressed against the metal barriers beneath me and also against the glass of the shopfronts lining two sides of the square.

We're supposed to accurately recall more from our adolescence and early adulthood than from any other period of our lives. I must be an exception to that rule. Years later, bringing that day back, I convinced myself that Robbie Clayton was there. I saw him everywhere. On the bus. On the balcony. In that room of gilt, where we sat on thick-legged chairs and admired the dark burgundy carpet and matching curtains. I was sure he'd drunk champagne out of the bottles passed between us. I was sure I'd offered a bottle to him; he was sitting on one chair and resting his plaster cast on another. I was sure I said to him: 'You're as much a part of this as the rest of us.' I'm sure he said: 'I know. Don't worry about me.'

It's a false memory, a slip into wishful thinking. My mind created it because I so much wanted it to be true. False memories begin when the original dulls or gets rubbed out, partially or completely, by others. Your emotions are responsible for filling in the gap, reconstructing an event so it fits with the way you want to remember things. It allows you to dismiss something you don't want to think about.

Robbie couldn't have been there. He didn't leave hospital until late that same afternoon. He didn't arrive back until everything was over – the streets empty, the revellers in pubs or at home again, the team splintered into its little cliques. There was no welcome party waiting on the doorstep for Robbie. Nothing but the cold wind of failure blew about him.

Any photograph of the team taken that day would have confirmed for me who was missing. Either I didn't look or I pretended not to notice because I felt guilty about enjoying myself without him. I soaked up a moment that was all about me. I didn't give a thought to the man who had made my career possible.

I doubt the rest of the team thought about Robbie either, but that's no excuse for what I did. We ought to have thought about him. We should have considered his feelings. Instead, we didn't talk about them or him. We conceived the event as a tragedy, which made it a taboo subject to be avoided. Robbie had discovered he wasn't indispensable. We thanked our lucky stars that we had yet to discover that truth about ourselves. We muttered quietly: 'There but for the grace of God,' and we moved on. Robbie's misery would only have got in the way of our celebrations, marring them. And thinking about him would have made no difference and changed nothing.

So we let him slide away, that day and afterwards.

For that reason, Robbie knew more acutely than I ever did how much football matters. You'd have learnt from him about how the game makes you feel – player and fan alike. The purpose. The pride. The honour. The sense of belonging. The fact you're part of something so much bigger than yourself. On those subjects, he would have been the prize authority. The game, which gave Robbie so much for so long, took something from him in the end. That's why he could have judged it coldly, the sentimentality stripped completely away. His argument, and the passion he generated to express it, would have meant more than anyone else's, especially my own, because it stemmed from loss rather than achievement.

But none of us had bothered to ask him.

12

THE POLICE ASKED ME whether I'd identify the body.

The man I saw didn't look like Robbie Clayton. He could have been anybody. I'd expected to find him as though his face was composed in sleep. But he was bloated and his skin was marbled and discoloured. There were cuts and abrasions on his hands and on his right foot, which had shed its shoe.

They said he'd been in the water for four to five hours before the boat had been sent to drag him out. They also said that he must have walked from Willoughby Hall to the river and thrown himself in from the centre of the bridge. I asked whether he'd been facing the stadium when he did it, but they couldn't be certain. A fisherman, awake before the fish, had found him snagged against another bridge further down the river, not far from the training ground.

When I saw Jonjo Whelan at my door, I'd immediately thought of Frank Mallory. I assumed he had died. I'd asked Jonjo to repeat what he'd said because I couldn't take it in. After he did, it was as though he'd slammed his fist into my chest. He came inside, and we sat on the sofa in dumbfounded silence – I don't know for how long – before either of us could speak Robbie's name again. I tried to remember the very last thing Robbie had said to me; whether, indeed, he'd spoken at all after turning his back on Davie Collins and walking away. I couldn't think of anything. No last words for the ages.

The police handed me a plastic bag containing his belongings: a hotel key, a wallet with £55 inside it, a pen and the commemorative coin he'd been given at the banquet. They'd already been to his hotel. There was no note, but they'd found Robbie's brown holdall, which I'd seem him carrying the day before. Inside, buried beneath yesterday's newspapers, was his Footballer of the Year statuette and the replica Cup winner's medal the club had given him. I have no idea why he'd brought them. Nor do I know who Robbie intended to inherit them afterwards. The police gave them to me.

The truth came out quickly. About the pub, repossessed three months before. About Beth, who had left six months before that;

no one knew where she'd gone or how to contact her; someone thought she might be in Spain. About Robbie, living in a bedsit with one good suit and two pairs of shoes. I imagined a small room with cheap furniture, the white rings of cups or mugs burnt into the wood, and a grimy net curtain at the window. I also imagined the empty days he spent in it. His possessions were crammed into two suitcases.

After I left the hospital morgue, I went directly to the ground. The news of Robbie's death was still quite fresh, but already fans had constructed a shrine to him. Scarves were tied to the lattice-work of the bridge. Someone had found a colour photo of him, taken from an old magazine, and pasted it onto cardboard. This had been fixed firmly to the rail of the bridge too. There were flowers, wrapped in crinkly cellophane, scattered on the pavement and also across the embankment steps below. Candles had been brought and lit, already burnt down to the wick or blown out in the breeze that ruffled the water below.

The world carried on normally. The traffic over the bridge, throwing out exhaust fumes. The chug of pleasure boats down the river. The white-collar workers sitting on the grass with their packed lunches. The fishermen. The dog walkers. The joggers who never smiled.

I went into my office, taking Robbie's brown holdall with me. I laid it beside the chair which he'd occupied 24 hours before. I sat down in it, aware of the indentation his back had made against the cushion. I ran my hands across the soft arms, gripping the edges the way his hands had done.

There was so much I didn't know and would never find out.

Every fresh start had led to a dead end for Robbie, who'd found no way to make another new beginning. But he didn't let on, and so none of us knew how difficult things had become for him or how hard he'd tried to change them. I only realised how well he'd worn his disguise after death removed it. Robbie hadn't seemed like a muddled heap of pain and perplexity. I'd seen no trace of crisis in him. As I sat there, silent and alone, I remembered his blustery confidence and also his lies, which I believed were told with good intent; he hadn't wanted to burden anyone.

I knew the story about replaying the Cup final on the parkland of Willoughby Hall – and the spat between Davie Collins and me – would not appear in that weekend's newspapers. Not now. Collins would stay silent because he was sharp enough to know the repercussions of speaking out. He'd have been forced to explain things. If his baiting of Robbie appeared in cold type, he would be blamed for tipping him over the edge. He'd be a pariah.

Something Collins had said, shortly before we got on the bus to go to the banquet, came back to me. He was looking around the directors' room, his gaze alighting on each face but lingering on Robbie's. 'Some of the lads have let themselves go. You know what's caused that? Disappointment. They convinced themselves that one match, a Cup final, would make their fortune and be enough to sustain them for years and years. They've measured their lives against a single success. Their expectations for it were too high.'

In that grand pronouncement, the old polarity still remained between Collins and Robbie and also Collins and me. We'd never be reconciled. We'd never find common ground. He didn't understand either of us.

I wanted Collins to suffer for it. I wanted him stoned and shamed. I wanted him to pay so punitively that he would feel something of what Robbie must have felt in those last days, those last hours. But I also knew it would serve no purpose, bring no consolation and ameliorate none of the shock, confusion, guilt or grief for me.

Collins may or may not have been to blame. He may or may not have been the last straw. We'll never know. That's the thing about suicide. You ask yourself questions that are – then and forever – unanswerable. The experts will tell you that suicide is complicated. That mostly there isn't one cause, but two or three, or even more. You can't say definitively which one in the end carried more weight than the others.

Robbie was a man of quiet feelings. He was also careful about sharing them. I didn't know whether he was lonely. I didn't know whether he judged his life purely according to what was absent from it. I didn't know whether the new difficulties he faced finally became too much for him – or whether everything could be traced back to Cup final morning, when high hopes turned into hard luck. How slim the margin is between realising an ambition and being denied it.

Robbie had been one thing, which was famous, and then become another, which was an ex-footballer about whom fans said: 'Whatever happened to . . .' or 'Didn't you used to be . . .'

I asked myself whether, if I'd known how much Robbie was hurting, I could have made a difference and saved him.

I didn't know that either.

In fact, all I knew for certain was this: Robbie had been one of the people who had changed me as a person, and it would take the rest of my life to get over the fact that he was gone.

That night, locking myself in the apartment, I spent three hours on the phone to Freyja. She'd never met Robbie. She knew him only from the stories and the anecdotes I'd told her.

'I don't know what else you could have done,' she said. 'You were pleased to see him. You made sure that you sat next to him at the banquet. You wanted him there on Sunday. You stuck up for him because you cared about him. You very nearly punched someone to prove it. You can't blame yourself and you shouldn't.'

'But I do,' I said. 'I do.'

Frank Mallory had a saying: 'If you're loyal, you're loyal. There's no halfway house where loyalty is concerned.' This, from the man I'd watched turn his head away from Robbie on Cup final morning, as though he was a passing stranger begging for money. How coldly he had done that. And how uncaringly he discarded Robbie afterwards. He was no use to Frank and so had ceased to matter to him.

I hated Frank for that. He'd left behind a wounded man. I hated myself still more for being exactly like him. My betrayal with Beth was unforgiveable, but at least it was fleeting and never repeated. My betrayal in the months and then the years that followed was far more damning because I was conscious of it – aware of every visit I didn't make, every invitation I didn't extend to him. I didn't write. I didn't phone. I made excuses for not doing so without ever believing in them. I told myself that I was focusing on my career, coping with my father's illness and then my own depression.

None of it withstood scrutiny. I ran away from Robbie, rather than towards him, out of shame. I'd been a bastard, the lousiest friend. To admit it properly would have meant confronting the most uncomfortable truth. I had more in common with Frank than I wanted to acknowledge.

The past is something you're supposed to grow out of. Some of us never can because we can't get over the mistakes we made.

EPILOGUE
A BALL AS WHITE AS THE MOON

As MORE TIME PILES up behind you, it becomes harder to bring back a moment exactly as it was. The first problem is that you've changed. You've lost touch with the many people you used to be. The things you felt and wanted back then are no longer the same, and your memory is skewered by the knowledge of what came next and also the consequences of it.

But, though 20-odd years have passed since Robbie Clayton died, I remember every detail about that season's last match against Middlesbrough.

I remember that I experienced no nerves whatsoever. I remember looking at my watch at 6 a.m. and calculating that everything, for better or worse, would be over by 6 p.m. I remember most of all the thoughts that ran through my mind. I decided it was probably for the best that I was leaving the club, hopefully with a minor success to my credit. Someone new would take over unencumbered by either my past or Frank Mallory's.

I would stay in the city for a few days afterwards. I would speak from some cold church pulpit at Robbie's funeral, picking my way as delicately as I could through the tragedy of his death. I would go back to Sweden and to Freyja, free of my home city.

We would take a boat from Stockholm and rent one of those lovely rust-coloured cottages again. We would hide there for a while.

I got to the ground absurdly early. TV crews were still unwinding cables. The police were putting out no-parking bollards. The programme sellers had still to arrive. The souvenir stalls had yet to be set up. There was only a trickle of fans on the bridge, most of them inspecting the cards attached to the flowers for Robbie. I drove past them, no longer able to look at the sadness of that scene.

For no other reason than because I could, and also because everything has a last time, I went to inspect the pitch. It was a warm, drowsy morning, as though mid-summer was almost upon us. Only a few rags of cloud troubled the sun. The day would get hotter. I had asked for the grass to be left a millimetre or two longer than usual. I had also asked for it not to be watered. I wanted the pitch to be hard and dry. I walked from box to box, testing the firmness of the soil with the heel of my shoe. When I came to the halfway line, I looked about the empty ground. For a second or two — no more — I saw the child I had once been. He was running onto the pitch, throwing that orange ball ahead of him and kicking it down the touchline. When Freyja had the baby, the first thing I'd buy for it would be an orange football.

Every big match emits energy, a crackle like an electrical charge. I knew it was there. I also knew everyone else was feeling it; I just couldn't feel it myself.

I'd idled through training the previous morning, my heart and my head never in it. Jason Deane was sorry I had lost my friend. He added how grateful he was to have met Robbie. Aaron Buchan said he knew how I must be feeling, which he didn't, but the gesture was sincerely heartfelt. Stefan Fournier was practical. He swore that he'd make the match as 'easy as possible' for me. 'We'll score quickly and take control,' he promised.

I had only one decision to make. I thought briefly about dropping Curtis Taylor. I told Jonjo Whelan: 'He's a liability and could cost us a point the way he cost us two at Liverpool.' Then, arguing against myself, I said: 'It's still more of a risk to throw in another goalkeeper now.'

All we needed was a point. But if both Derby and Sunderland lost, we could afford to lose as well. Derby were at Leeds. Sunderland were at home to Manchester City. No one expected either of them to win. No one expected Middlesbrough to beat us.

I didn't know how Middlesbrough had managed to get themselves relegated. Man for man, we were unequal to them in almost every department. We didn't have an experienced striker with a left foot to rival Ravanelli's. He was the 'White Feather', his hair steel-grey and his handsome face hide-brown from the sun. His trademark celebration – yanking the front of his shirt above his head – had become fashionable because he'd scored enough goals to make it so, even in a struggling team. I hoped he didn't fancy the game. I hoped he was thinking of next week and the

FA Cup final. Nor, apart from Fournier, did we possess anyone as inventive as Middlesbrough's two Brazilians: Juninho, the 'Little Fellow', and Emerson, who swept up behind or beside him. Middlesbrough had lost the League Cup final against Leicester City after a replay at Hillsborough. To lose two finals in one season would devastate them, so I wasn't sure whether they'd soft-pedal against us, saving themselves for next Saturday, or attack us ferociously with a nothing-to-lose insouciance.

In my office, piled on the desk, were the day's newspapers. For the first time in more than two decades, I'd barely given a thought to Frank Mallory. But, safely out of hospital, there he was on the back pages: he'd given an 'exclusive' interview to almost everyone about his relationship with Robbie. Frank had slipped effortlessly into his old groove of self-aggrandisement. The articles, billed as a tribute to Robbie, were actually all about Frank and his vanity, a determination to write history for his own benefit.

In one of those pieces, Frank was photographed in a wheel-chair. He held a photograph I had seen hanging in his hallway. He and Robbie were sitting together at the Football Writers' Association dinner, shortly before Robbie went on stage to receive his award.

Frank came out with more or less the same spiel he'd given me at his dining table. I could hear each sentence. He repeated all the claims that I knew were bullshit. Frank was adamant that he'd supported Robbie, often secretly, for the past 15 years. With a twist of spite, he added that he'd done this 'because others had ignored him'. Almost everything said was a lie, including the punctuation. He had stubbed out his Cup final team like a burnt-down cigarette.

He dwelt indecently on the story of the woman he'd once talked out of suicide on the bridge. He insisted Robbie had jumped from the same, a fact he couldn't have known for sure because no one did – not even the police. If he'd been there, said Frank, he could have talked Robbie down too. 'Only I could have done that,' he boasted.

I searched for the merest hint that he was aware of Davie Collins' attempt to humiliate Robbie, and also my attempt to step in and stop him. He evidently didn't know about that. I guessed the other players were ashamed of letting things go so far and then of not chasing after Robbie. No one had wanted to tell Frank about it. Not even Jonjo, who had only heard about the fracas second-hand from me.

There would be a minute's silence before the Middlesbrough match. The teams would wear black armbands. Frank said he intended to wear one too. He also planned to go onto the pitch – 'wheeling myself there if necessary' – to pay his respects alongside us to 'a truly great player and a greater man'.

Thinking again of Frank's cruelty towards Robbie, I felt an intense, righteous anger.

2

AS CONFLICTED AS MY emotions were about Frank Mallory, I nevertheless borrowed from him. He'd said all the right things before our FA Cup final. He'd used plain language. He hadn't dissolved into cliché. I've never liked the clichés of football. The way we say that goals are 'plundered', that a ball 'rasps' against the net, that defenders are 'no-nonsense'. In real life, we don't talk that way because we'd sound ridiculous. At Wembley, Frank had pared down every sentence and made them pithy. There were no epic flourishes, no soaring rhetoric.

I wanted everything to be that simple. The black suit I wore. The words I spoke. In the silence of our dressing room, just a quarter of an hour before we went out, I talked very slowly and for less than a minute. I knew I didn't have to rally us with clever words; I need only give a calm account of the facts.

We had the sympathy of the neutrals, who wanted us to 'win for Robbie' – even though some of them were unsure of who he was or what he had achieved.

I said: 'Here we are. At journey's end. Run as hard towards it as you've run for the past months. That's all I want from you.

Look after yourself and look after your friends out there. Don't be scared. Play as well as I know you can.'

I leant against the back wall, watching the players file into the tunnel and hearing them encourage one another. Jonjo Whelan and I waited until the tunnel was clear before we walked out of the dressing room. I felt the blasting, oven heat of the afternoon. The crowd greeted us with a solid din of white noise. Jonjo had to shout to say something he'd been waiting to tell me. 'You need to look at the directors' box,' he said, pointing towards it. At the end of the third row, on her feet and clapping, was Freyja. She was wearing a red dress and a pair of oversized sunglasses. Her hair was scraped back. 'She got here an hour ago,' explained Jonjo, still shouting. 'She took a train, a boat, another train and a taxi. She didn't want to tell you she was coming in case she didn't make it. You won't believe who organised everything for her. Jack Munroe. Perhaps he doesn't dislike you after all. Perhaps he's changed his mind about selling up.'

Frank came onto the pitch. He didn't use a wheelchair. He didn't even carry a stick. He was flat-footed and shuffled a little, however. It was as though he had lost his toes. He went to shake hands with some of the players and then stood next to me, holding the framed photograph of Robbie that I'd seen in the newspaper. His expression was completely blank, stripped of all emotion. What he was thinking was unknowable.

Just before the minute's silence began, he took a huge step to his right, as if wanting to distance himself from all of us. *It's all about him again*, I thought.

I envied Frank his ability to fake sincerity. It was a masterclass of acting. I also loathed him for it. When the minute's silence was over, he walked off, holding the photograph above his head, and didn't look back. He sat in the directors' box, a row behind Freyja. I fixed my gaze on him, waiting for a response. None came. He seemed entirely indifferent to both our survival and mine.

3

HOW UNBELIEVABLY WELL WE started.

If you hadn't seen the table, you wouldn't have known how much was at stake or appreciated the pressure we carried onto that field. In those first 10 minutes, Middlesbrough didn't know where to go or how to hide from us.

Three-quarters of the pitch was in bright sunlight, and we ripped across it. It was as though, before sending us out, I'd pressed some switch that had sprung the whole smooth mechanism of the team into gear.

I'd been distracted, out of it for three days as this immense game rolled towards me. If the team had noticed that, it hadn't bothered them. We were at the point of burying Middlesbrough and throwing the shovel on top of them. 'If we don't score now,' I said to Jonjo Whelan, 'we'll never score.'

In the 21st minute, Jason Deane was boxed in near the corner flag by two covering defenders. There seemed to be nowhere for him to go. He got his boot under the ball and lifted it into the air. Somehow – I still can't explain this – he took two sublime steps through a gap so narrow that most of us wouldn't have squeezed into it sideways. The defenders, unable to comprehend the suddenness of this, waited half a second too long before turning and giving chase. Deane retrieved the ball, sped away and rode an ugly tackle that, if he'd gone down, would have brought us a penalty. He finished the chance, which he'd created on his own. A low shot flashed into the far bottom corner.

His strike blew the roof off the ground. Deane had again shown that goal-scoring came to him intuitively. He stepped into the box as naturally as a man steps into his office.

I started screaming: 'Slow down. Take your time. Hold the ball.'

I was worried that we'd exhaust ourselves, wilt and then burn up under the sun. We did slow down; not, though, to our advantage. Everything was coming so easily that we began to get over-fancy, adorning every move with three or four touches too many. Middlesbrough were there to be killed off, but we wanted to do it in a way that was too elegant and too pretty.

I had set up a relay system of messages to tell me when anything happened at Elland Road or Roker Park. No system, though, was better than the crowd's reaction. If Derby or Sunderland scored or went behind, the moans or the cheering from our own fans would let us know. I heard nothing. Derby and Sunderland hadn't inflicted a blow. The only team that could hurt us was ourselves.

After half an hour, we nearly did that. Blackmore pushed a ball up to Ravanelli, who turned midway in our half and exploited our timid decision to stand aside, like a gentleman letting a lady go through a door ahead of him. The further forward Ravanelli went, the further we retreated. He ate up the space we conceded and was able to shoot – with that left foot – from 20 yards. Like the defence in front of him, Curtis Taylor didn't move. It was as though his feet were stuck in a tub of concrete. The shot hit the top of our right-hand post with such force that I thought the whole frame of the goal would collapse.

A minute later, Sunderland scored. Then Derby fell behind, leaking two goals in quick succession.

We ploughed on, a little more cautiously now.

Half-time was only a minute or so away when we caught Middlesbrough on the break. Deane held himself back, timing his run so well that the defenders were convinced he must be offside; they looked for the flag that would save them. An image rose in my mind: clean through, given a one-on-one chance that he seldom missed, I saw Deane chip the ball in. The game was ours. We'd saunter through the second half, gliding home.

The crowd, willing him on, prepared to celebrate. Deane was in full stride, approaching the 'D' at speed. But he never got there. He wanted to go faster than his hamstring would let him. He pulled up with a shudder, half a yard short of the box, as though a sniper had shot him in the back of his right thigh. He hopped a few steps before going down, the ball dribbling away.

Deane had shaken hands with Frank before the start of the game, but he'd refused to look at him while doing so. When the moment arrived, he'd turned his head away, making the snub very obvious. The expression on his face had reminded me of someone biting down on a bad tooth. In the dressing room, as his snapped hamstring was bound with white bandages, Deane apologised to everyone, as though he could have prevented the injury. 'I wanted to score so many times today that Mallory would get sick of lifting his arse off his seat to applaud,' he said.

4

I PLAYED IT SAFE. THAT was a mistake.

I used only one striker and one wide player, dropping an extra man into midfield to protect our lead. Without Jason

Deane, we struggled because the ball came back more rapidly at us. We couldn't hold on to it, which meant we couldn't hold back Middlesbrough either. The heat was beginning to go from the day, but the sky was still cloudless, and the opposition began to assert themselves for the first time.

Diminutive midfielders always look faster than they actually are. The rapid movement of their 'little' legs fools you into thinking that. In the first half, Juninho had been a butterfly. He'd floated slowly from one part of the pitch to another. Picking up his game, he was suddenly everywhere at great pace. Emerson tackled the life out of us, patrolling the channels. Nigel Pearson dominated anything pushed at him in the air. The Middlesbrough defence locked itself up as impregnable as a combination safe.

A worrying urgency came over us. We tried to do everything too fast, jumping around the pitch and scuttling back and forward, mostly without the ball. I think we hoped that hurrying up the game would make the minutes go faster, saving us from our ordeal. We ought to have done what good pros do: whittle away time, cling to possession, love the corner flag.

It takes a minute to score a goal and five minutes to change a match completely. I watched those minutes tick by on the electric scoreboard:

60 ... 70 ... 75 ... 80

We were almost there. Derby were no longer of any consequence to us. Their relegation required only an official stamp. Sunderland, a breath away from us, were our only problem.

Someone once said that 'the sound of a big football crowd baying its delight and its outrage has no counterpart'. I agreed with him then. Even the shabbier parts of our ground, grime still clinging to them from a decade ago, seemed brightly magnificent because of the atmosphere inside the stadium. The suspense was intolerable for Jonjo Whelan, who became wildly agitated. 'We haven't made a chance since the half began. They aren't taking possession. We're gifting it to them.'

As he said this, Middlesbrough won a fourth corner in rapid succession. The previous three had seen the usual jostling and shirt-tugging and digging of one another in the ribs. Each time we'd beaten back the attack. This corner fooled us. Juninho struck it flatter. The tactic confused Fournier, the ball skimming off his forehead at the near post. Pearson, powering in, stooped to meet the slack clearance. His header went through Curtis Taylor, who flapped his hands at it.

Nine minutes to go.

In sport, as in life, the 'ifs' are what you look back on. They stand out in the story of your life like exclamation marks. If Robbie Clayton's foot had landed two inches to the right of that hole on Cup final morning, he'd have played at Wembley; he wouldn't have missed the great event of his life. If I hadn't bust my knee at Stamford Bridge, I wouldn't have been forced to quit the game – and I wouldn't have come back from Sweden, because I wouldn't have gone there in the first place.

The goal undid us, tearing us into bits. Every 'if' possible crowded into my mind then. If Jason Deane hadn't got injured. If I'd chosen different tactics at half-time. If I'd dropped Taylor.

We couldn't get out of our own half. Middlesbrough were swarming all over us. Three minutes after the goal, Emerson played the ball in from the left, aiming at Ravanelli and finding us in disarray. Ravanelli had sufficient space to weigh up where to place his shot. Aaron Buchan came across to narrow the angle, lunging at him. The ball, which Ravanelli hit with his right foot, struck Buchan on the left knee. Taylor went the wrong way. He tried to scramble back, stumbled and stuck out a leg. I will *never* understand how Ravanelli's drive didn't go in. It came off the toe of Taylor's boot and spun over the bar, scraping off the paint. Taylor had no idea how he'd got to the ball or, immediately afterwards, where it had gone. He even looked for it in the net.

Sick with trepidation now, I hadn't wanted a game to end so much since the Cup final.

5

ERBY'S RESULT FILTERED THROUGH first. They'd lost 2–1. A minute later, Sunderland's game was over too. They'd won 3–1. I tried to tell Stefan Fournier, so he could tell everyone else.

We just had to cling on to be safe.

But Fournier was on the far touchline, losing the ball against Emerson and desperately scrapping to get it back. It was played square to Pearson, who struck the thing high upfield. It was more of a Hail Mary punt than a pass. Buchan jumped with Ravanelli. The tussle took place almost two-thirds of the way inside our half and near the right touchline. Buchan's header went as far as the centre circle. The whistle went: he was penalised for fouling the striker. Buchan protested, pointlessly. Ravanelli had fouled him, he said. He slapped his hand against the air in a show of disgust and mimed how Ravanelli had bent himself almost double and backed into him. I kicked a water bottle out of my technical area.

Juninho trotted over to take the free kick. Everyone was hovering on the edge of the box. They looked at one another – shouting, pointing, shoving, either attempting to claim a few feet of space for themselves or trying to close that same space down.

The referee went among the players to restore order. When this didn't work, he blew his whistle a few times. He looked twice at his watch, calculating how much time to add on. He checked with the linesman, who nodded at him.

We were in the 94th minute.

In those situations, you can't help but think about what might happen. Juninho, over-eager, might fluff his kick. Wanting to reassert himself, Buchan might tug at someone's shirt or miss his header. Taylor might come for the cross and not claim it. For tossing a free kick into a packed area is like a spin of the roulette wheel. You can't know for sure where the ball will land, how it will bounce and settle. You can only wait until it does, hoping it falls right for you.

Juninho made us wait. Picking the ball up, he rubbed it against the front of his shirt. He repositioned the kick – an inch forward, two inches back, another two inches to the side. He calibrated the desired trajectory and force in his mind.

I turned around very quickly and looked at the directors' box. I saw Freyja, the anxiety on her face very clear. I saw Frank, his emotions held so firmly in check that no one would have known whether he wanted us to stay up or go down. When I turned towards the pitch again, Juninho was taking a step towards the ball.

How steeply it rose off his boot. How much lift he got from the minimum of swing and effort.

At the top of its flight, the ball seemed to stop and hang against the sky. It continued to hang there, as brilliantly white and whole as a full moon. If someone had taken a photograph then, they would have captured everything good about football: the thrill of it . . . the splendour of the grass . . . the faces of a packed crowd, decked out in full colour . . . every head tilted upwards . . . the ball about to succumb to gravity . . . the result 90 seconds from being decided . . . an entire season behind us.

Jonjo Whelan appeared at my shoulder. 'Tell me we're going to clear this. Tell me we're going to make it,' he said.

The ball began to fall towards our penalty spot. I looked across at Jonjo and said:

'Of course we're going to make it,' I said. 'Of course . . .'

6

IT WAS NUDGING 1 A.M. Sunday had turned into Monday. I hadn't noticed.

I'd slid down the sofa. I was using the coffee table as a foot-stool. I didn't know how much I'd had to drink since the game had ended, but there were two empty wine bottles on the floor and another, half full, stood beside them.

For umpteen hours, I'd pressed rewind, pause and play – mostly reliving and re-analysing the game's last minute. I'd freeze the TV picture at the very moment Juninho's free kick was about to drop out of the sky.

On each occasion, just as the film was about to spool forward, I'd said quietly in my mind: 'Robbie Clayton would have got to that ball first. He'd have headed it into the back of the stand.'

Freyja came out of the bedroom, unable to sleep because I was still awake. 'Switch the TV off. You need to call it a night,' she said, pulling at the silk belt of her dressing gown. 'There's no use going over everything again. How many times have you watched it? You'll drive yourself mad.'

Gently, she tried to take the remote control out of my hand.

'Five more minutes,' I pleaded. 'I'm still thinking.'

7

WHENEVER FRANK MALLORY SHARED his opinion about set pieces, he'd tell me: 'Look for the idiot.' The idiot was the defender who lost concentration. Someone who'd doze off and ball-watch, letting the man he was marking drift away. Someone who'd wander about, absent-mindedly, and stand in a daft place. Someone too slow to react, becoming a useless spectator. Someone too bullish who would clumsily obstruct his own team mate – the only player capable of clearing the bloody thing. 'There's always one idiot,' insisted Frank.

We had two.

Whenever I pressed the play button, Curtis Taylor would pelt off his line towards the penalty spot. He'd been the hero when the toe-end of his boot had denied Ravanelli. Still hyped up, emboldened by that achievement, Taylor wanted too much to be the hero again.

But he was only half of our problem.

As captain, Aaron Buchan believed the saviour's role ought to belong to him. Buchan was supposed to be minding Ravanelli, but he saw nothing other than the ball and so bulldozed his way towards it, mistaking stupidity for unparalleled daring. Unaware of who was around him, Buchan hammered into Stefan Fournier, unbalancing the Frenchman as well as himself. The goalkeeper had already come so far that he couldn't turn back, which was the only reason he kept going. Buchan and Fournier fell against Taylor, who made a pointless grab at the ball, missing it completely before smacking into the turf. The three of them toppled over like bowling pins.

From half a dozen different angles and in agonising slow motion, I saw:

The unprotected goal and Taylor's desperation to get back into it.

Ravanelli peeling away to the back post.

The desperate lunge he made towards the chance.

And the ball as it bounced over his boot and skipped harmlessly away, striking the advertising boards.

Somehow, we'd survived.

I didn't know how. Each time I replayed the free kick, I flinched a little, expecting the outcome to be different. I was waiting for Ravanelli to punish us.

It was a shave so close that it almost took our skin off. It also made the difference between staying up and going down actually measurable. 'A foot,' calculated Jonjo Whelan, a long while afterwards. He had held his hands apart like a fisherman demonstrating the size of a miserable catch.

The TV cameras had isolated scenes from the chaos that I had missed from the touchline: Fournier blowing out his cheeks in relief and then wiping the dust from his hair and the front of his shirt; Taylor tugging Buchan off the floor before slapping him on the back (neither player, knowing himself culpable, looked at the other); Ravanelli standing on the spot where the chance had capriciously eluded him, still wondering where the ball had gone.

Something aural – even the sound of a loved one's voice – is more difficult to store in the memory than something visual. But the noise that reverberated around the ground rose to such a level then that I felt it beneath my feet and through my body, which is how I will always remember it.

The game was over.

I walked away from the bench, anxious to escape the crush to come. I was still walking when Taylor clipped a short goal kick to Fournier, who simply stood on the ball and waited for the whistle. When it came, a second later, he flicked the ball into his hands and then thumped it high and long, a souvenir for any fan prepared to claim it.

Jonjo screamed just one word: 'Yes' which I could hear above everything else. My future had dominated so much of the build-up that everyone seemed to have forgotten what the match, which was his last, meant to Jonjo too. He sprinted onto the field. He was immediately lost, like every player, amid our fans, who had jumped the perimeter wall in a benign invasion.

I looked upwards into the stand, searching for Freyja, but I couldn't find her. When I got to the end of the tunnel, she was waiting for me near the dressing room. 'I started crying and now I can't stop,' she said. The door at the end of the corridor was open. I saw Frank. He was coming down the steps from the directors' box, clutching the handrail tightly. I thought he would turn right towards me, but instead, after a flicker of a glance was exchanged between us, he hurried in the opposite direction as quickly as his weak legs would carry him. Frank's bitterness, his jealousy and his lack of magnanimity demonstrated how different he was from the managers he most envied. He was no Stein, no Busby and certainly no Shankly. He lacked their dignity. I wondered what he truly despised the most: his own failure or my success? If I hadn't been obliged to go into the directors' box myself – the supporters were insisting that I make an appearance there – I'd have chased after Frank and demanded to know.

Even without a trophy to brandish, it felt like the aftermath of the FA Cup final.

The pitch was a mass of people, a great spread of red and white. The only grass still visible encircled the far corner flags. You'd have thought we had won the Premier League rather than merely avoided relegation from it.

I waved and clapped and bowed to the fans, who reciprocated by chanting repeatedly:

'CALLY MUST STAY'

In football, where you rise again and fall again, you have to make the most of times like that. They roll in so rarely, and the feeling you get from success never lingers. In only ten weeks the game would cross into a new season, and the old one would already be history, waiting to be forgotten. The match would soon count for very little; only the romantics and sentimentalists would continue to care about it.

Knowing this, I shook hands and swigged champagne. I accepted the scarves admirers draped around my neck, a small ceremony of honour. Those who were closest to me must have realised I was going through the motions. I was only pretending to be perfectly happy. My far-away look was the giveaway. I smiled, but I couldn't celebrate wildly or wholeheartedly, the way winners are supposed to do.

The result meant a lot to me, but far less than it would have done 48 hours before. I was thinking about Robbie Clayton. I always would.

After all the players and the coaching staff had struggled to get up from the pitch to the directors' box, arriving in twos and threes with more champagne, I was able to slip away and eventually sweep up the last of my possessions from Frank's office. It didn't take long. As I stuffed everything into a single bag, I thought of my first day back in the city, how I'd walked from the Market Square to the bridge to stare at the ground and look down the river. Then, I was an unfancied manager of an unfancied team. Now, and for a week or two more at least, I had a reputation to protect. I had achieved what no one else had believed possible. How quickly three months had passed. How they had changed me, perhaps forever.

I closed the door to Frank's office very softly. As it clicked shut, I heard the fans chanting my name again.

'You know what's going to happen, don't you?' asked Freyja. 'The new owners will see the scenes out there and ask you to carry on. You've made it impossible for them to do anything else. You'll get the call tomorrow, I'm certain of that. You'll need to decide tonight whether you'll say yes. Will you say yes?'

I gave her the only answer I could.

'Honestly, I don't know'.

Author Notes and Acknowledgements

I owe a profound debt to Jon Riley, who commissioned and edited *Injury Time*. I ought to tag one other important thing. Jon is a life-long Spurs supporter. I'd say he has *almost* forgiven me for the 'poetic licence' I have taken with his beloved team's recent history. Or perhaps not.

Other thanks go to Jasmine Palmer for her work on the proofs.

For the umpteenth time, I also want to acknowledge the insight and unstinting support of my agent, Grainne Fox.

As ever, nothing would get done without my wife, Mandy. Mind you, that fact applies to every facet, big or small, of my life.

No, I'm not exaggerating . . .